Telepresence in Training

Series Editor
Jean-Marc Labat

Telepresence in Training

Edited by

Jean-Luc Rinaudo

WILEY

First published 2018 in Great Britain and the United States by ISTE Ltd and John Wiley & Sons, Inc.

ISTE Ltd
27-37 St George's Road
London SW19 4EU
UK

www.iste.co.uk

John Wiley & Sons, Inc.
111 River Street
Hoboken, NJ 07030
USA

www.wiley.com

Library of Congress Control Number: 2018957301

British Library Cataloguing-in-Publication Data
A CIP record for this book is available from the British Library
ISBN 978-1-78630-342-4

Contents

Chapter 7. Co-construction of Tangible, Dispersed and Multi-semiotic Spaces through the Use of a Telepresence Robot 145

Dorothée FURNON

Chapter 8. The Telepresence Robot in Universities: Between Subjectification and Unlinking 163

Jean-Luc RINAUDO

Introduction

Thinking About Telepresence in Training

The techniques used in distance learning or hybrid education are increasingly complex because of technical innovations and technologies that have been harnessed. At the same time, the analyses undertaken by researchers to examine the uses, practices, conclusions, implications and unexpected features of these techniques have become even more complex [BAR 13]. Research into the effectiveness of a technological approach to teaching and learning has demonstrated limitations [CHA 03]. Researchers who have focused on the digital are now researching the way in which these techniques can have meaning for different actors (learners, teachers, creators, decision-makers, etc.). It is within this comprehensive and heuristic research effort that the contributors to this work are situated.

The development of computing and communication technologies for teaching, training and learning contributes to the adjustment of the markers that enable the easy classification of the types of instructional system: on the one hand, in the classroom, and on the other hand, remotely. Thus, from the origins of distance education, which we can date back to Viviane Glickman, beginning with the invention of the postage stamp in Great Britain [GLI 02], through the 1980s, the distance learner is situated in a space and time that are completely different from that of the educator. With the first techniques for synchronous online exchanges such as chat, the distance learner remains in a different location from the educator, but they share the learning environment in cyberspace simultaneously. The notions of presence and absence must therefore be re-examined, which Geneviève Jacquinot has notably undertaken [JAC 93]. These investigations should be continued for virtual

Introduction written by Jean-Luc RINAUDO.

classroom tools or telepresence robots, because they make it possible for educators and learners to share the same time and space, most often in groups. The diverse forms of telepresence in education, distance learning and the support of students, notably in the formulation of their research essays, in the use of personal learning environments, etc., are developing rapidly. They provide the opportunity to reformulate the investigations and give rise to serious questions. For example, how should we think about the hierarchy of presence and absence in these techniques [JAC 93] in order to make possible "the presence of the absent" [PER 14]? What effects do forms of telepresence have on the process of mediation? What effects do they have on group learning dynamics? How does it transform collaborative work? What effect does telepresence have on the perception of the body? What new forms of education, teaching and research work can now occur?

This book follows a symposium that brought together researchers, primarily in education sciences, during a meeting of the *Réseau international de recherche en éducation et formation* (RÉF) in July 2017 at the *Conservatoire national des arts et métiers* (CNAM) in Paris. It was the first time that a symposium was dedicated to the theme of telepresence in the RÉF framework. Hailing from five different countries, the contributors presented their analyses of the techniques they studied and of the practices of students and teachers from diverse theoretical frameworks on which they conducted their recent or current research. This work therefore aims to highlight telepresence in training. The challenge of combining analyses substantiated by different theoretical foundations can lead to a risk of diffusion; on the contrary, we think that it is through this cross-disciplinary approach that the complexity of learning environments can be approached. Furthermore, the authors of the texts presented here are not all situated at the same distance from their objects of investigation. In an interview for the journal *Distances et médiation des savoirs*, I indicated that we have to shed light on the relationship of the proximity we have to the objects of research, ranging from complete engagement to absolute exteriority [RIN 16]. This book brings together texts written by educators, practitioners implicated in the techniques they present and analyze, and researchers who have greater degrees of distance from the objects they study. Nevertheless, our aim here is not to underestimate the contribution of practitioners to this work of analyzing telepresence, but rather to indicate from where these different authors express themselves in order to make it possible to understand how they construct their understanding of the situations they are investigating.

The work is composed of three parts. The first part brings together three chapters concerning telepresence and student support.

In Chapter 1, Brigitte Denis begins with the assumption that one of the stakes for distance learning in adult education is to establish techniques that respond to the needs of learners, to respect andragogical principles and to provide a quality pedagogical and ergonomic environment. Moreover, guidance is an essential factor in the implementation of such techniques. By achieving a feeling of presence [JAC 02] and providing socio-emotional, cognitive, organizational and meta-cognitive support to the learner that may encourage the perception of different kinds of proximities, it influences perseverance and the achievement of its objectives. Brigitte Denis addresses mediation between e-tutors and learners in a hybrid learning system. The five e-tutors in this system were asked about their perceptions of the features that develop the feeling of telepresence in learners during their interactions with the latter. The analysis of the results demonstrates and puts into perspective certain factors that are likely to foster these feelings.

In Chapter 2, Gustavo Angulo and Cathia Papi, researchers at Teluq (an open university at the University of Québec), provide a literature review of collective work in the training of researchers. When knowledge is increasingly considered to be the foundation of modern economies, the training of researchers takes on first-order importance in order to galvanize social development. However, this initiation into the research profession, which often begins with the production of a thesis during graduate school, is long and difficult for students on campus as well as at a distance [IRA 14, RIT 12]. Digital possibilities allow for the consideration of new forms of support. Among them, collective work in virtual learning spaces that is considered as communities is often planned to foster a feeling of presence and to stimulate the development of knowledge and competence [CRO 08, PIC 11, SIN 11]. But what are the unique characteristics of these communities for educating researchers? Based on a systematic analysis of studies published during the last 10 years, Angulo and Papi examine forms of telepresence and their influence on these collective dynamics.

In Chapter 3, Ann-Louise Davidson and Nadia Naffi, researchers at Concordia University in Montreal, aim to present a reflexive analysis of their experiences in supporting students enrolled in an online undergraduate education degree program and the systems they designed to support the learning process in a problem-based approach. After the presentation of the context, the authors provide a brief overview of the literature concerning theoretical concepts that underlie their support within a problem-based learning approach to online courses. They mention the challenges of co-design, co-production and co-teaching of university courses that are entirely online concerning social media. Taking into account the implications of online courses, they address the challenge of problem-based learning from a pedagogical perspective based on socio-constructivism. To support students through authentic and meaningful learning experiences, they have involved them in social media. It is from these authentic experiences that they engaged in a co-reflection about their practices, in view of the elements that activate them and those that act as levers in the learning process.

The second part brings together two chapters about telepresence in teacher education, written respectively by two educators from high-level professional schools in Switzerland, Romaine Carrupt (Chapter 4) and Stéphanie Boéchat-Heer (Chapter 5).

Chapter 4 presents exploratory research that aims to better understand the contributions and limits of telepresence collaboration, via virtual classes, using a professional training system for hybrid teaching. From this perspective, Romaine Carrupt compares the discourses produced by teachers during initial education, during a mutual analysis in a virtual classroom, and in person, in order to understand the degree to which the reference to different kinds of knowledge is differentiated according to the context that may or may not be relayed by the virtual class. What emerges from this analysis is that interactions in the virtual classroom are primarily oriented towards scientific knowledge, while the experiential dimension takes precedence during in-person sessions.

In Chapter 5, Stéphanie Boéchat-Heer presents the results of a study devoted to the evaluation of the place occupied by telepresence in teacher education, in support activities and in collaborative work. More precisely, she evaluates the general perception and the feeling of self-effectiveness of teachers in this practice, as well as the strategies of self-regulation that have been implemented. This study follows a comprehensive approach and relies on the analysis of a corpus of data collected via a questionnaire and semi-directed interviews. The self-regulatory strategies of teachers allow for an understanding of the dimensions in play in the attitude of support for telepresence work and for the ability to reply more fully to the educational needs of teachers and to support them in this process. These results engender reflection about the very technique of support for telepresence work, and open the discussion about the contributions and limits of such a practice.

The final part brings together four contributions from researchers who study a technique using telepresence robots in education at an engineering school, at a university or even in a doctoral seminar.

In Chapter 6, Françoise Poyet provides exploratory research that relies on a digital university initiative in the Rhône-Alpes region (UNR-RA 2015). During 2015–2017, experiments that made it possible to test telepresence robots in pedagogical situations were conducted with students whose physical handicaps prevented them from easily moving around on their university campuses. The data collected via an interview with about 10 users allowed for the exposure of the existence of a new ontophany [VIA 13] induced by the telepresence robot. This research offers the opportunity to analyze the relationship that is established between users and the robot and to reflect on the emergence of an authentic symbiotic interaction between them [BRA 09]. Specifically, Françoise Poyet considers the particular incarnation of a remote student's body via the robot based on the hypothesis that the proprioceptive appropriation of the robot by the student directly impacts the perception of his real body and, beyond that, his own physical schema. She then discusses the notions of expanded, prolonged and fixed corporality.

In Chapter 7, Dorothée Furnon proposes an expansion on the preceding chapter, beginning with the idea that the development of the use of telepresence robots in teaching leads to a rethinking of the way in which the action is co-constructed in an environment whose mediation is human, digital, technical and technological. Her study attempts to understand the way in which students and teachers develop new spaces of meaning during interactions mediated by a telepresence robot in an educational context. She analyzes two pedagogical situations in which actors find themselves confronted with the necessity of reconfiguring common spaces of intelligibility by transforming digital objects into instruments of perception to attain mutual intelligibility.

In Chapter 8, in an analysis based on an approach to psychoanalytical orientation, I propose a text in which I study the reality of the psyche, in the Freudian sense, experienced by students who benefit from the telepresence system to overcome their inability, which is temporary but lasting for several weeks, to get to class. Here I pinpoint experiences that are suitable for subjectification and others favoring unlink in the psyche.

Finally, in Chapter 9, Christine Develotte proposes to explain the implementation of a technique specifically designed to provide research data about telepresence in a doctoral seminar. She first presents the context of this reflexive research, which proposes researchers and apprentice-researchers as objects of study. She briefly describes the background, the participants, and the in-person and remote communication modalities. She then deals with the technical environment for the collection of data and the sessions that were selected to be filmed. She lingers more specifically on the complexity of the multimodal communication that can take place between different participants depending on the tools used. She then specifies the theoretical framework from which three research angles emerged, and the technico-methodological decisions made to recover different kinds of data (videos, interviews, written texts). This is followed by a discussion of the scientific stakes of this kind of system, as well as the questions that it could raise, particularly in the area of educational science.

Finally, we cannot conclude this introduction without specifically thanking Jacques Wallet, who agreed to write the postface.

References

[BAR 13] BARON G.L., "La recherche francophone sur les "technologies" en éducation : réflexions rétrospectives et prospectives", *Sticef, 20*, vol. 20, 2013, accessed January 2018 at: http://sticef.univ-lemans.fr/num/vol2013/16-baron -reiah/sticef_2013_NS_ baron_16p.pdf.

[BRA 09] BRANGIER E., DUFRESNE A., HAMMES-ADELE S., "Approche symbiotique de la relation humain-technologie : perspectives pour l'ergonomie informatique", *Le travail humain*, vol. 72, no. 4, pp. 333–353, 2009.

[CHA 03] CHAPTAL A., *L'efficacité des technologies éducatives dans l'enseignement scolaire. Analyse critique des approches française et américaine*, L'Harmattan, Paris, 2003.

[CRO 08] CROSSOUARD B., "Developing alternative models of doctoral supervision with online formative assessment", *Studies in Continuing Education*, vol. 30, no. 1, pp. 51–67, 2008.

[GLI 02] GLIKMAN V., *Des cours par correspondance au e-learning*, PUF, Paris, 2002.

[IRA 14] IRANI T.A., WILSON S.B., SLOUGH D.L. *et al.*, "Graduate student experiences on- and off-campus: Social connectedness and perceived isolation", *International Journal of E-Learning & Distance Education*, vol. 28, no. 1, accessed January 2018 at: http://www.ijede.ca/index.php/jde/article/view/.

[JAC 93] JACQUINOT G., "Apprivoiser la distance et supprimer l'absence ? Ou les défis de la formation à distance", *Revue française de pédagogie*, vol. 102, pp. 55–67, 1993.

[JAC 02] JACQUINOT G., "Absence et présence dans la médiation pédagogique ou comment faire circuler les signes de la présence", in GUIR R. (ed.), *Pratiquer les TICE. Former les enseignants et les formateurs à de nouveaux usages*, pp. 104–113, De Boeck, Brussels, 2002.

[PER 14] PERAYA D., "Distances, absence, proximités et présences : des concepts en déplacement", *Distances et médiations des savoirs*, vol. 8, 2014, accessed January 2018 at: http://journals.openedition.org/dms/865.

[PIC 11] PICARD M., WILKINSON K., WIRTHENSOHN M., "On online learning space facilitating supervision pedagogies in science", *South African Journal of Higher Education*, vol. 25, no. 5, pp. 954–971, 2011.

[RIN 16] RINAUDO J.-L., "Entretien avec Jean-Luc Rinaudo", *Distances et médiations des savoirs*, vol. 13, 2016, accessed January 2018 at: http://dms.revues.org/1370.

[RIT 12] RITTER E., Non-completion in thesis required master's degree programs, PhD thesis, Eastern Illinois University, 2012, accessed January 2018 at: http://thekeep.eiu.edu/cgi/viewcontent.cgi?article=1790&context=theses.

[SIN 11] SINDLINGER J., Doctoral Students' Experience with Using the Reflecting Team Model of Supervision Online, PhD thesis, Duquesne University, 2011.

[VIA 13] VIAL S., *L'être et l'écran*, PUF, Paris, 2013.

List of Abbreviations

BYOD:	Bring Your Own Device
eT:	e-Tutor
F2F:	Face-to-Face (in person)
GDTPI:	Gestion de dispositifs techno-pédagogiques innovants
HEP-VS:	Haute école pédagogique du Valais
HQP:	Highly Qualified Personnel
ICT:	Information and Communication Technologies
ICTE:	Information and Communication Technologies in Education
ITPS:	Innovative Techno-pedagogical System
LMS:	Learning Management System
MEN:	Ministère de l'Éducation nationale
PCL:	Problem-centric Learning
PCLO:	Problem-centric Learning Object
TPS:	Techno-pedagogical System
VC:	Virtual Class

Part 1

Telepresence and Student Support

Feelings of Telepresence and Proximity: the Perspectives of E-tutors on a Hybrid Learning Environment

1.1. Introduction

Educational techniques integrating the use of digital technologies, whether it is in person, remote or a combination of the two, have been implemented in most educational fields. The presence of an e-tutor constitutes one of the key elements for maintaining the learners' motivation to pursue their distance education [DEN 03] because the interactions between them make it possible to bring about a "feeling of presence at a distance" [JAC 02] and of proximity [ROD 11].

The present contribution is anchored in the analysis of a hybrid learning system, namely a university certificate for the management of innovative techno-pedagogical environments (MITPE), whose target audience consists of educators who teach innovative techno-pedagogical system (ITPS) specific to their context.

After having briefly established the notions of telepresence and "proximities of distance", and having described our instructional system (context, objectives, epistemological options, actors, techno-pedagogical mediatization and so on), we will focus on the process of mediation between e-tutors and learners, and, more specifically, on the feeling of presence at a distance (or telepresence) and of proximity felt by the e-tutors in relation to

Chapter written by Brigitte DENIS.

their students. Based on the analysis of interviews with e-tutors, we will examine the way in which they think their interactions through the student's "roadbook" procure a feeling of telepresence within the system, the nature of this feeling, and the conditions that foster its emergence or its failure to emerge. The results of this exploratory study will then be discussed and put into perspective.

1.2. Telepresence and proximities in remote interactions

Each of the dimensions of this distance (place, action, time) represents for the learner a risk of estrangement, of rupture with the system, with the community of participants, or even with the learning task in process. It is therefore necessary to provide strategies in order to avoid or minimize these risks connected to the lack of physical presence between teachers and learners.

1.2.1. Overcoming absence with telepresence

In a hybrid or completely remote system, different modalities of interaction with the learner are generally envisioned in order to compensate for the distance. The availability of knowledge via a process of mediatization, and especially the circulation of signs of the instructor's presence and/or of the learners transmitted via the use of more or less interactive technological tools, allows for a certain degree of "presence at a distance" [JAC 93]. However, we should not think that technological mediation is sufficient for overcoming absence.

It is important to consider the way in which we can integrate presence into distance within such systems. Indeed, the distance dissolves in telepresence [PER 11]. Consequently, we can consider, for example, how the teacher or tutor can be psychologically or mentally present all while being physically absent [JAC 93, JAC 02]. This preoccupation should be integrated into the process of instructional engineering [ROD 10], more specifically in the education of e-tutors. These e-tutors can in effect be or become close to learners without encountering them physically.

In addition, in many systems that integrate distance, emphasis is placed on the social dimension of learning. The proximity of the learner to their peers rests on a positive attitude towards collaboration, resource sharing, debate and solidarity. The peers are considered to be opportunities for learning. This social dimension to learning is found in Jézégou [JÉZ 10], according to whom telepresence constitutes a space for mediatized social interaction thanks to virtual reality technology; telepresence interactions contribute to the elimination of absence. This author considers presence in learning environments integrating collaborative activities or in online learning communities to be the result of the pedagogical presence (coordination, activities, moderation, etc.), which itself results from remote interactions between the learner and instructor or e-tutor, who aim to support socio-affective and socio-cognitive presences (interactions between learners).

This leads us to think about telepresence in terms of the learner's proximity to the set of agents (human and non-human actors)[1] in the learning system in which he is engaged: "[...] it is important, as soon as a system is designed, to provide elements that promote the emergence of the feeling of proximity, because engagement in learning activities is dependent on the effective proximity (experienced as such) of the system [PAQ 11]. Thus, the apparent diffusion of the elements of place, action, and time is not a synonym for remoteness and can even promote links of proximity. The participants in a distance learning system share a single learning 'space', even though it is done in a mediatized and asynchronous way" [BRA 14, p. 2]. By dissolving the constraints of space and time, some artifacts allow for synchronous communications (e.g. chat, videoconferencing) or asynchronous communication (e.g. email, shared documents) between e-tutors and learners, and they can orchestrate the perception of the feeling of telepresence and sustain engagement in learning activities. However, it is not only the creation and the provision of artifacts allowing for the development of targeted competences by the system, but especially a reflexive process with regard to their use and the interactions that make it possible to feel the proximity of distance.

---

1 An agent is defined by the ability to act, to have an influence and a level of intensity, during a course of action. Agents can be both human and non-human (objects, resources, structural entities, values, epistemological and pedagogical options, etc.). For example, the learner's roadbook plays a role in the learning process.

1.2.2. *Experiencing the feeling of proximity at a distance*

In a blog post entitled "*De la proximité en formation à distance*" (on proximity in distance education), Rodet [ROD 11] examines certain links of proximity from the learner's position: to what and to whom should the distance learner be close? He distinguishes seven points of view in terms of proximity: the learner's distance from himself, his peers, his tutor, the instructional designer, the institution and the knowledge contents.

Among these links of proximity, we are particularly interested, in the context of this study, in the proximity of the learner to himself (reflexive expression about his learning process) and his proximity to his e-tutor.

On the one hand, we will focus on the e-tutor's perception with regard to the fact that the learner should be "able to take a big-picture view of his ways of learning, his cognitive preferences and his emotional relationship to the act of learning" [ROD 11] and on the evolution of his project – in other words, on the metacognitive tasks anchored in the education he is pursuing. The development of reflexivity constitutes, in effect, one of the competencies targeted by the current training system. The learner's reflexive process about his learning process and about the development of his project, as well as his communication with his e-tutor in this regard, are supported by filling out a roadbook. The artifact connected to this activity is chosen by the learner or proposed by the e-tutor (e.g. shared document, e-portfolio, etc.). It can be assimilated into a portfolio for learning and evaluation. Effectively, this e-portfolio "is presented as a structured collection of data chosen by the author based on his targeted objectives. It is not necessarily shared with others; its main function is the author's reflexive analysis of his own activities" [MAI 08, p. 53].

On the other hand, it is the feelings of telepresence connected to a more or less significant proximity between e-tutor and learners that will be studied through the remarks made by e-tutors following their remote interactions with their students. In addition to the roles undertaken to develop this proximity, we will highlight certain variables in the instructional relationship, such as the fact that a learner who is close to the e-tutor dares to call upon the latter, perceiving a climate of confidence, or the way in which the e-tutor watches over the cultivation of this climate in order to promulgate the signs of presence and to respond to the learner's requests.

1.3. Research question

This work consists of an exploratory study of the feeling of presence and of perceived proximity by e-tutors within the implemented hybrid system. Our research question is the following: "According to the e-tutors (eT) for the MITPE certificate, which remote interactions with learners, via the maintenance of a roadbook, contribute to the development of a feeling of presence and proximity within the hybrid learning system?"

The recommended roles in the e-tutor's profile are supposed to contribute to the feeling of telepresence (on the pedagogical, socio-affective, cognitive and metacognitive levels) in the MITPE learning system. We will examine the elements the e-tutors highlight to describe their feeling of telepresence with their students.

1.4. Presentation of the system

In order to contribute to a response to the need for education in terms of the integration of information and communication technologies (ICT) in an innovative techno-pedagogical system, a university certificate program was created in 2016–2017 under the leadership of the *Centre de recherche sur l'instrumentation, la formation et l'apprentissage* (CRIFA) at the University of Liège in partnership with two higher learning institutions, the Albert-Jacquard and Henri-Spaak high schools in Belgium. This certificate is intended to coordinate the participant's progress so he will be led to understand and to manage the changes in his techno-pedagogical project.

In the following, we will present the targeted competencies for learners and the target audience to which the certificate in MITPE is directed, as well as the organization of this hybrid system.

1.4.1. *Targeted competencies and target audience*

This training concerning the use of the management process for the implementation of innovative techno-pedagogical systems aims to develop the following competencies in the learner:

– to analyze techno-pedagogical systems through the systemic analysis of its structural and functional aspects;

– to manage change in this context by taking into account the approach and the dynamic of implemented innovation and by implementing its practices (models, analysis tools, etc.);

– to analyze his professional practices through tools that assist with reflection in order to formalize his learning and his professional development.

Three primary audience types are targeted, with the condition that the participant implements, alone or as part of a team, a techno-pedagogical system that aspires to train learners (e.g. students, staff members) or his colleagues. It is concerned with training actors such as:

– professors, technical or pedagogical personnel resources, higher education administrators, etc.;

– teachers, cybermedia center managers, administrators, etc. of other educational levels (elementary, secondary and education for social advancement);

– educators or training administrators from various contexts (associations, companies, public digital spaces, training centers, non-governmental organizations, etc.).

1.4.2. *Organization: a hybrid techno-pedagogical system*

This certificate includes four modules: (1) definition and analysis of a techno-pedagogical system (TPS); (2) implementation of an innovative TPS; (3) evaluation and management of the TPS; and (4) end of certificate work. Our chosen epistemological approach is socio-constructivist. Moreover, the certificate is based on andragogical principles: student projects, immediately transferable learning, management of the training process by the adult, references to previous experience for learning new things, pedagogical methods enabling discussion, sharing, and the construction of knowledge, taking prerequisites into account and so on.

The training that is the object of this study occurs over a five-month period. Activities take place primarily remotely and are tutored. This allows the participants to engage in a distance learning experience (as learners) within a hybrid system. The latter is situated in the "ecosystem" configuration according to the typology of Burton *et al.* [BUR 11].

1.4.2.1. *Face-to-face activities*

Synchronous, collective meetings (approximately every five weeks) take place over three in-person days and two virtual classes (by half-groups), equivalent to about 30 hours. The face-to-face activities consist of framing and discussing the key concepts that punctuate the training (e.g. learning system, systemic approach, innovation, regulation). This provides an opportunity to present certain theoretical notions and software programs in a structured and fairly condensed manner and to undertake their exploration in a seminar setting (e.g. project planning). The in-person course also provides the opportunity to spotlight and to accumulate constructive criticism from peers and instructors, or to cooperate in order to begin or to deepen his thinking about the project from a particular point of view (e.g. adequacy of activities and of the choice of pedagogical tools in the context of the pursued objectives).

1.4.2.2. *Focus on remote activities*

Ninety percent of the activities will take place remotely. A certain number of hours is attributed to module-related work, then to the work of the participant in the context (application) and framework of his roadbook, and finally to the report of his end-of-certificate work. Activities that take place remotely are generally individual, but some are cooperative. All of these are directly linked to the learner's project.

In addition to a first activity of an initial consultation of accessible resources on the distance learning platform and an activity including the first two phases of the LQRT method (Lecture, Question-Response, Test), namely reading a document and asking questions in a forum dedicated to this purpose within the Learning Management System (LMS), six remote activities (or tasks) are scheduled (see Figure 1.1). Their goal is to lead the learner to formalize his process, taking into account his context and the interactions between the human (and non-human) actors used at different systemic levels. They focus on: (1) the outline and description of the techno-pedagogical environment (TPE); (2) project planning; (3) analysis of the latter from diverse e-project management models; (4) analysis of the e-project in terms of Strength/Weaknesses/Opportunities/Threats (generally known by the acronym SWOT); (5) analysis of the management process of the innovative techno-pedagogical system and its results, leading to potential regulations; and (6) production of an end-of-certificate work in the form of a synthesis.

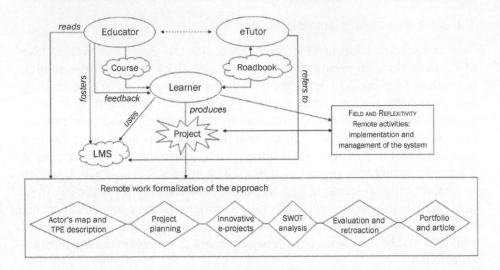

Figure 1.1. *Learners' activities and links between agents*

A file is available via the certificate's LMS for each of the activities. This file describes the instructions for the work to be done remotely. The targeted objectives are described there, as are the activity meaning, its steps, the resources to be used to complete it, the evaluation criteria and the formal elements (document format, deadline, estimated number of hours to complete the task). This mediating artifact aims to support the involvement of the learner in his work. These reference points can nevertheless be the object of precise requests via interactions with his designated e-tutor. During the implementation of the project in the field, the participant is led to take contextual complexity into account, as well as to engage in reflection and actions entailing the participation of different actors. The roadbook is regularly updated with the learner's reflexive commentary (shared with the e-tutor).

1.5. Learning system agents

This system involves diverse agents (human and non-human actors). On the one hand, we will focus here on the actors engaged in the phases of design, implementation–animation activities and management of the learning system, particularly on the aspects connected to the learning–teaching process. Since our learning system is hybrid, the in-person sessions continue to be completed through work linked to the participant's personal project.

Moreover, this project involves other actors in the field (e.g. colleagues, training students), whom we will not mention here. In addition, the learners' profile mentioned above (see target audience) will be defined more precisely in the methodological portion of this study. Furthermore, we will briefly present the types of artifacts used in the virtual environment through which the learners progress.

1.5.1. *Creator-directors*

The design and production team primarily consists of a core of three people, each from a partner institution. They are experts in Information and Communication Technologies in Education (ICTE) who have extensive experience in training (future) educators and in the introduction of ICT in educational contexts.

A techno-pedagogical engineering process, some of whose elements can generate a feeling of presence within this learning system, is implemented before and during the training in order to support the teaching–learning process.

Referring to the competencies targeted by the training program, these techno-pedagogues have tackled the creation and/or mediatization of activities and resources. They designed pedagogical scenarios integrating ICTs [DEN 06], implemented either during synchronous sessions (in person – virtual classes) or remote, asynchronous activities. They have chosen the technological tools that will be used during learning activities, in-person and at a distance. They have created the didactic resources that will be useful for training. Activity files, videos, written documents (syllabus, articles, etc.) and the roadbook are also examples of non-human actors that create a link between student and system or supervisor.

The goal of this approach is to bring the learner closer to the designer by allowing him to identify and understand his intentions as well as the requirements connected to the proposed activities. "This proximity depends therefore on the way in which the objectives of the training, the modalities chosen, and the general structure of the training course are exposed in the system's resources" [ROD 11].

The designers often post the activities and resources online, sometimes with the help of another person. "On this score, it seems important to allow the learner to have as much visibility as possible of the entirety of the course from the beginning of the training, if not before" [ROD 11].

1.5.2. *The supervising team*

The certificate's supervisors are experts (professors, researchers, lecturers, tutors, etc.) who moderate and support the participants along their path. Among these human mediators, we can distinguish between two categories of contributors: moderators/educators and e-tutors.

1.5.2.1. *Moderators/educators*

Moderators/educators are in sync with the creation team, especially because most of the former are part of the latter group as well. In effect, apart from limited recourse to an external contributor from the partner University of Liège-CRIFA and other high schools, they are the ones who will implement the MITPE training system. They are (co)responsible for one or more modules (or courses). In this framework, their intervention falls under the initiation of course sessions in person or remotely (virtual classes), the evaluation of work (feedback to the students), the provision of explanations following questions addressed to them by students or that the e-tutors pass on, the management and use of technical resources supporting the organization of individual and group work of the module participants (forum, e-mail, online shared documents, announcements, etc.). In addition, they interact with the e-tutors with regard to the students' development during team coordination meetings.

1.5.2.2. *E-tutors*

E-tutors intervene only to monitor students at a distance. In this system, each learner is supported for the duration of their course by an accredited e-tutor.

The recruitment of e-tutors (eT) takes place in several stages. The coordinators call on people experienced in the domain of ICTE and distance instruction. A short internal training course follows, which leads to a relative consensus concerning the recommended intervention in the training system, given the pursued objectives. This phase is part of the instructional engineering process described by Rodet [ROD 10] and, more specifically, of the training of remote tutors [DEN 03]:

– appeals to eT candidates;

– training of eTs and consensus about their intervention profile;

– presentation of the eTs and types of potential interventions to the learner;

– monitoring of remote interactions;

– meeting between eTs and the supervising team;

– repeat of the monitoring phases for remote interactions and another meeting between the eT and supervising team.

The formalized and detailed roles constitute the e-tutor's reference profile and will be communicated to the learners. They will thus be informed about the types of interactions they can expect from their e-tutor and will be able to distinguish the e-tutor's specific roles from those of the moderators/ educators responsible for the course. They will consequently know to whom they should address themselves and on what topics. During the training course, two meetings are scheduled between all the e-tutors and the educators in order to discuss the monitoring of students.

The establishment of e-tutoring here targets the provision of presence at a distance, that is, of a pedagogical, cognitive and socio-affective nature. The e-tutor's profile, established and communicated during this session of the MITPE certificate, is based on the main categories of the following interventions, which themselves are made up of more specific behaviors: welcome and start-up (e.g. getting to know each other), technical support (e.g. providing technical help), pedagogical support (e.g. occasionally explaining or giving additional theoretical references), socio-affective and motivational support (e.g. encouragement, rapid response), organization of work (e.g. reminders of due dates, understanding of instructions), interactivity (e.g. stimulation of communication between peers) and reflection (e.g. clarification of reflections about the learning process). Over time, a relationship should arise from these socio-cognitive interactions between the student and his accredited e-tutor.

It is a question, in the definition of Gounon et al. [GOU 04] of planned, proactive instruction. In effect, the pace and the intervention profile are specified for this training system. This recommendation is even more important since it is the e-tutor who is supposed to support the learner in his reflexive process with regard to his training and the implementation of his project.

1.5.3. *Types of recurring artifacts*

A recurring structure within each module brings together the categories and the artifacts of the same type. To this are added different tools for communication and sharing, for production, for planning and activity management and for reflexivity. Most of these kinds of non-human actors stem from the LMS in which the courses are implemented.

Different kinds of tools are moreover mobilized in training during face-to-face or remote meetings in order to execute the proposed activities (collective or individual). Some tools are proposed (e.g. "app of the day" during the in-person days) in order to foster the learners' techno-pedagogical culture (see Figure 1.2).

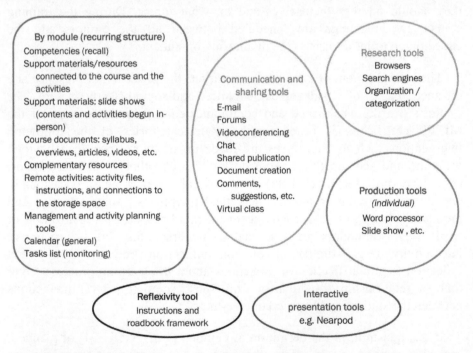

Figure 1.2. *Primary tools and technology services used in the certificate system*

1.6. Methodology

We asked e-tutors to highlight the components of the feeling of telepresence and the conditions linked to its development through their interactions with their learners.

1.6.1. *Data collection*

1.6.1.1. *Target audience: e-tutors*

The study focuses on the set of e-tutors (N=5) who are part of the MITPE certificate. Their previous experience in e-tutoring for similar certificates varied from 0 to 3 years.

The 2016–2017 cohort included 11 enrolled learners, including five professors from higher education, two university research-educators and four educators connected to training programs (distance learning service, non-profit association, professional training institute for small- and medium-size businesses). They work in a variety of domains: paramedical training, educational technology, computing, social sciences, higher education, distance learning and office automation. Of these, seven completed all of the activities and obtained the certificate, one participant decided to split his curriculum over two years, two did not turn in all of their work (including the end-of-certificate work), and another withdrew because his project was no longer topical.

These students implemented a variety of projects: production of an e-portfolio related to identity and professional development; high-fidelity simulation lab for nursing; community of practice activities in the health domain; online course deployment, etc.

Depending on availability, an e-tutor was assigned to monitor one to four learners.

	eT1	eT2	eT3	eT4	eT5
Experience	First year	Third year	Fourth year	Second year	Fourth year
Number of learners	2 A1, A2	4 A3, A4, A5, A6	1 A7	2 A8, A9	2 A10, A11

Table 1.1. *Experiences of e-tutors and designated students*

1.6.1.2. *Method*

The data concerning the e-tutors' perspectives was collected via semi-structured interviews that lasted approximately a half-hour. The interviews were recorded and analyzed for contents targeted by our research question. We are concerned here with the e-tutors' reported practices and depictions.

From the recounted situations, we first investigated what e-tutors associated with the feeling of telepresence (or presence at a distance). Since the roadbook is the mediating artifact for communication between the e-tutor and the student, we have also collected some data related to this. Then, we asked the e-tutors about their perceptions about the impact of their interactions with students in order to see how they could, according to them, be connected to the feeling of telepresence. We also identified different conditions and limits for e-tutoring, situations experienced as positive or negative ("critical moment(s)"), the elements indicated as useful for the conservation or stimulation of motivation, engagement, and perseverance for the student and the e-tutor. The interview guide is found in the appendix.

1.6.2. *Limitations*

Different limitations can be identified as follows:

– other communication modalities between students and e-tutors exist in additional annotatable, shared documents, for example the exchange of e-mail. These texts were not subjected to content analysis; only the examples mentioned by the e-tutors having been taken into account;

– this exploratory study relies on a limited number of subjects, although all of the system's e-tutors were questioned;

– the content analysis could be deepened, and a triangulation of the data collection could be effectuated. The e-tutors' opinions should be related to those of the students.

1.7. Results

After having examined the interaction modalities (synchronous/asynchronous, in-person/remote) between e-tutors and students, as well as the media that supports them, we will present the clues provided by the answers to our research question.

1.7.1. *Interaction modalities and media*

In general, interactions were asynchronous and took place via the mediation of the roadbook, and, to a certain extent, by e-mail. The roadbook is generally a document written and shared in Google Docs, where all of the e-tutors (at least at the beginning) provided their comments and responded to questions. Thus, eT3 noted his replies in another color and added a comment about which the student was automatically notified (A7). For his part, eT3 used mail two or three times (lateness, recall or reply to an urgent question about work), in order to ensure "direct contact". On the contrary, eT4 did not use this process with A9; in the end, they decided to use a word processing document that A9 sent via e-mail, which allowed eT4 to note that the document had been updated. In his interactions with A10, eT5 used Google Docs and the comments mode, once by integrating chat, as well as a few contacts via email: "Collaborative publishing makes it very easy to get in touch in the same space. This decreases the constraints and makes it possible to get to the important things" (eT5). Furthermore, eT1 and eT2 used a shared directory (Dropbox) to access the roadbook. Only A11 never made an entry into the roadbook, despite reminders and rare exchanges with eT2.

In addition, some e-tutors (eT1 and eT4) had the opportunity to meet their students in person; we will return to this later. eT2 also received a request for a meeting from A6, but eT2 was not there when A6 came to the university. There were no other requests, "otherwise, I would have agreed to or been ready to respond to another request", she specified. We should note that one of the e-tutors mentioned that "the fact of talking without seeing the person isn't a limit – in fact, it's better. That way, we didn't base anything on the person's physical appearance" (eT3).

1.7.2. *Conditions and types of exchanges between e-tutors and students*

According to the tutors who were asked, the perception of a feeling of presence by the students depends on different variables, including the exchange modalities and the intervention types implemented.

1.7.2.1. *Conditions and types of exchange: e-tutor's proactivity or reactivity, pace of exchanges with the student*

According to e-tutors, the feeling of presence perceived by the student is linked to the latter and to the e-tutors' interventions. Thus, for example, as eT5 underlined: "It really depends how the instruction is going; I think that one student isn't like another; so the guidance can be completely different depending on the student's needs, and also depending on the tutor".

Some e-tutors were more or less proactive. One of them considered himself to be better situated for replying than for spontaneous interventions (as, for example, requests).

There were times when, in a concerted fashion, there was a relaxation of the pace of interactions (a pause for personal or professional reasons). Some had to contact their students repeatedly in order to maintain contact, with or without success. For most of the e-tutors, the pace of exchanges was weekly at the beginning of the training, then less frequently, or almost not at all, for some. The decrease in this pace generally depends more on the learner than on the e-tutors. On both sides, there were generally professional constraints that affect this pace. According to some e-tutors (eT3 and eT4), some students experienced an accumulation of constraints (full-time work, the MITPE project, family responsibilities, or even a change in professional circumstances).

The fact that there were no or few interactions during some periods may be due to the e-tutor and/or the student. Thus, an e-tutor was uncomfortable because she had forgotten to ask about her student. She went for two and a half months without thinking of getting in touch, although they had agreed on a two-week break. She told herself: "I didn't do my job … Maybe I missed a message." In the end, there had been no message. She wrote to her student to explain the situation and to say that she had "returned". The latter (A7) replied that she had as well, and their interactions started up again.

In addition, an e-tutor highlighted the necessary conditions for playing her part: having a minimum number of exchanges with the student. She did not get a response from one of her students, despite several attempts at contact: "I 'harassed' A11 through multiple means of communication for weeks […] A minimum response from the student is required!" (eT5). This same e-tutor underlined that "what is a bit difficult is this desire for availability that one places on oneself as a tutor." This causes a "degree of pressure on the tutor. Sometimes, it comes at an inconvenient time, when we're already swamped with something else; we'd like to reply in four hours, but time flies. This difficulty is a downside of availability."

Mutual engagement is considered to be the foundation for the eT–student relationship: "As in every system, a certain degree of engagement is required on the part of the student and the tutor [...] It's a prerequisite (as it is in person)" (eT5). Two e-tutors expressed their disappointment that they had not be notified personally that their student had withdrawn (report for the following year) (eT5 for A10) or that they would not complete the certificate at the end of the year (unsubmitted end-of-certificate work) (eT1 for A2).

The pace of exchanges was not mechanical. It could be affected by the e-tutor's perception of the need to communicate (risk of drop-out, student knowledge, etc.). With some students, the e-tutor can get the impression that his e-mails "lead to overload, although the goal is support."

In addition, the fact of encountering one's student from time to time (the case for eT4, who saw A8 during other classes) can diminish the number of interactions intended to show that the e-tutor is there and to communicate the idea that he can be relied on.

1.7.2.2. *Types of intervention and presence*

According to the questioned e-tutors, a minimum number of interactions are necessary to produce a feeling of presence and to perceive the proximity between e-tutors and students. These can be of different kinds: "socio-affective", "motivational", "cognitive" and "pedagogical" are the adjectives used to describe the e-tutor's telepresence.

1.7.2.2.1. Motivational or socio-affective support

For his part, eT5 described motivational support as a "feeling of framing, of feeling somewhat protected by the framework. Not feeling lonely about work, feeling supported, being followed up on, sustains motivation."

The e-tutor provides support in particular when the student indicates difficulties, for example, for personal reasons (such as "the need for time to devote to one's children, to take a break"). He shows himself to be comprehensive and tries to maintain motivation without putting on too much pressure.

This year, the e-tutors agreed that they had less recourse to socio-affective support than in other years.

1.7.2.2.2. Pedagogical or cognitive support: learning support

Some tutors describe their "cognitive or pedagogical" presence (eT1, eT2 and eT4). This consists of indicating to the student that he is going in the right direction in his work – without correcting them. In other cases, they provided explanations related to the course contents (or models), either in response to a request or after having observed an inaccurate understanding of the material. They replied to the questions that were asked, sometimes referring to other readings. Sometimes, the e-tutor transferred the question to the instructor or went back himself to the reading in order to reply.

The e-tutors also gave feedback about reflexivity, about the need to better organize one's thoughts or about the way in which ideas were presented. Pathways or suggestions regarding the project also came from e-tutors. These exchanges varied in depth depending on the e-tutor and the student in question.

The perception of presence was perceived in a bilateral manner following the sending of feedback and the student's reaction to it (eT1 and eT3).

1.7.3. *How do e-tutors provide the feeling of telepresence from a distance?*

E-tutors brought up different behaviors that are likely to achieve this kind of feeling.

1.7.3.1. *Initial contact*

The initial contact was considered to be very important. Sending a welcome message, introducing yourself, negotiating the way to communicate and to operate, etc. made it possible to begin the dialogue. The first contact in writing with the student provided the opportunity to adjust depending on the style of the individual's responses. This can also be achieved by showing a short introductory video for each e-tutor during the first in-person meeting. This makes it possible to show who is the e-tutor for each student: "They see their face and the way in which they speak." It is a jumping-off point for better coming to know each other.

One of the e-tutors went to meet his students at the beginning, during an in-person class session. He suggested making this a requirement at the beginning and at the end. This point of view was clarified by another: "A meeting with the person (in person), is good, but not necessarily right at the beginning. At the beginning, it's better to have an informal exchange; the video can also be useful for building an image of the e-tutor."

1.7.3.2. First-name basis between e-tutors and students: symmetrical, uninhibited and humane relationships

Three of the five e-tutors brought up the fact of being on a first-name basis with students as promoting the feeling of presence.

Thus, eT1 said he was there to share with the student. There is "no high position in relation to the student [...] We move forward together." The relationship was symmetrical (sharing information, questions, etc.). As for eT4, he considered that not being connected to the grading process put students at ease. The person was free to say whatever they want, which was very positive: "The relationship has to be friendly and uninhibited for it to work (for example, if the student wants to complain, about instructions – as during the previous year, during the remote, collaborative activity when one person in the group wasn't doing any work, not being afraid to complain, or even when it's about the instructor, if necessary, not being afraid to say so (as long as it's constructive) even though it can have an impact on grading" (eT4).

One of the eTs indicated that he wanted to show that he was as "humane as possible" (eT3). From the beginning, eT3 gave her students some personal information. She used simple and natural language, except when she provided explanations about theoretical points (reframing). However, how much can emotional proximity take hold? What should the e-tutor's reaction be when a student "recounts in an e-mail everything that's happening in his life?" (eT2).

1.7.4. Impact of the eT's interventions/interactions

The impact of instructional interventions was mixed. E-tutors sometimes found traces of it in the roadbook. They were asked about the role they played. These reflections hold clues for implementing "best practices" in e-tutoring.

1.7.4.1. *No or little impact*

One of the e-tutors did not have the same experience or perception as his students. With respect to one of them, he considered that he had "no impact with regard to his student's progress" (eT1). He attributed this to the fact that "she knew where she was going and how she was going to get there. She didn't need help, or even a welcome."

Another e-tutor did not know how to position herself for this year. The previous year, she had the impression that her interactions had a positive impact, that it had helped her students to get started and to ask herself questions. This time, she said she had submitted a question about a particular topic and proposed to the tutee to review part of the material, as well as providing complementary documents, but she "didn't find any trace of reply in the roadbook. Maybe 'the effects are visible in the work?'" (eT2). She didn't feel "seen as a source of support, but rather [as] a constraint." She felt she had "less influence on the students than during the previous year. The socio-affective link was barely present, even though it was initiated via e-mail." Nevertheless, she realized that other e-tutors must also have sent reminders.

Another situation: one student's roadbook was not structured, which did not comport with her e-tutor's work style. The latter's suggestion that she divide the roadbook into different parts was followed at first, but then the student "went back to a mix of ideas, sometimes with a small title." However, eT3 let her do as she wished, because she did not want to "impose her way of working."

For his part, eT4 considered that he had not "had a socio-affective impact", which "had been the case during the previous year" with his students.

1.7.4.2. *Perception of project progress and the student's reflection*

When the student's project advanced thanks to external support or to that from the e-tutor, the latter expressed positive feelings: "When there's a release, for example, A5 found external support" or "It's good news for her reflection and her work. She's moving forward, which makes me happy" (eT2).

The perception of the connections between the addressed content and the project bore witness to the student's evolution.

The effect of the e-tutor's interventions can be sources of gratification: "Any time you can make a comment and when you see that the person evolves afterward. When you ask a question to try to help them go a bit further in terms of reflexivity [...] afterward, this helps them take stock, to do something with it, to think; doing it over, I would do it like that. You see a change, a sort of added-value for your intervention. It's very gratifying" (eT5).

In addition, the positive comments formulated by his student concerning their remote interactions and the fact of having met during document exchange at the end of the year were positively perceived: "A7 came to see me, gave me feedback, she said I was great, that she had been helped, she had been able to stay on course..." (eT3).

1.7.4.3. Suggestions taken into account

With regard to improvements, eT1 suggested expanding the spectrum of A1's system by creating "video clips and adding the senses (five senses)." This had an impact on the pedagogical reflection supplied in the roadbook. This educator indicated that she "provided a critical eye at the pedagogical level", by putting her experience at the service of the student's responses. These interactions were followed by additions to the roadbook.

1.7.4.4. Project or conceptual clarification

When the e-tutor asked the student for an explanation of his project, he generally received a direct response, which probably led to a clarification of the project.

One of the e-tutors thought that he had an "impact, especially at the level of the learning process." He cited the example of A9, who had written a reflection about a model (systemic analysis). This learner asked herself a question and made a mistake about the model; eT4 intervened, and afterwards, this reflection was applied to her work: "At the level of content, she reused elements she asked me about". This e-tutor considered himself to be a "support for the learning process at the level of what is seen in the certificate."

For his part, eT5 picked up the case of a former student with whom he had interacted; these interactions had allowed him to monitor his project step by step. Furthermore, he had also, on this occasion, learned things (e.g. contents). In addition, "learning took place about the instruction and its benefits for students. It was very satisfying for both."

1.7.4.5. *Proximity to instructors*

Support from educators was indicated twice, particularly when there was no response or some doubt about the reaction: "A strength is the proximity to educators; the tutor knows that there will be a rapid response to his questions […], the e-tutor's support was comforting" (eT1).

1.7.4.6. *E-tutor's availability and reaction time*

Extensive availability and rapid reaction (without which he may miss the request) were among the e-tutor's strengths. It is nevertheless necessary to set certain limits on this point.

1.8. Discussion

Following the analysis of the words from the MITPE certificate e-tutors, a series of points concerning the feelings of telepresence and proximity were extracted.

As with other hybrid systems referred to as "ecosystems" in the typology by Burton *et al.* [BUR 11], a frequent and diverse use of technological tools by the students was established. The remote interactions with the e-tutor did not escape from this. In this frame, they were supported by different tools for communications (e.g. e-mail) and production (such as an online shared document). Because the choice of these tools and the way of using them were negotiated at the beginning between the learner and the e-tutor, they could be used to engage the telepresence relationship; this can be accomplished as soon as the first meeting.

As one might expect, the students each had their own characteristics. One student was not like another. Some were more proactive than others and engaged more or less intensely in the relationship with their e-tutor. This intensity also varied at different times. The pace of these exchanges, which was weekly on average at the beginning of the training, sometimes became more infrequent for some students. Individual variables (personal or professional, project, individual characteristics) [CHA 98] explained some of these situations. Thus, the student's scheduling constraints or workload can become obstacles to good progress in terms of interactions and the development of a close link with their e-tutor. A climate of confidence can subsequently be difficult to establish between them. If the student does not take advantage of the opportunity for support from his e-tutor or does not perceive his roles and his benevolent character, the feeling of telepresence or proximity will probably not be produced, which can go hand in hand with the student's disengagement from the training process.

It is therefore the responsibility of the e-tutor to perceive and to take into account what is happening remotely, outside of the activities during which the students encounter their teachers, in order to create this proximity and to not ruin the student's feeling of telepresence, confidence and support, and thus to avoid potential disengagement [JAC 93]. Therefore, during the eT's internal training, the e-tutors are required to be proactive. It is the e-tutor who, if the student does not send out signs of life, does not meet expectations with regard to reflexivity or does not dare to ask via the roadbook (or another means of sharing and communication), should connect with the student, show signs of presence and re-describe his roles in relation to the latter.

The requirement for regular filling out of the roadbook aims to coordinate the tutoring relationship. Nevertheless, this regularity can be the subject, in a concerted manner between the two parties, of a certain degree of flexibility. This bore witness to a close link between the e-tutor and the student, a relationship of confidence that is being woven. This relationship was also established when the e-tutor showed himself comprehensively (psychological and emotional presence) when the student indicated he was having difficulties. The feeling of telepresence was also expressed through a contextualized, proactive instruction, that is, when the e-tutor detected a problematic situation [GOU 04] and reacted to it spontaneously, e.g. by correcting an error of comprehension of the material. In fact, in distance education as in other learning situations, the more feedback that is provided immediately, the more it is appreciated for pursuing and progressing in what has been begun.

E-tutors noted that some students developed a reflexive process easily enough, and also that others had difficulty, or did not see the utility, or at least a need to formalize it. Lenoir [LEN 12] highlighted that reflexive practice is "linguistic: it occurs through words, which can be interior; dialogic: one can't reflect without talking to someone else, which can also be another 'self' (interior language); and social: the result of social interaction, including when I speak to myself". Sometimes, a simple prompt was enough to kick off this metacognitive process and to share, via the roadbook, their perspective about their learning styles with the e-tutor. This process, recommended by the system's designers and educators and supported by the e-tutor, bore witness to a certain degree of proximity between the student and himself. It is nevertheless necessary to remember that a reflexive practice is not the prerogative of all. To develop it, several tracks of questions were supplied (such as the roadbook framework), brought up, and sometimes even expanded on by the e-tutors. As for the latter, as one of them mentioned, deepening their training with regard to reflexive analysis would probably be an asset for better meeting this objective.

In addition, knowing the students' projects well and being attentive to their personal characteristics (e.g. editorial style, domain) as well as their evolution stimulated the feeling of presence at a distance. Several e-tutors called their students by first name and vice versa, which bore witness to a certain familiarity and proximity. From there to thinking, as some e-tutors do, that an uninhibited and symmetrical relationship could be established between e-tutors and students, particularly when the e-tutor is not responsible for student evaluations, and that each could learn from the other, opinions diverge. This opinion is not held by all of their colleagues or by some students. Although andragogical principles and the choice of a socio-constructivist approach, which underlie this training system, encourage the establishment of symmetrical relationships and an egalitarian climate in which "opinions, ideas, personalities, and behaviors can be different, but [in which] each person thinks that the opinions and ideas of the other deserve respect and attention" and where the educational relationship "is underpinned by the desire to understand the other's point of view, to incorporate as one the situation's important elements" [BAG 12], the fact remains that these two kinds of actors have separate roles that will also tend to characterize their complementary and hierarchical relationships. In effect, students may feel a hierarchy, for example because the e-tutor's task is to monitor anything that is implicated in his learning process and his project, to stimulate metacognitive behaviors in this regard, or even because they consider that the e-tutors have recognized competencies with regard to using and implementing ICTEs, competencies that their students are in the process of acquiring or developing.

In addition, if, in some situations, e-tutors question themselves about the kind of behavior to adopt in a situation, they consult the "eT reference profile" approved at the beginning of the training. They often found an answer to their questions there; if not, they spoke to the coordinator or presented their questions during meetings between e-tutors and the supervisory staff. The latter were perceived positively, because they made it possible not only to take stock of the students' progress, but also to deliver their questions, and to compare their points of view with other eTs as well as with teachers. This proximity to the teachers was highlighted as a strength of the system. The e-tutor felt supported as a participant in a community of tutors.

1.9. Conclusion and perspectives

This exploratory study reveals a series of factors that, according to e-tutors, contribute to the feeling of telepresence at a distance. E-tutors experienced and considered the development of a feeling of presence thanks to the pedagogical, cognitive or socio-affective support that they provided to their students.

The questions asked during interviews with e-tutors made it possible to extract and reinforce the roles taken on by the latter with regard to their students, as well as to understand some conditions, inputs and limits of e-instruction in this system. Tracks for developing or maintaining a feeling of telepresence and proximity with oneself (reflexivity) emerging from the interactions between the e-tutors and students have been extracted.

All of the e-tutors considered themselves trained for the tasks assigned to them. As necessary, they referred to the e-tutor's intervention profile that they had decided to adopt. Their feeling of effectiveness varied depending on the student under consideration. Sometimes they saw a real impact following their interactions with students, and sometimes none or little. The complexity due to context and individual variables, primarily with regard to the students, partly explains this impression.

The mediatization process that constituted the creation of a roadbook, a tool that was seen as providing an opportunity that could be used in order to develop signs of presence (the supervisor being thus "psychologically" [JAC 93] or "mentally" [JAC 02] present, all while being physically absent), only partially supported its results. Some tracks can be envisaged for structuring it, all while leaving some freedom to the learner as to how to complete it. Nevertheless, technological mediatization, by itself, will not make it possible to develop the students' competencies with regard to the reflexive analysis of their practices. The task of putting in place and stimulating a reflexive process, an activity that was still relatively unfamiliar to some students, relied primarily on the e-tutor. Following the latters' training process, in order to share their observations about reflexivity and the ways to arouse it in students, can probably influence the maintenance of the roadbook in the way that the designers and teachers of the system expect.

The observations reported in this study are far from generalizable. It is important to take into account the aforementioned limits, particularly with regard to triangulating data collection and analysis. In fact, in a hybrid system where students meet infrequently and manage their activities in the framework of their project, interactions with the e-tutor are so important in supporting their progress.

1.10. Appendix: e-tutor interview guide

In the presentation of the results, in order to focus on the present research question, some data has not been used. Thus, the responses to question 5 are only partially included. The responses to some questions have been consolidated (Q 11 and 12 with Q 6). In addition, the questions concerning eT training and a review of the implementation of their interventions were not addressed in this study.

1) Do you think the eT (in MITPE, in your case, with this year's students) created a feeling of "telepresence" or "presence at a distance"? (N.B. as planned/experienced).

2) If the feeling of presence existed: was it felt by students? Thanks to what?

- Specify the type(s) of presence engendered by your interventions (pedagogical/affective/cognitive presence + examples).

3) How was this feeling of presence transmitted?

4) What are the modalities of this telepresence? (Tools? Contents? Pace of exchanges?).

5) Were the interactions via the roadbook more or less regular with your students, according to you?

    - Was filling out the roadbook perceived as necessary by students? Or just "obligatory"?

    - E-learner's points of view on the maintenance of the roadbook? What meaning did they attribute to it? (utility, value of the task, ease)

6) What is according to you, the impact of your interactions with your students?

    - At the level of...

    - Links to the feeling of presence at a distance.

7) What are, according to you, the conditions for optimal e-instruction?

8) What are, according to you, the limits of e-tutoring in this learning environment (MITPE)? Furthermore (e.g. in the TAD certificate), was this different?

9) What is your training as an e-tutor?

10) Can you locate yourself in relation to the list of reference behaviors established together? (See the consensual profile)

    - Check the list, comment on it.

    - Adjustments to contribute?

11) Can you mention a moment or a difficult situation you experienced during your tutoring?

    - Illustrate it.

    - How was it overcome or resolved?

12) Can you describe a moment or situation of abundance about eTs?

1.11. References

[BAG 12] BAGUETTE C., SEUTIN C., KERSTENN F. *et al.*, "Les relations symétriques et complémentaires", *Espace d'échanges sur la systémique du site IDRES*, 2012, accessed October 2017 at: http://www.systemique.be/spip/spip.php?article810.

[BRA 14] BRASSARD C., TEUTSCH P., "Proposition de critères de proximité pour l'analyse des dispositifs de formation médiatisée", *Distances et médiations des savoirs*, vol. 5, 2014.

[BUR 11] BURTON R., BORRUAT S., CHARLIER B. *et al.*, "Vers une typologie des dispositifs hybrides de formation en enseignement supérieur", *Distance et savoirs*, vol. 1, no. 9, pp. 69–96, 2011.

[CAR 92] CARRÉ P., PEARN M., *L'autoformation dans l'entreprise*, Éditions Entente, Paris, 1992.

[CHA 98] CHARLIER B., *Apprendre et changer sa pratique d'enseignement : expériences d'enseignants*, De Boeck, Brussels, 1998.

[DEN 03] DENIS B., "Quels rôles et quelle formation pour les tuteurs intervenant dans des dispositifs de formation à distance ?", *Distances et savoirs*, vol. 1, no. 1, pp. 19–46, 2003.

[DEN 06] DENIS B., VANDEPUT E., "Le scénario pédagogique : outil d'expression des compétences TOP des enseignants. Scénariser l'enseignement et l'apprentissage : une nouvelle compétence pour le praticien ?", *8ᵉ Biennale de l'éducation*, Lyon, France, 11–14 April 2006.

[GOU 04] GOUNON P., LEROUX P., DUBOURG X., "Proposition d'un modèle de tutorat pour la conception de dispositifs d'accompagnement en formation en ligne", *Revue internationale des technologies en pédagogie universitaire*, vol. 1, no. 3, pp. 14–33, 2004.

[JAC 93] JACQUINOT G., "Apprivoiser la distance et supprimer l'absence ? ou les défis de la formation à distance", *Revue française de pédagogie*, vol. 102, pp. 55–67, 1993.

[JAC 02] JACQUINOT G., "Absence et présence dans la médiation pédagogique ou comment faire circuler les signes de la présence", in GUIR R. (ed.), *Pratiquer les TICE. Former les enseignants et les formateurs à de nouveaux usages*, pp. 104–113, De Boeck, Brussels, 2002.

[JÉZ 10] JÉZÉGOU A., "Créer de la présence à distance en e-learning. Cadre théorique, définitions et dimensions clés", *Distances et savoirs*, vol. 8, no. 2, pp. 257–274, 2010.

[LEB 08] LEBRUN M., DESCHRYVER N., CHARLIER B. *et al.*, "Learn-Nett, un réseau pour la formation des enseignants. Une communauté de pratique ?", in C. CHARNET, C. GHERSI, J.-L. MONINO (eds), *Le défi de la qualité dans l'enseignement supérieur : vers un changement de paradigme-XXVe colloque de l'Association internationale de pédagogie universitaire (AIPU)*, Montpellier, France, 19–22 May 2008.

[LEC 00] LECLERCQ D., Dispositifs d'Apprentissage et Modèles Appliqués aux Nouvelles Technologies (DIAMANT), internal document, Service de technologie de l'éducation, Université de Liège, 2000.

[LEC 98] LECLERCQ D., DENIS B., JANS V. *et al.*, "L'amphithéâtre électronique. Une application : le LQRT-SAFE", in LECLERCQ D. (ed.), *Pour une pédagogie universitaire de qualité*, pp. 161–186, Éditions Mardaga, Liège, 1998.

[LEN 12] LENOIR Y., "Réfléchir dans et sur sa pratique, une nécessité indispensable", Université de Sherbrooke, 2012, accessed January 2018 at: https ://www.usherbrooke.ca/crcie/fileadmin/sites/.../Analyse_re__flexive-Outil1.pdf.

[MAI 08] MAILLES-VIARD METZ S., ALBHERNE-GIORDAN H., "Du e-portfolio à l'analyse du produit et du processus de conception du projet personnel de l'étudiant", *Revue internationale des technologies en pédagogie universitaire*, vol. 5, no. 3, pp. 51–65, 2008.

[PAQ 11] PAQUELIN D., "La distance : questions de proximités", *Distances et savoirs*, vol. 9, no. 4, pp. 565–590, 2011, DOI : 10.3166/ds.9.565-590

[PER 11] PERAYA D., "Un regard sur la "distance", vue de la "présence"", *Distances et savoirs*, vol. 9, no. 3, pp. 445–452, 2011.

[PER 14] PERAYA D., "Distances, absence, proximités et présences : des concepts en déplacement", *Distances et médiations des savoirs*, vol. 8, 2014, accessed June 2017 at: http://dms.revues.org/865.

[ROD 10] RODET J., "Propositions pour l'ingénierie tutorale", *Tutorales*, vol. 7, pp. 9–22, 2010.

[ROD 11] RODET J., "De la proximité en formation à distance", *JRodet Conseil : digital learning,* 2011, accessed January 2018 at: https://sites.google.com/site/jacquesrodet/Home/essai/delaproximiteenformationadistance.

Reinforcing Telepresence in Research Training with Learning Communities: Remote Collaboration between Student-Researchers

2.1. Introduction

The importance of research training in postgraduate education has elicited particular interest from several researchers in education science, as suggested by the growing number of publications on the subject [BAP 11, BUT 05, DEU 08, MAN 07, TAH 12]. Important practical efforts have also been dedicated to the improvement of its quality. A large part of the literature relative to research training has emphasized the complexity of supervising student work [LEE 07]. Some studies have focused on questions such as the vague, different and sometimes incompatible expectations of students and teachers [CAD 00], problems in interpersonal relationships between them [IVE 05], the diversity of roles filled by teachers [LEE 08], the absence of policies or guidelines to help students [KIM 14] and the feeling of isolation experienced by the latter [IRA 14]. These difficulties seem to intensify when the training takes place in a distance learning context.

From the outset, it is necessary to shed light on what we are calling a "student-researcher". For us, he/she is a researcher-in-training undertaking, with the supervision of research director, a project whose duration varies

Chapter written by Gustavo ANGULO and Cathia PAPI.

from country to country, the area of study, as well as several personal and professional factors. The student-researcher (we will also use the term "apprentice-researcher") must be enrolled in a graduate degree program, that is, a master's program or a doctorate. By writing a master's thesis or doctoral dissertation, graduate students reconstruct the work carried out as part of their research project.

Literature about research training takes into account the difficulties encountered by students who are being initiated into the profession of academic researcher, especially when they produce a thesis or dissertation. In effect, the student's passage from student to apprentice-researcher is not painless for most, because they lack experience regarding scholarly research and often undertake their projects with impressions that are not always a good fit with the reality of academic research. This lack of awareness about the scientific process often leads to difficulties in the conduct of research projects and the fulfillment of master's theses.

In general, three categories of difficulties associated with training in the research process in higher education can be identified. The first type of difficulty is related to the affective dimension. In this category, we find, for example, feelings of isolation and lack of self-confidence. The second category is related to the complexity inherent in the definition of the research project and, consequently, of the documentary research process. The third category includes difficulties associated with the writing of scholarly texts and, in general, of all kinds of scientific communications. These difficulties partially explain the late submission of theses [AHE 04] and the low graduation rate [RIT 12], particularly in graduate-level distance programs [JEP 04].

Writing a thesis requires competencies in methodology, which are not developed before the graduate level [WIS 03]. Similarly, it is necessary to exercise resilience to failures and tolerance of ambiguity, which are essential personal skills for the development of a critical and creative work. [LOV 05]. The formulation of a thesis also requires perseverance in an uncertain activity [STY 00], which will only seem correctly done at the end of the process and for which we only have a few referents [CAR 05]. In effect, the completion of a thesis is an iterative process [MON 08] that presupposes exchanges about intermediary texts with interlocutors well versed in the art of research. The process requires repeated revisions of our work and considering the norms of the research culture in the field. This is even more difficult for the neophyte researcher because of his/her inexperience as scholarly author. As a result, relying on feedback from people who are similar to the target reading audience for the thesis will help develop the communication competencies of the student-researcher.

In this context, peer support in a community has been examined as a support strategy [FOR 08, GRE 06, PAL 10]. It fosters horizontal feedback, which contributes to the identification and resolution of problems in student research projects and the textual products with which they are associated. It also creates a safe space for submitting their work for verification by an audience, which thus becomes a "testbed". It propels the co-creation of criteria for self-management of work quality. Finally, it encourages the interaction between peers to compensate for the lack of a support context among apprentice-researchers [BAN 03, HOR 03].

We thus propose to focus on the challenges raised by the fulfillment of graduate research work (i.e. masters in Québec or master 2 in Europe), and to problematize the perspective of collaboration between student-researchers in learning communities by shedding light on the multidimensional approach to the concept of distance proposed by Jacquinot [JAC 93], and then to present the difficulties that pedagogical distance can induce and the way research has addressed the issue of creating presence as an attempt to reduce this distance.

2.2. Multidimensional approach to distance learning

The fundamental objective of distance learning (DL) is to make training programs accessible to the public that encounters obstacles to attending learning institutions at fixed times [MOO 11]. Distance learning is characterized by spatial distance between the teacher and students, as well as between the latter and their peers, which entails a variable degree of asynchronicity between teaching and learning activities [GLI 02]. This spatio-temporal representation of distance has been the traditional framework used to analyze pedagogical phenomena that take place in the context of distance learning [PER 11].

In a paper that has strongly inspired reflection on the subject, Jacquinot [JAC 93] recognized several distances that have been derived from a rupture of spatial co-presence between the teacher and students. Other dimensions of distance are added to previously mentioned geographic and temporal distances, which can be technological, socio-cultural, socio-economic or pedagogical. Although they impose constraints, these distances also bring advantages that provoke innovations in the pedagogical relationship [JAC 10]. The challenge is then to "tame" them because they seem to bring added value; however, at the same time, they are likely to have counterproductive effects. Let us discuss some aspects associated with these distances.

Geographic and temporal distances facilitate access to resources independent of place and time, but they also require a high degree of self-regulation, a competence that is not always sufficiently developed in beginners of distance learning. Thus, much importance is given to the management of temporal distance between requests from the student and replies from the institution [JAC 93]. Therefore, synchronous meetings, whether they are F2F or virtual, are multiplying at the expense of the flexibility associated with asynchronicity in distance learning. Nevertheless, they are considered to be a key element of support and a determinant of student success [MCB 09]. This dichotomy between the flexibility on which many projects are based and the constraints imposed by synchronous meetings was reported by Peraya [PER 14] as one of the limits of distance learning.

Jacquinot [JAC 93] also described a technological distance between the development of tools (both hardware and software) and pedagogical needs. This distance seems to be more significant these days, considering the accelerated evolution of technological scenarios. However, the potential of distance learning relies not only on the availability of technological solutions, but also on the potential for adapting them to pedagogical needs and integrating them pertinently into learning scenarios [PER 06].

Relative to socio-cultural and socio-economic distances, the will to reduce these gaps has provided the foundation for distance open universities. In principle, they target the public that is ill-suited to traditional modes of education, or even excluded from the system, particularly at the higher education level. However, in fact, most of individuals who have benefited from the advantages of distance learning already have a certain level of university training and are opting for this training modality in order to further specialize in a field [CHR 13, POM 14].

Pedagogical distance refers to the distance between the sources of knowledge and information and those who want to learn and assimilate them [JAC 93]. In other words, pedagogical distance is defined as the non-presence of the mediators of knowledge or learning, particularly of students or the teacher. This concept brings together the central idea of the theory of transactional distance [MOO 11]: distance is not simply a question of geographical separation but also primarily a pedagogical phenomenon. What is important is the effect of this separation, particularly regarding the interaction between students and the teacher, on the design of pedagogical systems and on the organization of human and technological resources.

Our interest is focused on this distance because it is at the heart of the pedagogical relationship. However, it seems to be difficult to reduce it given the interdependence of the different dimensions of distance [TRO 10]. Thus, one of the major challenges of distance learning consists of finding a balance between these dimensions while maintaining a tolerable level of pedagogical distance. Several questions are raised in this regard: what are the potentially harmful elements of this distance, and how can their effects be mitigated? What benefits can it bring? How can we take advantage of these potential advantages? In what way can we negotiate a compromise between the threats and the opportunities that it includes? Let us examine the way in which creating presence in distance learning has been explored as a potential solution for the difficulties engendered by pedagogical distance.

2.3. Modulating pedagogical distance: what presence should be created?

The concept of distance on which the DL phenomenon is founded thus encompasses several meanings. The pedagogical dimension of this distance is the subject of our interest, given the strong influence it exercises on the learning experience. We show here the difficulties that pedagogical distance can induce, and we will also examine the way in which research has tackled the issue of creating presence in distance learning as an attempt to reduce pedagogical distance.

Pedagogical distance, which is considered as limited access to educational resources, includes all of the dimensions that increase the perception of distance from the sources of knowledge as well as the communication gap between people who take part in the learning experience

[JÉZ 02]. The scale of this gap is a function of the degree of educational dialogue, on the one hand, and of the structure level, on the other hand. Consequently, pedagogical distance determines the level of autonomy required from students in order to modulate this distance [BOU 00].

The student's autonomy refers to the capacity to make decisions concerning his/her own learning process. The promotion of skills such as self-managing the learning process, resource seeking and self-evaluation of progress can be a quality criterion for distance learning programs [MOO 11]. A certain level of pedagogical distance is therefore tolerable, or even desirable, because it favors the development of the student's autonomy as well as self-management competencies [JÉZ 08].

However, a high level of pedagogical distance can bring about a certain number of difficulties. For example, Baker [BAK 10] noted that a low perception of immediacy and of pedagogical presence is a predictor of discouragement. Sahin [SAH 07] observed a relationship between an insufficient level of support and student dissatisfaction. Sun, Tsai, Finger, Chen and Yeh [SUN 08] added other factors that lead to student dissatisfaction: the student's attitude towards distance learning as well as the low perception of relevance to teaching and evaluation.

Several studies, for example, by Martz, Reddy, and Sagermano [MAR 04] or Starr-Glass [STA 13], have suggested that a low level of interaction with the teacher and peers is the main determinant of the degree of pedagogical distance. These studies have stated that the communication gap between students and between them and the teacher can lead to disengagement from a meaningful learning process. Similarly, Chang and Kang [CHA 16] stated that a lack of interaction is the main impediment to the development of the ability to work in a team. In his study, Rovai [ROV 02] reported that the feeling of isolation is considered to be one of the harmful consequences of neglecting pedagogical distance.

The measure of pedagogical distance is therefore a function of the degree of presence and the activity of valid interlocutors in a learning experience. It is a question of modulating absence; in other words, it is a question of ensuring an adequate level of presence in the learning environment that makes it possible to overcome the difficulties brought about by pedagogical distance without compromising the autonomy and self-management of students. Thus, educational environments used in distance learning are likely to make it possible to "tame distance" [JAC 93] by using synchronous and asynchronous communication modes and, having done so, to disseminate social interaction between actors in these environments [JÉZ 12]. This vision of distance learning relies on the principle stating that presence results "from some forms of social interaction between students and between the teacher and the students when the latter are engaged in a remote, collaborative process within a digital communication space" [JÉZ 10, p. 259].

Research confirms that the feeling of membership in a community can not only modulate the level of pedagogical distance that is considered to be acceptable, but also favor perseverance in studies, the flow of information between students, the availability of support, the engagement with the group's objectives, the cooperation between members of the group and satisfaction regarding the group's efforts [BEN 05, FOU 03, LEE 06, LOI 14]. Furthermore, participation in a community allows students to benefit from a socio-affective climate that is favorable to social and emotional projection through the intermediary of the means of communication used [GAR 00]. This social dimension of presence in distance learning is influenced by the context of communication (including factors such as motivation, familiarity, skills, engagement and activities) as well as the usage time of media.

Arbaugh [ARB 08] suggested that in an online or hybrid training experience, a deep and meaningful learning process is built within the community by the interaction between the social, cognitive and educational dimensions of presence. Thus, the reinforcement of presence in distance learning using learning communities seems to be a plausible strategy to operate the levers and brakes associated with pedagogical distance.

According to Arbaugh, the social dimension of presence in a learning community includes three elements: open communication, emotional expression and group cohesion [ARB 08]. Open communication is associated with the creation of an environment that is conducive to free expression. In order for social presence to thrive, students should feel free to express themselves openly [GAR 08]. Emotional expression refers to the sharing of emotions and camaraderie [GAR 08]. Humor and self-disclosure are two examples of emotional expression in a community. Group cohesion and interaction both concern social presence and the learning process

[ARB 05]. Collaborative learning activities favor the establishment of social presence and the reinforcement of community [RIC 03, ROV 02].

Nevertheless, social interaction is insufficient to attain the pedagogical objectives of a learning community. The highest levels of learning require rich discussion in order for the students to engage in a reflexive and continuous discourse leading to the construction, confirmation and critical reflection of meaning [GAR 07]. This cognitive dimension of presence is the central element of critical thinking, which is considered to be a process as well as a major outcome of teaching in higher education [GAR 07]. Four phases of increasing complexity characterize cognitive presence: first, an initiating event allows the participants to recognize a problem and to question themselves; second, students use several sources of information to explore problems, exchange ideas and discuss ambiguities; third, by participating in learning activities, students integrate ideas, create solutions and reflect on content; and finally, in the resolution phase, they describe the applications of created knowledge.

Arbaugh [ARB 07] identified the development of cognitive presence as the most demanding of the three dimensions of presence. To go beyond the exploration phase and in order to attain the highest levels of thought, Meyer [MEY 04] suggested strategies such as the establishment of a discussion schedule, moderation of the discussion and modeling, which leads the discussion to the educational dimension of presence.

The educational dimension of presence, for its part, is defined as "the design, facilitation, and orientation of the cognitive and social process with the goal of producing learning outcomes that are personally meaningful and pedagogically valid" [AND 01]. The educational process starts before the beginning of the learning experience with its planning, and continues for the entire experience with the roles of facilitation and orientation.

Our reflection draws its origin, therefore, on the one hand, from the results of research that suggest that collaborative work within a community can favor the negotiation of a compromise between the threats and opportunities that pedagogical distance brings. On the other hand, our questions are rooted in the need to manage non-presence in the context of distance research training. Having already elucidated the first elements of the problem, let us now discuss the difficulties connected to remote support of student-researchers.

2.4. Increasing presence in the research learning process through distance learning: how to problematize collaboration between student-researchers at a distance?

We have examined the way in which research has explored the encouragement of participation in communities as a means for "taming" pedagogical distance. Let us now look at the difficulties relative to learning about the scientific research process in postgraduate education, particularly in the context of distance learning.

Over the last few decades, teaching in higher education has experienced a large increase in part-time students, partly because of the rapid expansion of distance learning and so-called "open" universities [EVA 02, EVA 04]. For the faculty, this has led to difficulties related to the remote supervision of student research [MIT 08]. These difficulties can arise from personal, emotional or psychological problems, and can be associated with the teaching style offered or even be specific to the research.

Learning to conduct research at the postgraduate level is a complex process that includes several dimensions and that poses major challenges for students and the teachers supervising them; moreover, pedagogical distance can act as a catalyst for difficulties relative to the research learning process [SIL 16].

One of the challenges endemic to research training in higher education lies in the establishment and maintenance of fruitful relationships between supervisors and student-researchers [MAI 09]. F2F exchanges are generally perceived as being essential for constructing such a relationship [KLE 12]. However, productive, remote relationships have always been established in scholarly communities [STE 95], and the exchange of ideas, thoughts and data, founded on the written tradition, allows members of these communities to share and debate their work. Research training in postgraduate education consists in part of introducing the student to the practices of the scholarly community; nowadays, this includes the use of current means of communication [LEE 08].

Florida [FLO 03] asserted that although modern and "creative" knowledge-based economies function through communication technologies by relativizing spatio-temporal limits, context remains a vital element for members of these societies and communities. If they can have robust professional and social relationships online, their daily existence is rooted in the particular context where they live. This dichotomy suffuses teaching in postgraduate education in general; nevertheless, the balance is different for distance learning in postgraduate education [NAS 14].

The difficulties related to pedagogical distance can be a major obstacle even for the most motivated students. Because of its very specific and specialized orientation, research in postgraduate education relies on a base of reading, thinking and writing that are primarily solitary [MIL 02]. It is clear that the sense of isolation felt by students and supervisors can be deeper in the context of distance learning [WIL 11], although it can be intense enough for any student in a master's or doctoral program [JSM 11]. In higher education, success relies as much on the capacity for sustained, systematic and solitary efforts as on intellectual aptitude.

Thus, the challenge consists of exploring the relationship needs of remote student-researchers in order to offer appropriate strategies for networking and support. Evans *et al.* [EVA 04] suggested that the strategies that work best with undergraduate students off campus will not be as fruitful for some students in postgraduate education. The possibilities they offer for connection are considered to be insufficient, and the frequency of requests is considered to be excessive. Therefore, support mechanisms for student-researchers should be able to respond to a wide variety of needs and expectations [NOR 13]. To this end, there can be no formula that subordinates the practices, personalities and values of the people involved in the student–supervisor relationship. Several systems rely largely on the capacity of the supervisor to interpret, adapt and successfully direct the demands of this relationship [ELE 09, KET 09, LEE 07, LEE 11, REM 12, WIS 12].

Support for learning about the research process in the context of distance learning thus constitutes a very promising research direction that includes the analysis of the needs of student-researchers and their supervisors as well as the design of practical frames of reference. These approaches should reflect the nature of higher education, the diversity of the interests of students and supervisors, and the particularities of the relevant field of study.

In order to reduce the effect of difficulties relative to the process of learning how to conduct scientific research, several solutions have been explored: for example, training professors how to supervise research, training students in research methods and changing supervisory approaches to increase presence (see, for example, [NOR 13]). The models for directing research work founded on a group approach are increasingly being investigated in doctoral studies [BOU 05, CRO 08, FLO 12, FOR 08, GRE 06, OLS 09, PAL 10, PAR 09, WEG 16, WIS 07], where the literature reveals a growing tendency to encourage the collaborative approach for research training, while such studies remain rare in master's level programs [CHO 14, JOH 95, WIC 14].

The relationship between the student and the supervisor in remote research training constitutes a very interesting path for exploration. This also applies to the construction and maintenance of a learning community within postgraduate education. In effect, such communities can be considered as a bridge towards scholarly communities in the disciplinary fields of students [ROC 12]. We can assume that the construction of communities of remote student-researchers is similar to the construction of other learning communities. However, in this regard, Parker [PAR 09] suggested that pedagogical approaches in postgraduate education operate in a significantly different way.

It is important to recognize that students in postgraduate education are people with a high level of education. For students pursuing research-oriented master's programs, passing tests in traditional courses is generally not particularly difficult [LOV 05]. On the contrary, they face a greater challenge concerning the fulfillment of research work whose final project will be evaluated by members of the scientific community. Munich [MUN 14] affirmed that student-researchers appreciate activities that support their research project, but that they do not like activities that seem incidental to the pursuit of their objectives.

Studies carried out with doctoral students [FOR 08, GRE 06, LEE 06, PAL 10] have suggested that student-researchers are generally very receptive to community activities that include authentic and fruitful tasks, and that they are, on the contrary, generally reticent about participating in activities that only serve to construct community. In order to develop effective support strategies, there exists a rich potential for research on expertise, needs and orientations of master's students at a distance, as well as on the relationship that they adopt with their studies.

The development of research programs in postgraduate education in the context of distance learning entails an understanding of the nature of higher-level study and expected production by students. These products are very different from those conducted in class [LOV 05]. In effect, research training entails significant individual efforts, even in laboratory science, where a student's research is part of a team project. Essentially, a student in a research-oriented master's program should apply theoretical knowledge and methodological competencies to undertake a study with scientific rigor [MON 08]. Although making an original contribution to knowledge is not a *sine qua non* condition for the master's thesis (Quebec) or the master 2 (Europe), the student must show that he/she is capable of directing scientific research with precision.

The development of learning communities in a remote postgraduate program should thus recognize the tension that exists between a communal exercise and the individualist imperative to appropriate knowledge and research know-how in the relevant domain [SAM 06]. As a result, in the construction of a community of remote student-researchers, the needs of the members and the requirements that are imposed on them must be organized within the process and the materials, as well as in different personal, social and professional contexts [DYS 06]. These questions constitute a growing area of research in diverse disciplines and domains.

Several aspects of these communities of apprentice researchers draw our attention. Thus, the problem can be posed in several ways. First, the effect of peers on the progressive improvement of student learning and on the latter's autonomy is a subject that previous researchers have not examined thoroughly. Are these communities temporary structures that support students in the development of high-level competencies required for scientific researchers? Can interaction with peers compensate for the effects of transactional distance between the student and the experienced researcher?

Second, the complementarity of individual and community approaches is an aspect that has been minimally tackled until now [DYS 06, SAM 06]. Student research projects often address fairly distinct subjects. Nevertheless, they often experience the same difficulties and share uncertainty about the scientific research process. In what way can a community complement personalized supervision provided by the professor?

Third, several questions arise concerning the professor's role in the community. Knowledge of the degree of negotiation in teaching presence between the professor and students remains insufficient. What level of structure should be provided? What are the effects of a pedagogical design that can be adapted to the pace and needs of the student or of a fixed structure with, for example, established activities and a meeting calendar? The literature does not make reference to the institutional status of these communities. Should their implementation be recorded in the faculty policy or should it be the professor's discretionary decision-making?

Fourth, several essential aspects associated with the perception of utility of these systems deserve further analysis. Several studies on the interaction between students in online training systems have highlighted a low interest level among many students in communicating with their peers [AND 05, AND 10, CHO 09, ISA 06, POE 06]. In this context, how can we sustain a rich and productive dialogue within the community? How can active participation, engagement and the appropriation of the learning space be encouraged? In what way can the most reticent students be persuaded to participate in work within the community?

Several other elements have not been sufficiently studied, such as the heterogeneity of skills acquired as researchers, the difference in the pace of each member's learning process, the dissimilarity of perspectives with regard to collaborative work, as well as their impact on the community's effectiveness. In order to take advantage of this plurality, it will be necessary to adapt a model of peer support. As a hypothesis, the proximity of students who are at a more advanced stage of the program will facilitate the acquisition of knowledge and the development of competencies for inexperienced students, and consequently will reduce the transactional distance from the professor.

Another aspect that has been insufficiently addressed refers to the limits of collaboration in a context that is often characterized by competition, such as higher education. We must recall that research positions are not numerous, especially in the university environment. This foments rivalry between people pursuing the same goal, which does not always fit, let us admit it, with collaboration, sharing and mutual aid. This deserves questioning: where is the border situated between community support and personal affirmation independent of others? At what point does a peer stop being a comrade and become an opponent?

With respect to the integration of technology into interaction systems for student-researchers, a literature review allowed us to highlight that research in this field emphasizes four purposes on which these structures are based [PAP 17]. First, some studies have emphasized that these techno-pedagogical systems aim to reduce the difficulties related to the geographic dispersal of peers [SLO 14, SUS 06]. Second, online communities of researchers in training are considered to be strategies to enhance the learning experience [WIL 11]. Third, establishing a relationship between apprentice-researchers, which is made possible by communication technologies, is explored as a way to break isolation by supporting interaction [KEV 13]. Finally, the design of some of these systems relies on their potential to support the acquisition of knowledge and the development of competencies in scientific research [HAN 15].

Similarly, there arise other questions related to the choice of tools and applications that are best adapted to the main objective pursued by the community, in order to provide a platform for mutual aid on the cognitive, social and emotional levels for student-researchers in postgraduate education. The adoption of technologies leads to the consideration of several aspects (political issues in some cases) that cannot be circumvented. For example, this includes requirements relative to the use of tools determined by the institution [WIL 13]. On the one hand, some decision-makers impose the use of proprietary software and discourage the use of open source code or free software. On the other hand, the socio-economic environment that surrounds some universities sets the conditions for technological choices and requires an openness to the use of open access tools. It is also important to interrogate the implications of these decisions on the establishment of a community that responds to its members' needs.

2.5. Further questions

Given what has already been stated, we must note that the study of communities of student-researchers in postgraduate education in distance learning constitutes a very promising field of research with a wide scope. For our part, we are particularly interested in establishing the conditions for the success of a community that aims to support second-year master's students in their research work and in the writing of their theses. Several questions will guide our short-term research agenda:

1) With regard to research training in master's programs in a distance learning context, to what extent does the augmentation of global presence using a learning community contributes to modulating pedagogical distance?

2) How does interaction with peers within a learning community support the academic research learning process?

3) What activities favor effectiveness in work with peers with the goal of reinforcing learning about the research process for master's students at a distance?

The first question aims to establish the impact of a learning community for remote student-researchers on the modulation of the effects of pedagogical distance. The second question aims to determine how interactions between students can support the development of competencies as academic researchers, the acquisition of in-depth knowledge about research in their discipline and the adoption of a critical gaze for examining the complex realities of the relevant field of study. Finally, the third question derives from an interest in identifying the practices that allow a community of online student-researchers to be considered as having a fruitful pedagogical strategy, which also leads us to question the best process for encouraging participation in the community and maintaining it over time.

2.6. Conclusion

Communication technologies seem promising for interesting solutions to "tame" distance through telepresence. Although we have shown a propensity to respond to learning needs through the design of support materials that will be accessible asynchronously, two factors accelerate the adoption of synchronous communication tools to aid student-researchers: on the one hand, the need for remote university training in postgraduate education, increased in part by professional geographic mobility and, on the other hand, the ubiquity and the banalization of synchronous communication systems.

Jutras and Desjardins [JUT 14] observed a tendency among professors to reproduce the same dialogical dynamic during virtual encounters that take over synchronous communication technologies such as F2F meetings. However, the authors proposed the hypothesis of a change in practices when technologies are integrated into the context of higher education. New forms of collective support can be offered thanks to the use of ICT, for example through virtual seminars on research-specific subjects, interactive virtual workshops and thematic virtual meetings [CRO 08, PIC 11, SIN 11].

Finally, we propose a "working definition" about what an online community of student-researchers consists of. In our view, this community designates a group of graduate students who aim to develop competencies as academic researchers, to acquire extensive knowledge about research in a particular domain and to develop critical thinking about the complex realities of a discipline. Group members accomplish learning activities in collaboration, either synchronously or asynchronously, using information and communication technologies.

Initially, this definition seems minimalist and immature. Nevertheless, it is necessary to consider that it is only a point of reference to initiate our analysis. Empirical verification will allow the evolution of this conceptual proposal into a more complex and theoretically consistent form.

2.7. References

[AHE 04] AHERN K., MANATHUNGA C., "Clutch-starting stalled research students", *Innovative Higher Education*, vol. 28, no. 4, pp. 237–254, 2004.

[AND 01] ANDERSON T., LIAM R., GARRISON D.R. *et al.*, "Assessing teaching presence in a computer conferencing context", *JALN*, vol. 5, no. 2, 2001, accessed January 2018 at: http://auspace.athabascau.ca/bitstream/2149/725/1 /assessing_teaching_presence.pdf.

[AND 05] ANDERSON T., "Distance learning – social software's killer ap?" *The Open & Distance Learning Association of Australia*, 2005, accessed January 2018 at: https://auspace.athabascau.ca/bitstream/handle/2149/2328/distance _learning.pdf?sequence=1&isAllowed=y.

[AND 10] ANDERSON T., POELLHUBER B., MCKERLICH R., "Self-paced learners meet social software: An exploration of learners' attitudes, expectations and experience", *Online Journal of Distance Learning Administration*, vol. 13, no. 3, 2010.

[ARB 05] ARBAUGH J.B., "Is there an optimal design for on-line MBA courses?", *Academy of Management Learning & Education*, vol. 4, no. 2, pp. 135–149, 2005.

[ARB 07] ARBAUGH J.B., "An empirical verification of the community of inquiry framework", *Journal of Asynchronous Learning Networks*, vol. 11, no. 1, pp. 73–85, 2007.

[ARB 08] ARBAUGH J.B., "Does the community of inquiry framework predict outcomes in online MBA courses?", *The International Review of Research in Open and Distributed Learning*, vol. 9, no. 2, 2008, accessed January 2018 at: http://www.irrodl.org/index.php/irrodl/article/view/490.

[BAK 10] BAKER C., "The impact of instructor immediacy and presence for online student affective learning, cognition, and motivation", *Journal of Educators Online*, vol. 7, no. 1, 2010, accessed January 2018 at: http://eric.ed.gov/?id=EJ904072.

[BAN 03] BANYTIS F., "The research higher degree student professional development program at Flinders University", Partners in Learning: 12th Annual Teaching Learning Forum, Perth, Australia, 11 and 12 February 2003.

[BAP 11] BAPTISTA A.V., "Challenges to doctoral research and supervision quality : A theoretical approach", *Procedia – Social and Behavioral Sciences*, vol. 15, pp. 3576–3581, 2011.

[BEN 05] BENBUNAN-FICH R., HILTZ S.R., HARASIM L., "The online interaction learning model : An integrated theoretical framework for learning networks", in HILTZ S.R., GOLDMAN R. (eds), *Learning Online Together: Research on Asynchronous Learning Networks*, Lawrence Erlbaum Associates, Mahwah, 2005.

[BOU 00] BOUCHARD P., "Autonomie et distance transactionnelle dans la formation à distance", in Alava S. (ed.), *Cyberespace et formations ouvertes : vers une mutation des pratiques de formation*, pp. 65–78, De Boeck, Brussels, 2000.

[BOU 05] BOUD D., LEE A., "'Peer learning' as pedagogic discourse for research education", *Studies in Higher Education*, vol. 30, no. 5, pp. 501–516, 2005.

[BUT 05] BUTTERY E.A., RICHTER E.M., FILHO W.L., "An overview of the elements that influence efficiency in postgraduate supervisory practice arrangements", *International Journal of Educational Management*, vol. 19, no. 1, pp. 7–26, 2005.

[CAD 00] CADMAN K., "'Voices in the air': Evaluations of the learning experiences of international postgraduates and their supervisors", *Teaching in Higher Education*, vol. 5, no. 4, pp. 475–491, 2000.

[CAR 05] CARLINO P., "¿Por qué no se completan las tesis en los postgrados ? Obstáculos percibidos por maestrandos en curso y magistri exitosos", *Educere*, vol. 9, no. 30, pp. 415–420, 2005.

[CHA 16] CHANG B., KANG H., "Challenges facing group work online", *Distance Education*, vol. 37, no. 1, pp. 73–88, 2016.

[CHO 09] CHOMIENNE M., MARCEAU F., "Un environnement de réseautage social pour apprendre au Cégep@distance", *Revue internationale des technologies en pédagogie universitaire/International Journal of Technologies in Higher Education*, vol. 6, nos 2–3, pp. 63–70, 2009.

[CHO 14] CHOY S., DELAHAYE B.L., SAGGERS B., "Developing learning cohorts for postgraduate research degrees", *The Australian Educational Researcher*, vol. 42, no. 1, pp. 19–34, 2014.

[CHR 13] CHRISTENSEN G., STEINMETZ A., ALCORN B. *et al.*, *The MOOC Phenomenon: Who Takes Massive Open Online Courses and Why?*, SSRN Electronic Journal, 2013, accessed January 2018 at: https://papers.ssrn.com /abstract=2350964.

[COL 12] COLOMBO L., "Grupos de escritura en el posgrado", *VIII jornadas de material didáctico y experiencias innovadoras en educación superior*, Universidad de Buenos Aires, Argentina, 2012.

[CRO 08] CROSSOUARD B., "Developing alternative models of doctoral supervision with online formative assessment", *Studies in Continuing Education*, vol. 30, no. 1, pp. 51–67, 2008.

[DET 04] DETURE M., "Cognitive style and self-efficacy : Predicting student success in online distance education", *American Journal of Distance Education*, vol. 18, no. 1, pp. 21–38, 2004.

[DEU 08] DEUCHAR R., "Facilitator, director or critical friend? Contradiction and congruence in doctoral supervision styles", *Teaching in Higher Education*, vol. 13, no. 4, pp. 489–500, 2008.

[DYS 06] DYSTHE O., SAMARA A., WESTRHEIM K., "Multivoiced supervision of Master's students: a case study of alternative supervision practices in higher education", *Studies in Higher Education*, vol. 31, no. 3, pp. 299–318, 2006.

[ELE 09] ELEY A., MURRAY R., *How to Be an Effective Supervisor: Best Practice in Research Student Supervision*, McGraw-Hill Education, 2009.

[EVA 04] EVANS T., HICKEY C., DAVIS H., "Research issues arising from doctoral education at a distance", *Research in Distance Education*, vol. 6, pp. 120–131, 2004.

[EVA 02] EVANS T., "Part-time research students: Are they producing knowledge where it counts?", *Higher Education Research & Development*, vol. 21, no. 2, pp. 155–165, 2002.

[FLO 03] FLORIDA R., *The Rise of the Creative Class*, Pluto Press, Melbourne, 2003.

[FLO 12] FLORES-SCOTT E.M., NERAD M., "Peers in doctoral education: Unrecognized learning partners", *New Directions for Higher Education*, vol. 2012, no. 157, pp. 73–83, 2012.

[FOR 08] FORD L., BRANCH G., MOORE G., "Formation of a virtual professional learning community in a combined local and distance doctoral cohort", *AACE Journal*, vol. 16, no. 2, pp. 161–185, 2008.

[FOU 03] FOUCAULT B., METZGER J.-L., PIGNOREL É., "Les réseaux d'entraide entre apprenants dans la e-formation : à la recherche d'espaces d'échanges et de communication", *2ᵉ colloque de Guéret. Les communautés virtuelles éducatives : pour quelle éducation ? pour quelles cultures ?*, Guéret, France, June 2003.

[GAR 00] GARRISON D.R., ANDERSON T., ARCHER W., "Critical inquiry in a text-based environment: Computer conferencing in higher education", *The Internet and Higher Education*, vol. 2, nos 2–3, pp. 87–105, 2000.

[GAR 07] GARRISON D.R., ARBAUGH J.B., "Researching the community of inquiry framework: Review, issues, and future directions", *The Internet and Higher Education*, vol. 10, no. 3, pp. 157–172, 2007.

[GAR 08] GARRISON D.R., VAUGHAN N.D., *Blended learning in higher education : Framework, principles, and guidelines*, John Wiley & Sons, Hoboken, 2008.

[GLI 02] GLIKMAN V., *Des cours par correspondance au e-learning : panorama des formations ouvertes et à distance*, PUF, Paris, 2002.

[GRE 06] GREEN R., "Fostering a community of doctoral learners", *Journal of Library Administration*, vol. 45, nos 1–2, pp. 169–183, 2006, available at: https://doi.org/10.1300/J111v45n01_09.

[HAN 15] HANNA A., "Enhancing collaboration between research supervisors and students using Learning Management Systems (LMS): Pedagogical perspectives", *International Journal of Research in Open Educational Resources*, vol. 2, no. 2, pp. 81–91, 2015.

[HOR 03] HORTSMANSHOF L., CONRAD L., "Postgraduate peer support programme : enhancing community", *HERDSA Annual International Conference*, Christchurch, New Zealand, 6–9 July 2003, accessed January 2018 at: http://www.researchgate.net/profile/Louise_Horstmanshof/publication/29453164_Post graduate_Peer_Support_Programme_Enhancing_Community/links/09e4150c00c f4bdc72000000.pdf.

[IRA 14] IRANI T.A., WILSON S.B., SLOUGH D.L. *et al.*, "Graduate student experiences on- and off-campus: Social connectedness and perceived isolation", *International Journal of E-Learning & Distance Education*, vol. 28, no. 1, 2014, accessed January 2018 at: http://www.ijede.ca/index.php/jde/article/view/856.

[ISA 06] ISABELLE C., VÉZINA N., FOURNIER H., "Un environnement 3D qui favorise le sentiment d'appartenance en situation de formation à distance", *Canadian Journal of Learning and Technology/La revue canadienne de l'apprentissage et de la technologie*, vol. 32, no. 2, 2006.

[ISM 11] ISMAIL A., ABIDDIN N.Z., HASSAN A., "Improving the development of postgraduates' research and supervision", *International Education Studies*, vol. 4, no. 1, p. 78, 2011.

[IVE 05] IVES G., ROWLEY G., "Supervisor selection or allocation and continuity of supervision: Ph.D. students' progress and outcomes", *Studies in Higher Education*, vol. 30, no. 5, pp. 535–555, 2005.

[JAC 93] JACQUINOT G., "Apprivoiser la distance et supprimer l'absence ? Ou les défis de la formation à distance", *Revue française de pédagogie*, no. 102, pp. 55–67, 1993.

[JAC 10] JACQUINOT G., "Entre présence et absence", *Distances et savoirs*, vol. 8, no. 2, pp. 153–165, 2010.

[JEP 04] JEPPESEN C., NELSON A., GUERRINI V., *Diagnóstico y perspectiva de los estudios de posgrado en Argentina*, IESALC/UNESCO-Ministerio de Educación, Ciencia y Tecnología de la República Argentina, Buenos Aires, 2004.

[JÉZ 02] JÉZÉGOU A., "Formations ouvertes et autodirection : pour une articulation entre libertés de choix et engagement cognitif de l'apprenant", *Éducation permanente*, vol. 152, pp. 43–53, 2002.

[JÉZ 08] JÉZÉGOU A., "Apprentissage autodirigé et formation à distance", *Distances et savoirs*, vol. 6, no. 3, pp. 343–364, 2008.

[JÉZ 10] JÉZÉGOU A., "Créer de la présence à distance en *e-learning*", *Distances et savoirs*, vol. 8, no. 2, pp. 257–274, 2010.

[JÉZ 12] JÉZÉGOU A., "La présence en *e-learning* : modèle théorique et perspectives pour la recherche", *International Journal of E-Learning & Distance Education*, vol. 26, no. 1, 2012, accessed January 2018 at: http://www.ijede.ca/index.php/jde/article/view/777.

[JOH 95] JOHNSTON S., "Building a sense of community in a research master's course", *Studies in Higher Education*, vol. 20, no. 3, pp. 279–291, 1995.

[JUT 14] JUTRAS F., DESJARDINS F., "Pratiques d'encadrement à distance des mémoires et des thèses : l'état des connaissances", *Mutations de l'accompagnement dans les formations en ligne*, Rouen, France, 8–10 October 2014.

[KET 09] KETTERIDGE S., SHIACH M., "Supervising research students", in FRY H., KETTERIDGE S., MARSHALL S. (eds), *A handbook for teaching and learning in higher education: Enhancing academic practice*, 3rd edition, pp. 166–185, Routledge, New York, 2009.

[KEV 13] KEVANY K.M., LANGE E., COCEK C. *et al.*, "Online graduate programs and intellectual isolation: Fostering technology-mediated interprofessional learning communities", in WANG V. (ed), *Handbook of Research on Technologies for Improving the 21st Century Workforce: Tools for Lifelong Learning*, pp. 302–321, IGI Global, Hershey, 2013.

[KIM 14] KIMANI E.N., "Challenges in quality control for postgraduate supervision", *International Journal of Humanities Social Sciences and Education*, vol. 1, no. 9, pp. 63–70, 2014.

[KLE 12] KLEIJN R.A.M., DE MAINHARD M.T., MEIJER P.C. *et al.*, "Master's thesis supervision: Relations between perceptions of the supervisor–student relationship, final grade, perceived supervisor contribution to learning and student satisfaction", *Studies in Higher Education*, vol. 37, no. 8, pp. 925–939, 2012.

[LEE 06] LEE J., CARTER-WELLS J., GLAESER B. *et al.*, "Facilitating the development of a learning community in an online graduate program", *Quarterly Review of Distance Education*, vol. 7, no. 1, pp. 13–33, 2006.

[LEE 07] LEE A., "Developing effective supervisors: Concepts of research supervision", *South African Journal of Higher Education*, vol. 21, no. 4, pp. 680–693, 2007.

[LEE 08] LEE A., "How are doctoral students supervised? Concepts of doctoral research supervision", *Studies in Higher Education*, vol. 33, no. 3, 2008, accessed January 2018 at: http://epubs.surrey.ac.uk/484/.

[LEE 11] LEE A., *Successful research supervision: Advising students doing research*, Routledge, London, 2011.

[LOI 14] LOISIER J., *La socialisation des étudiants en FAD au Canada francophone*, document, Réseau d'enseignement francophone à distance du Canada (REFAD), 2014.

[LOV 05] LOVITTS B., "Being a good course-taker is not enough: A theoretical perspective on the transition to independent research", *Studies in Higher Education*, vol. 30, no. 2, pp. 137–154, 2005.

[MAI 09] MAINHARD T., VAN DER RIJST R., VAN TARTWIJK J. *et al.*, "A model for the supervisor–doctoral student relationship", *Higher Education*, vol. 58, no. 3, pp. 359–373, 2009.

[MAN 07] MANATHUNGA C., GOOZÉE J., "Challenging the dual assumption of the always/already autonomous student and effective supervisor", *Teaching in Higher Education*, vol. 12, no. 3, pp. 309–322, 2007.

[MAR 04] MARTZ W.B., REDDY V.K., SANGERMANO K., "Looking for indicators of success for distance education", in HOWARD C., SCHENK K., DISCENZA R. (eds), *Distance Learning and University Effectiveness: Changing Educational Paradigms for Online Learning*, pp. 144–162, Information science publishing, Hershey, 2004.

[MCB 09] MCBRIEN J.L., CHENG R., JONES P., "Virtual spaces: Employing a synchronous online classroom to facilitate student engagement in online learning", *The International Review of Research in Open and Distributed Learning*, vol. 10, no. 3, 2009, accessed January 2018 at: http://www.irrodl.org /index.php/irrodl/article/view/605.

[MEY 04] MEYER K.A., "Evaluating online discussions: Four different frames of analysis", *Journal of Asynchronous Learning Networks*, vol. 8, no. 2, pp. 101–114, 2004.

[MIL 02] MILLS J., "Intellectual isolation, geographical isolation and information overload of academics at a rural university: An information-seeking perspective", *Rural Society*, vol. 12, no. 3, pp. 263–272, 2002.

[MIT 08] MITCHELL T., CARROLL J., "Academic and research misconduct in the PhD: Issues for students and supervisors", *Nurse Education Today*, vol. 28, no. 2, pp. 218–226, 2008.

[MON 08] MONGEAU P., *Réaliser son mémoire ou sa thèse : Côté jeans et côté tenue de soirée*, PUQ, Quebec, 2008.

[MOO 11] MOORE M.G., KEARSLEY G., *Distance education: A systems view of online learning*, Wadsworth Cengage Learning, Belmont, 2011.

[MUN 14] MUNICH K., "Social support for online learning: Perspectives of nursing students", *International Journal of E-Learning & Distance Education*, vol. 29, no. 2, 2014, accessed January 2018 at: http://www.ijede.ca/index.php/jde/ article/view/891.

[NAS 14] NASIRI F., MAFAKHERI F., "Postgraduate research supervision at a distance: A review of challenges and strategies", *Studies in Higher Education*, vol. 40, no. 10, pp. 1–8, 2014.

[NOR 13] NORDENTOFT H.M., THOMSEN R., WICHMANN-HANSEN G., "Collective academic supervision: A model for participation and learning in higher education", *Higher Education*, vol. 65, no. 5, pp. 581–593, 2013.

[OLS 09] OLSON K., CLARK C.M., "A signature pedagogy in doctoral education: The leader-scholar community", *Educational Researcher*, vol. 38, no. 3, pp. 216–221, 2009.

[PAL 10] PALIKTZOGLOU V., ROGERS C., SUHONEN J., "Design challenges of developing an online PhD supervision community", *Proceedings of the 5th Annual South-East European Doctoral Student Conference*, pp. 401–411, SEERC, Thessaloniica, 2010.

[PAP 17] PAPI C., ANGULO G., BRASSARD C. *et al.*, "¿ Por qué comunicarse en formación a distancia ?", *Revista internacional de Tecnología, Ciencia y Sociedad*, vol. 6, no. 1, pp. 23–32, 2017.

[PAR 09] PARKER R., "A learning community approach to doctoral education in the social sciences", *Teaching in Higher Education*, vol. 14, no. 1, pp. 43–54, 2009.

[PER 11] PERAYA D., "Un regard sur la 'distance', vue de la 'présence'", *Distances et savoirs*, vol. 9, no. 3, pp. 445–452, 2011.

[PER 14] PERAYA D., "Distances, absence, proximités et présences : des concepts en déplacement. Distances et médiations des savoirs", *Distance and Mediation of Knowledge*, vol. 2, no. 8, 2014.

[PER 06] PERAYA D., "La formation à distance : un dispositif de formation et de communication médiatisées. Une approche des processus de médiatisation et de médiation", *Calidoscópio*, vol. 4, no. 3, pp. 200–204, 2006, available at: http://www.revistas.unisinos.br/index.php/calidoscopio/article/view/6005/3181.

[PIC 11] PICARD M., WILKINSON K., WIRTHENSOHN M., "An online learning space facilitating supervision pedagogies in science", *South African Journal of Higher Education*, vol. 25, no. 5, pp. 954–971, 2011.

[POE 06] POELLHUBER B., CHOMIENNE M., L'amélioration de la persévérance dans les cours de formation à distance les effets de l'encadrement et de la collaboration, Report, Cégep@ distance, 2006.

[POM 14] POMEROL J.-C., Les universités à l'heure des MOOC, Flyer, université Pierre et Marie Curie, 2014, available at: http://www.printempsunt2014 .univ-lorraine.fr/files/2014/07/pr%C3%A9sentation-MOOC-pomereol.pdf.

[REM 12] REMENYI D., MONEY A., *Research Supervision for Supervisors and Their Students: Research Textbook Collection*, Academic Conferences Limited, Kidmore End, 2012.

[RIC 03] RICHARDSON J., SWAN K., "Examing social presence in online courses in relation to students' perceived learning and satisfaction", *JALN*, vol. 7, no. 1, February 2003, accessed January 2018 at: https://www.ideals.illinois .edu/handle/2142/18713.

[RIT 12] RITTER E., Non-completion in thesis required master's degree programs, PhD thesis, Eastern Illinois University, 2012, accessed January 2018 at: http://thekeep.eiu.edu/cgi/viewcontent.cgi?article=1790&context=theses.

[ROC 12] ROCKINSON-SZAPKIW A.J., "Investigating uses and perceptions of an online collaborative workspace for the dissertation process", *Research in Learning Technology*, vol. 20, no. 3, pp. 267–282, 2012.

[ROV 02] ROVAI A.P., "Building sense of community at a distance", *The International Review of Research in Open and Distributed Learning*, vol. 3, no. 1, 2002, accessed January 2018 at: http://www.irrodl.org/index.php/irrodl /article/view/79.

[SAH 07] SAHIN I., "Predicting student satisfaction in distance education and learning environments", *Turkish Online Journal of Distance Education*, vol. 8, no. 2, 2007.

[SAM 06] SAMARA A., "Group supervision in graduate education: A process of supervision skill development and text improvement", *Higher Education Research & Development*, vol. 25, no. 2, pp. 115–129, 2006.

[SIL 16] SILINDA F.T., BRUBACHER M.R., "Distance learning postgraduate student stress while writing a dissertation or thesis", *International Journal of E-Learning & Distance Education*, vol. 31, no. 1, 2016, accessed January 2018 at: http://www.ijede.ca/index.php/jde/article/view/958.

[SIN 11] SINDLINGER J., Doctoral students' experience with using the reflecting team model of supervision online, PhD thesis, Duquesne University, 2011.

[SLO 14] SLOAN D., PORTER E., INGERSLEV K. *et al.*, "Using e-learning to support international students' dissertation preparation", *Education + Training*, vol. 56, nos 2–3, pp. 122–140, 2014.

[STA 13] STARR-GLASS D., "From connectivity to connected learners: Transactional distance and social presence", in WANKEL C., BLESSINGER P. (eds), *Cutting-edge Technologies in Higher Education*, vol. 6, pp. 113–143, Emerald Publishing, Bingley, 2013.

[STE 95] STEPHEN T., HARRISON T., The Electronic Journal as the Heart of an Online Scholarly Community, communication from the department of scholarships, 1995, accessed January 2018 at: http://scholarsarchive.library .albany.edu/cas_communication_scholar/5.

[STY 00] STYLES I., RADLOFF A., "Affective reflections: Postgraduate students' feelings about their theses", in KILEY M., MULLINS G. (eds), *Quality in Postgraduate Research: Making Ends Meet*, pp. 203–214, University of Adelaide, Adelaide, 2000.

[SUN 08] SUN P.-C., TSAI R.J., FINGER G. *et al.*, "What drives a successful e-Learning ? An empirical investigation of the critical factors influencing learner satisfaction", *Computers & Education*, vol. 50, no. 4, pp. 1183–1202, 2008.

[SUS 06] SUSSEX R., "Technological options in supervising remote research students", *Higher Education*, vol. 55, no. 1, pp. 121–137, 2006.

[TAH 12] TAHIR I.M., GHANI N.A., ATEK E.S.E. *et al.*, "Effective supervision from research students' perspective", *International Journal of Education*, vol. 4, no. 2, 2012, accessed January 2018 at: http://www.macrothink.org/journal/index.php /ije/article/vieFile/1531/1682.

[TRO 10] TROPE Y., LIBERMAN N., "Construal-level theory of psychological distance", *Psychological Review*, vol. 117, no. 2, pp. 440–463, 2010.

[WEG 16] WEGENER C., MEIER N., INGERSLEV K., "Borrowing brainpower – sharing insecurities. Lessons learned from a doctoral peer writing group", *Studies in Higher Education*, vol. 41, no. 6, 2016.

[WIC 14] WICHMANN-HANSEN G., THOMSEN R., NORDENTOFT H.M., "Challenges in collective academic supervision: Supervisors' experiences from a master programme in guidance and counselling", *Higher Education*, vol. 70, no. 1, pp. 19–33, 2014.

[WIL 11] WILLEMS J., FARLEY H., ELLIS A. *et al.*, "Supervising higher degree research (HDR) candidates at a distance: What do emerging virtual world technologies have to offer?", *Proceedings of Education 2011 – 2021 Summit: Global Challenges and Perspectives of Blended and Distance Learning*, Australia: Distance Education Hub (DEHub) / Open and Distance Learning Association of Australia (ODLAA), accessed May 2017 at: http://www.dehub.edu.au/summit2011/, 2011.

[WIL 13] WILSON S., "Open source in higher education: How far have we come?", *The Guardian*, 28 March 2013, accessed July 2018 at: https ://www.theguardian.com/higher-education-network/blog/2013/mar/28/open-source-universities-development-jisc.

[WIS 03] WISKER G., ROBINSON G., TRAFFORD V. *et al.*, "Recognising and overcoming dissonance in postgraduate student research", *Studies in Higher Education*, vol. 28, no. 1, pp. 91–105, 2003.

[WIS 07] WISKER G., ROBINSON G., SHACHAM M., "Postgraduate research success: Communities of practice involving cohorts, guardian supervisors and online communities", *Innovations in Education and Teaching International*, vol. 44, no. 3, pp. 301–320, 2007.

[WIS 12] WISKER G., *The Good Supervisor: Supervising Postgraduate and Undergraduate Research for Doctoral Theses and Dissertations*, Palgrave Macmillan, London, 2012.

3

Facilitating Problem-Based Learning: A Reflective Analysis

3.1. Introduction

This chapter aims to present a reflexive analysis of our experiences in supporting students enrolled in an online education baccalaureate program, and the systems that we designed to foster learning using a problem-based learning approach. After the presentation of the context, we provide a brief overview of the literature concerning the theoretical concepts that underlie our support of the students using a problem-based learning approach in online courses. We report on the challenges of co-designing, co-producing and co-teaching of university online courses about social media. Considering the implications of online courses, our team focused on problem-based learning (PBL) grounded in a socio-constructivist pedagogical perspective. To support students through authentic and meaningful learning processes, we offered them telepresence on social media. We engaged in co-reflection based on our experiences to improve the course over a four-year period. We therefore present a reflection about our practices with regard to the elements that create pedagogical tension and those that, in our experience, act as levers in the learning process.

Chapter written by Ann-Louise DAVIDSON and Nadia NAFFI.

3.2. Context

In several countries, higher education is going through a revolution caused by several factors such as globalization and internationalization, democratization of education, the principles of new public management, changes in the methods of financing university establishments, privatization, the crisis in the academic profession, changes in student demography, digital technologies and distance learning [ALT 09]. The current conditions and the evaluation and ranking criteria for higher education establishments are forcing universities to be more competitive in research as well as in the academic programs and services offered to students. In certain cases, quality is measured in terms of academic reputation, the student–teacher ratio, publications by professors and the international student–teacher ratio [IRE 15].

In this context, the function of the production of knowledge, of scientific publication and of knowledge mobilization takes up a large part of professors' energy, who therefore have less and less time to devote to pedagogy. This situation is problematic to say the least, since the report from the Organization for Economic Cooperation and Development (OECD) [OEC 16] shows a strong correlation between competencies in literacy, numeracy, and problem-solving in environments with a strong technological component and employability. In this context, students show a glaring need for training that is adapted and relevant to the new social reality [ALT 09], which requires increased efforts to make university courses relevant. Indeed, across the world, companies are transforming rapidly, and the labor market offers precarious conditions to workers who are often hired on fixed contracts or on call. Students often come back for postsecondary studies with a job (or two or three), a family and a panoply of conditions that make it impossible for them to study full-time.

In Canada, current conditions increase the need for universities to train highly qualified personnel (HQP) with tomorrow's skills. In particular, in 2001, the Conference Board of Canada announced that the labor market was waiting for a wave of future employees with three groups of skills. The first group, the fundamental skills, includes elements such as communication, information management, using numbers, and thinking and solving problems. The second group, personal management skills, includes elements such as demonstration of positive attitudes and behaviors, being responsible, being adaptable, engaging in learning continuously, and working safely. The third group, teamwork skills, includes working with others and participating in complex tasks and projects.

Sixteen years later, the relationship to technology has become more complex, and all of the work surrounding employability skills has become exponentially more complicated, since a large percentage of interactions take place through technological interfaces. The massive adoption of the Internet in 2001, the development of the social web (2.0, 3.0, 4.0, etc.), the omnipresence of technologies and the mobility of interfaces has had an impact on a large part of individuals' personal and professional lives. The boundaries between work and personal life have become blurred; information (sometimes false) is produced and circulates at the speed of thought, and the traditional communications barriers due to distance are being erased.

While most universities were in the race for massive open online courses (MOOCs), we have undertaken teaching in the online education baccalaureate program (Educational Studies and Digital Technologies) at the University of Ontario Institute of Technology (UOIT) because, on the one hand, they make it possible to offer training that is adapted and flexible for a student population that seeks to become HQP, and, on the other hand, they provide the opportunity for an in-depth reflection about the teaching component of our profession.

For several years, we have therefore engaged in producing synchronous and asynchronous online courses in a problem-based learning approach. This chapter highlights a quick landscape of the literature and the theoretical foundations of the problem-based learning approach, followed by a report about our class, and ending with our co-reflections as a professor, for one, and as course lecturer, for the other.

3.3. Problem-based learning and problem-based learning objects

Problem-based learning (PBL) is a concept that was developed during the 1960s by the medical school at McMaster University. Initially, the goal was to better prepare new doctors for the complexity of their work. On the heels of McMaster's medical school, several researchers became interested in PBL because the concept can be used as a pedagogical approach: it allows students to be more active in their learning processes by looking into complex problems in collaborative groups, and it allows teachers to adopt the role of discussion facilitators rather than the role of information transmitters [HAS 01, SAV 10]. In PBL, the contents are a means to accomplish a task or to resolve a problem. This approach is diametrically opposed to the traditional function of content that students must memorize to pass their tests.

PBL was designed to help students develop a more flexible knowledge base, to improve their ability to collaborate, and to develop their ability to resolve problems and to manage their learning processes themselves [BAR 86, NOR 92]. Hmelo-Silver [HME 04] mentions that in PBL, students become better team members because they exercise their capacity for dialogue and negotiation throughout group work.

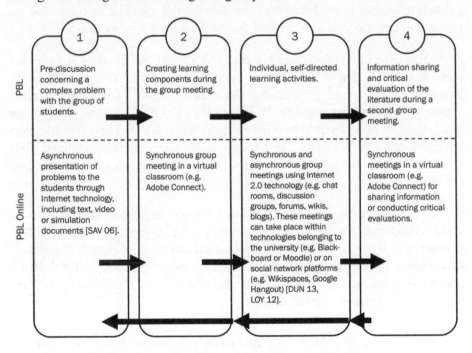

Figure 3.1. *The process of classic PBL and online PBL (inspired by [DUN 13, LOY 12, SAV 06])*

To be more consistent with these foundations, Loyens, Kirschner and Pass [LOY 12] suggested steps for engaging in the PBL process (Figure 3.1), with discussion at the beginning of the cycle and resource sharing at the end of the cycle, with the idea of iterative cycles until work is submitted. In the context of online learning, the cycle is slightly modified [DUN 13, LOY 12, SAV 06]. The second part of Figure 3.1 shows the differences between classic and online PBL. In the first step, resources are shared online, which means students have the opportunity to begin the discussion in asynchronous mode when the interface allows them to access shared resources. Online work therefore becomes much more collaborative and less individual (especially, in step 3). Since groups are formed from the beginning, the learning process is much more iterative, and the students do not need to wait for the second group meeting to discuss the resources they have found.

According to several researchers, PBL is established more efficiently when the pedagogical material has been planned in advance in the form of case study videos [KUR 09, PED 08] or problem-based learning objects (PBLO) [VAN 10]. A PBLO is a small digital unit that contains analytical questions, a context, or a case and questions for synthesis discussions. It can be presented in the form of a slide show or a video. The analytical questions serve to direct the student's attention to contextual analysis. The questions for synthesis are presented to raise questions about the student's initial concepts about the subject. Since memorization is not the objective of PBL, the purpose of PBLOs is to initiate conversations between students and the person who is in the facilitator role.

The use of PBLOs is especially relevant in the context of an online course [VAN 10]. Van Oostveen et al. [VAN 10] even suggested that PBLOs contribute to motivating students because they offer complex contexts from which problems emerge. These problems are identified by the team, which should use the strength of collaboration since the challenge is multidimensional, touching on, for example, the social, psychological, technological and political spheres.

3.4. The use of technologies and underlying competencies

Regarding the typology of information and communication technology (ICT) competencies for education, several attempts have been made to identify the types of competencies to be developed in teachers and students. We have adopted the model created by Desjardins [DES 05] because it relies on the categories of interactions with ICTs that can be generalized outside of the educational system and because it distinguishes the categories of competencies according to the class of interaction undertaken by the user. According to Desjardins, the subject, who thinks, perceives and acts through interactions with an interface or a technological object (technical competencies), can communicate with other subjects (social competencies), consult or produce information objects (informational competencies) and delegate a task to the computer as a cognitive tool (epistemological competencies).

With the technological developments of the last decade, it has become increasingly difficult to isolate these categories of competencies because the use of digital technologies generally involves multiple combinations of these interactions and, consequently, with the associated competencies. Nevertheless, the model seemed relevant to us for isolating the categories of interaction with technologies in our course and for engaging in a reflection about what students must do, that is, participating in the course through an entirely digital environment.

3.5. Description for an online course designed and developed with a problem-based approach

Our work was carried out in the context of a baccalaureate-level course entitled "Digital Communication Technologies". It was part of the required courses for the baccalaureate program in "Educational Studies and Digital Technologies" at the University of Ontario Institute of Technology (UOIT). The model adopted by program designers consisted of courses designed within a PBL approach delivered entirely online. All of the courses in this baccalaureate program included three components: 1) weekly tutorials in synchronous mode; 2) daily discussions in asynchronous mode, with several interfaces such as a learning management system, a microblogging site, a social networking site and a professional networking site; and 3) PBLOs in video format for each session provided through a YouTube channel.

During the design and development of this course in 2012, about 15 students were enrolled. The course today includes three sections for a maximum of 90 students (30 students per section), in part because the bandwidth limits the virtual class environment in terms of participants using video camera and microphone. Since, in a PBL approach, students must work together, and since class time should serve to facilitate discussion rather than to transmit content, this inherent technological limit is desirable for preserving the quality of conversations.

The course was therefore designed while taking space-time constraints into account. Our team taught from Montreal and the students were located throughout Canada, but especially around the city of Toronto. Working in multiple time zones was a challenge, primarily because it was necessary to consider the mature population who was working, in many cases, full-time. The class was therefore designed for interactions in both synchronous and asynchronous mode for students whom we would never meet physically. We used technologies for which UOIT had a license, Adobe Connect and Blackboard, but we also used YouTube for the videos, Facebook, Twitter and LinkedIn for asynchronous communications, and Google Drive for work requiring collaborations between students.

To create the course, rather than taking the content that underpinned the course description as a starting point, we thought about the experience we wanted to provide to the students to develop the overarching course competency, which was to "learn to exploit communications technologies productively and safely in education". We therefore took this competency as a starting point for designing the assignments, beginning with an analysis of the students' needs and developing the learning materials according to the problems that the student groups would identify from the presented context.

To design the contexts leading to the identification of problems, we wrote stories based on non-fiction characters, using pseudonyms. We therefore wrote the story of a plumber near retirement who can no longer keep his company afloat because his competitors are on social media; the story of a Venezuelan immigrant who has not been able to find work since arriving in Canada, in part because he does not have the required technological competencies; and the story of a language school owner who must transition from in-person teaching to online teaching. We wove together the stories by mixing in other characters and several events that provided the students with more contexts. We then created personas to ensure emotional proximity so that the story would be attached to a person for whom the students had to prepare training material connected to communication technologies in order to solve an authentic problem. We transformed the stories into videos that were uploaded to YouTube[1].

We then imagined the student learning experience and group work, and we created an iterative evaluation process. For this purpose, it was necessary to design a process by which the identification of problems online was

---

1 A summary of these videos, summarized for recruitment purposes, is available online at: https://www.youtube.com/watch?v=I_4FniFTz8A.

documented in preparation for a final evaluation (Figure 3.2). We inserted the YouTube link to the videos into our Facebook page, and we asked the students to begin discussion threads to explore the problems and to form teams based on their interests in asynchronous mode. We followed the discussions as closely as we could with the teaching assistant but, given the informal environment, we also asked for a peer formative evaluation. We offered our formative evaluation to help students improve their approach to discussion. Finally, we asked the students for their self-evaluation concerning their participation in the discussions, which we used to inform the final evaluation of their work.

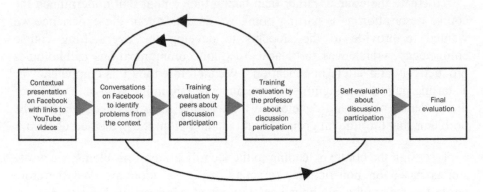

Figure 3.2. *Discussion about contexts and training evaluation loop*

Because lack of participation or collaboration in group work is often a source of frustration, we prepared a self-evaluation rubric for group work that students had to submit in each evaluation cycle. This rubric consists of questions related to the frequency and efficacy of communication with the group, the participation in group activities, resource sharing, task execution, decision-making, respect for others' ideas and empathy. Without wanting to claim that this rubric resolved all of our problems, it was a pedagogical design effort to allow the students to reflect on their role as collaborators and to become aware of their strengths and weaknesses.

More generally, we also had to think about a project evaluation process consistent with a PBL approach targeting the development of competencies. To ensure the development of the course competencies, that is, leveraging communication technologies productively and safely in education, we designed an iterative process in two loops so that the project, presented in two parts, could be examined by peers, the professor, and the team twice before the final evaluation for the course. Figure 3.3 shows this process, which begins with discussion about the project, the construction of work teams, and the two iterative evaluation loops for the two parts of the project until the work had to be submitted to the professors for final evaluation.

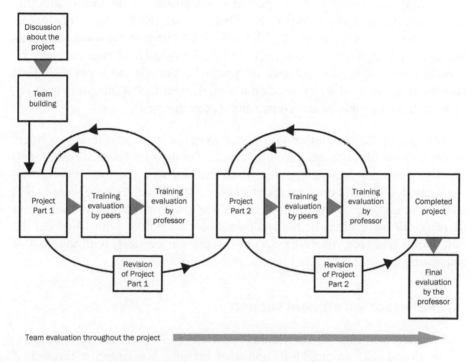

Figure 3.3. *The PBL project and its evaluation loops*

In addition, we added team evaluation throughout the project to ensure students' collaboration. We know that group work is not always easy and that, despite our intentions, the PBL approach does not guarantee the participation of all in an efficient collaboration.

3.6. Methodological framework for our reflection

As part of the study, we used a reflexive approach to ensure that we were offering the best support possible to students enrolled in an online course. To engage in the process of co-reflection in relation to our course, we had to find a way to identify our perceptions, that is, our own constructions of the meaning of our course design and its evaluation through the establishment of elements that we developed over a period of one year. To do this, we used an interview technique inspired by the Procter's qualitative grid [PRO 14], also called the "perceiver elements grid". The qualitative grid is a flexible tool for identifying and revealing a person's constructs. Constructs are the interpretations that allow him to anticipate events [KEL 55]. A qualitative grid is presented in the form of tables in which written or drawn descriptions are directly integrated into the cells. Although this method was designed by Procter for use in the context of research, therapy and psychological consultation, we used it to identify our own perceptions in our process of co-reflection on the topic of our course and its development.

Our use of the qualitative grid aimed to reveal our individual constructs as supervisors of the course on three levels. On the first level, we wanted to identify our individual perceptions as online teachers. On the second level, we wanted to identify our perceptions about our colleague (there were two of us) in the context of our online course. On the third level, we wanted to identify our perceptions of the students in our class. We both filled out the perception grid (see Appendix 3.9) to discuss our support, with the goal of improving our support for online students via co-reflection.

3.7. Reflection on student support

This course was a co-learning process in which we co-designed, co-developed and co-taught it, and also because we began a process of co-reflection about the meaning of how we support students in a PBL approach. Since we have worked together for several years, the intersections between the first two rows and the first two columns were collegial and pleasant points of discussion (please see the perception matrix in section 3.9). However, the reflection about other intersections was more serious and punctuated with assumptions that required us to spend more time discussing our perceptions about students and students with each other.

In our online course, we had certain expectations from students about which we were not fully aware. Although our intention was to offer a course that allowed students to take advantage of communication technologies in a productive and safe way, we faced several important elements of surprise.

The course included a double challenge that we took for granted: that of learning to work online and that of PBL.

Learning in an online course is inherently a different experience from that of a physically co-located course. It is not a question of entering the classroom with a notebook and a pencil (or with one's portable computer used as a notepad) to begin to understand the contents. To work online, students first need the necessary technological competencies, particularly those mentioned by Desjardins [DES 05]. According to this researcher, technological competencies are centered around four categories of interactions: technical interactions, informational interactions, social interactions and epistemological interactions. In the case of our students, some had never taken an online course, others did not know how to find information online, and many had no experience with online group work. Students who were not able to use technologies such as Adobe Connect, Blackboard, Facebook, Twitter, LinkedIn and GoogleDocs were paralyzed by their impediment in relation to others. Students who were not able to find information and to filter it in order to use it in context were unable to contribute to the collective construction of knowledge. Students who did not understand the expectations of interactions in social media and the requirements for keeping oneself up-to-date in discussions were unable to "keep their heads above water". Although this mixture of technical (or "manipulatory"), social and informational competencies was essential for our course, several students did not have these competencies.

Although the program delivery is done entirely within a PBL approach, there are several ways to interpret and use this approach. The perspective we adopted had the goal of preparing students with the necessary competencies to be integrated into the 21st Century labor market which, according to Savin-Badin [SAV 11], allows us to be prepared for professional activity. In this approach, knowledge is performative in the sense that it should serve to resolve real-life problems. This adopted perspective also had the effect of complicating the students' task because we changed the traditional rules of the learning process. In fact, in our course, we had taken on the role of discussion facilitator, and we avoided giving answers by using Socratic questioning, which forces students to call their choices into question. We also insisted that the students be active in their learning process, to ensure that the understanding of the problem to be solved, the modes of intervention, and the contents to be developed were entirely the construction of the individual students and their group. Furthermore, to be more consistent with PBL, we avoided offering content to be learned, which caused several students to feel a lack of reference points. All of the rules of the student's traditional role were changed and they had no other choice but to become more active in their learning process.

Admittedly, we initially designed our course without thinking about these two challenges: learning both online and in a PBL approach. With time and experience, we integrated these aspects into our course material and into our evaluation. First, we encouraged students to create a support structure for developing the three essential technological competencies that are prerequisite to the course. Second, we shared with them the expectations for a course in PBL so they would know their responsibilities and the facilitator's expectations. Third, we announced our evaluation criteria by sharing the rubric with them, but we were conscious that the students could not understand the criteria from the beginning. Hence, we integrated a looped evaluation process (see Figure 3.3).

On the students' part, we noted that several of them thought that an online course consisted of listening to videos, reading resources and doing the assignments, without worrying about their own telepresence and without expecting telepresence from the professors. Some had participated in online courses earlier and had not had to interact in synchronous or asynchronous mode with their professor and the other students. Since the course was advertised as a "tutorial" and not as a "lecture" during the first version of the course, some students believed that the tutorial was for those who had difficulty with the material and did not attend after the 10th week. We therefore changed the description to "compulsory weekly tutorial".

If attitudes about online courses can sometimes pose a problem, group work is almost always a problem. We took it for granted that, as adults, the students would know how to work together. On the contrary, group work was one of the greatest challenges [DAV 17]. Once the technology usage challenge had been resolved, the students understood that, in a PBL course, we would not give them answers and that they had to take charge of their learning process. The challenges of group work emerged rapidly, and they were mentioned in both synchronous and asynchronous communications. Through the years, we have seen every possible kind of problem. A student attended our course from a medical helicopter while waiting for take-off before his shift. Others attended the course during their lunch hour. Some had to put the course on "pause" because they were feeding their children, because the dog was barking, and so on. If all of the dimensions of life affect their asynchronous presence in the course, one hour a week, we quickly understood that group work was often almost impossible for some of them, which is problematic in a PBL approach. Hence, we created a group work rubric and a looped evaluation process (Figure 3.2). However, we also mention that the simple fact of integrating the evaluation rubric into group work did not resolve all of the problems. We had a case of intimidation in one group when some members threatened a female student with a bad evaluation if she did not do what they wanted, and she felt that she did not have the right to share her ideas. When such scenarios occurred, we had to be careful about how we interpreted the peer evaluation rubric to understand what was happening in the group. Since we interacted online, it was a bit more difficult to resolve such problems, and we were sometimes forced to separate students.

3.8. Conclusion

The approach we adopted in the course had important benefits that are worth mentioning.

The first benefit relates to our use of Facebook which resulted in the creation of a community of students who followed the course from the first year on. These students never left the Facebook group and, year after year, other students joined, as well as faculty members from the program. Although the Facebook group was public, students felt they were in a safe environment for discussing concepts and questions about the course. Since 2012, 406 members have joined this group. Within the Facebook discussions, students shared resources that were relevant for each semester, which meant that the community could benefit from them. The students from previous semesters remained in the group because they could update their knowledge and participate in discussions with new students. This robust participation in the Facebook group, even after the end of the course, can be explained by the fact that the questions studied in PBL rely on authentic real-life scenarios. The fact that former students remained also created stronger telepresence on the part of those students who had already completed the course.

We should add that online PBL forced the students to meet virtually, to interact together to produce documents in the framework of group work and to increase their exchanges through social media. If the adoption of PBL had a strong influence on the telepresence offered to students, we should add that the adoption of this approach also had an influence on our way of co-designing the course. Indeed, the creation of videos in a PBL approach destined for YouTube, the use of social media such as Facebook, Twitter and LinkedIn, and the online software such as GoogleApps are all aspects that contributed to the increase in exchanges and the strong telepresence in the course.

Despite the distance and the major challenge we offered students, we developed a very positive relationship with them. Several stayed in touch with us through the social media we used in the course. They invited us to the defense of their baccalaureate thesis (an end-of-program document in several Canadian universities), to their graduation (virtually), and we are continually updated on their professional progress. Three years later, we traveled by train to Oshawa to visit the EILab[2] facilities. In the Via Rail station at six o'clock in the morning, we took a selfie that we posted on Facebook, saying: "En route for UOIT to visit the EILab!" A group of students came to meet us in person. During their online program experience, they understood that the impressions they constructed of the person online might not correspond to the physical person, and they wanted to meet us face-to-face. We heard comments such as "Oh! Ann-Louise is tall! Oh! Nadia has long hair!" These anodyne details about the importance of meeting in person had no impact on the students' learning process, but the fact that we created an online community that remained intact after the course meant that students from past courses could contribute to discussions, both from a conceptual point of view and from the point of view of relevance to the course in their work. This proved to what extent the course's design was relevant. We are not insisting that an in-person meeting is essential, but, at a given time, for a community to survive, it is necessary to give personal time to social encounters so that exchanges can continue and so that connections can grow stronger, whether this is through virtual meetings or physically co-located meetings.

---

2 EILab is an international center on innovation for learning via digital means (see https://eilab.ca/).

Finally, our approach to co-reflection inspired by Procter [PRO 14] has allowed us to improve the course year after year. In thinking about our own perceptions and our positions with respect to students and groups of students, we have been able to use the experience to improve not only our online teaching approach, but also our approach to supporting students for increased comprehension.

3.9. Appendix: perception matrix

	Ann-Louise	Nadia	Students
Ann-Louise	What did Ann-Louise think about Ann-Louise's support in the context of the course?	What did Ann-Louise think about Nadia's support in the context of the course?	What did Ann-Louise think about the students' experience in the context of the course?
	Nadia	**Ann-Louise**	**Students**
Nadia	What did Nadia think about Nadia's support in the context of the course?	What did Nadia think about Ann-Louise's support in the context of the course?	What did Nadia think about the students' experience in the context of the course?

3.10. References

[ALT 09] ALTBACH P., REISBERG L., RUMBLEY L., *Trends in Global Higher Education: Tracking an Academic Revolution*, United Nations Educational Scientific and Cultural Organization, Paris, 2009.

[BAR 86] BARROWS H., *A Taxonomy of Problem-based Learning Methods. Medical Education*, Springer, New York, 1986.

[CON 00] CONFERENCE BOARD DU CANADA., Compétences relatives à l'employabilité 2000+, Survey, Ottawa, 2000.

[DAV 17] DAVIDSON A.-L., NAFFI N., RABY C., "A PCP approach to conflict resolution in learning communities", *Personal Construct Theory & Practice*, vol. 14, pp. 61–72, 2017, accessed January 2018 at: http://www.pcp-net.org/journal/pctp17/davidson17.pdf,

[DES 05] DESJARDINS F., "La représentation par les enseignants, quant à leurs profils de compétences relatives à l'ordinateur : vers une théorie des TIC en éducation", *La revue canadienne de l'apprentissage et de la technologie*, vol. 31, no. 1, pp. 27–49, 2005.

[DUN 13] DUNCAN M.J., SMITH M., COOK K., "Implementing online problem based learning (PBL) in postgraduates new to both online learning and PBL: An example from strength and conditioning", *Journal of Hospitality, Leisure, Sport and Tourism Education*, vol. 12, no. 1, pp. 79–84, 2013.

[HAS 01] HASLETT L., "1969 McMaster University introduces problem-based learning in medical education", in SCHUGURENSKY D. (ed.), *History of Education: Selected Moments of the 20th Century*, 2001, accessed January 2018 at: http://fcis.oise.utoronto.ca/~daniel_schugurensky/assignment1/1969mcmaster.html.

[HME 04] HMELO-SILVER C.E., "Problem-based learning: What and how do students learn?", *Educational Psychology Review*, vol. 16, no. 3, pp. 235–266, 2004, accessed January 2018 at: http://dx.doi.org/10.1023/B:EDPR.0000034022 .16470.f3.

[IRE 15] IREG Observatory, iREG Guidelines for Stakeholders of Academic Ranking, Guidelines, Brussels, 2015.

[KEL 55] KELLY G.A., *The Psychology of Personal Constructs*, vol. 2, Norton, New York, 1955.

[KUR 09] KURZ T., BATARELO I., MIDDLETON J., "Examining elementary preservice teachers' perspectives concerning curriculum themes for video case integration", *Educational Technology Research and Development*, vol. 57, no. 4, pp. 461–485, 2009.

[LOY 12] LOYENS S.M.M., KIRSCHNER P., PAAS F., "Problem-based learning", in HARRIS K.R., GRAHAM S., URDAN T. (eds), *APA Educational Psychology Handbook*, vol. 2, American Psychological Association, Washington, 2012.

[NOR 92] NORMAN G.R., SCHMIDT H.G., "The psychological basis of problem-based learning: A review of the evidence", *Academic Medicine*, vol. 67, no. 9, pp. 557–565, 1992.

[OEC 16] OECD, *L'importance des compétences : Nouveaux résultats de l'Évaluation des compétences des adultes*, Éditions OCDE, Paris, 2016, accessed January 2018 at: https://www.oecd.org/fr/competences/piaac/Limportance-des -competences-principaux-resultats.pdf.

[PED 08] PEDRETTI E.G., BENCZE L., HEWITT J. *et al.*, "Promoting issues-based STSE perspectives in science teacher éducation : Problems of identity and ideology", *Science & Education*, vol. 17, nos 8–9, pp. 941–960, 2008.

[PRO 14] PROCTER H., "Qualitative grids, the relationality corollary and the levels of interpersonal construing", *Journal of Constructivist Psychology*, vol. 27, no. 4, pp. 243–262, 2014.

[SAV 06] SAVIN-BADEN M., "The challenge of using problem-based learning online", in SAVIN-BADEN M., WILKIE K. (eds), *Problem-based Learning Online*, McGraw Hill, Maidenhead, 2006.

[SAV 10] SAVIN-BADEN M., HOWELL MAJOR C., *Foundations of Problem-based Learning*, McGraw-Hill Education, Berkshire, 2010.

[SAV 11] SAVIN-BADIN M., *Problem-based Learning in Higher Education: Untold Stories*, Society for Research into Higher Education and Open University Press, Philadelphia, 2011.

[VAN 10] VAN OOSTVEEN R., DESJARDINS F., BULLOCK S. *et al.*, "Towards a reconceptualization of online teacher professional learning: Problem-based learning objects (PBLOs)", *World Conference on Educational Multimedia, Hypermedia & Telecommunications*, pp. 1579–1588, Association for the Advancement of Computing in Education, Chesapeake, 2010.

PART 2

Telepresence in Teacher Training

Contribution of Virtual Classes to the Construction of Professional Knowledge for Teachers

4.1. Professional knowledge and virtual classes

This comprehensive chapter aims to better understand the contributions and limits of the use of virtual classes (VC) in a professional training system for teaching in secondary education I and II in Switzerland[1]. It examines the process of professional training in a formative approach, in a VC, centered on the mutual analysis of situations in the field and the articulation of different kinds of theoretical and practical knowledge [ALT 15].

Cognizant of the existence of numerous obscure areas in the construction of professional knowledge among teachers in training [MAU 11, ROG 11, TAR 15], we also examine the suitability of the system, its contribution to the acquisition of new professional knowledge and the management of practical experience. We try to determine, more specifically, whether the students' references to knowledge – scientific or experiential – during an analysis of practical techniques vary depending on the context that is mediatized by the VC or not. To this end, we compare the exchanges of students in VC and in person (PR).

Chapter written by Romaine CARRUPT.
1 Secondary education I concerns the last three years of obligatory education in France (from 12 to 15 years of age). Secondary education II concerns post-obligatory education: professional schools, general education schools, business schools and high schools.

After the presentation of the contextual framework for the research, we will clarify the conceptual framework, the object of study and the methodology adopted. Finally, we will reveal the results of the analysis and discuss them.

4.2. Hybridization of part-time training

Teacher training at the *Haute École Pédagogique du Valais* (HEP-VS) targets professionalization and is organized to alternate between training at the university and in the field. In order to facilitate the organization of part-time training and the integration of digital technologies, the training modalities are oriented towards hybridization [BUR 11, CHA 06]. The hybridization of the domains of training for secondary education thus alternates between university training – in person – and distance classes, supported by an e-learning platform and a telepresence tool, the VC.

4.3. Construction of professional knowledge in virtual classes

Our research is part of the field concerning computer-mediated training and hybrid training. We refer to the analysis of the social use of information and communications technologies (ICT) in training. We first specify the essential concepts and then articulate the concept of professional knowledge. Based on different works stemming from the teacher-training research field, we examine the mediating potential of the VC cognitive tool in professional training. We address the central points of the mediatization of a training activity in order to determine how much the use of a VC allows for the organization of interactions and conceptualization in a mutual analysis of practices. We formulate rules for the engineering of professional training using hybrid teaching. These are the axes of our exploratory research.

4.3.1. *A system for hybrid professional training*

A hybrid system alternates between different training modalities, in person and at a distance, and integrates the technologies in order to sustain teaching/learning [CHA 06]. It employs different forms of mediatization and mediation [CHA 06, PER 08]. The process of teaching consists of creating the necessary conditions for the modification of students' mental processes by the use of different psychological instruments [SCH 09], including technological tools. The specificity of a hybrid professional training system lies in its capacity to allow students to socially weave close connections between their previous knowledge and proposed knowledge in training. The process of professional training is produced in a dialectic between different dimensions of knowledge and situations that are rich in perception, favoring a subjectification of knowledge. A hybrid professional training system is situated, henceforth, in a didactic of professional knowledge, and implements integrative, interactive and reflexive activities [BUY 09, BUY 10, BUY 11a].

4.3.2. Synchronous communication in a virtual class

The concepts of video/visual/Web conference and virtual classes are rather unstable [SAV 13, WAL 12]. The term video or visual conference refers to communications mediatized by computer requiring a high-bandwidth connection as well as audio/video equipment. In the context of training, we retain the term "virtual class" through an analogy with a classroom.

The technical object utilized (Adobe Connect) allows for the organization of the VC via audio, video and written channels. It presents a variety of functionality facilitating exchanges (screen sharing, whiteboard, documents, written chat, note-taking and interaction tools such as emoticons). It offers different kinds of organization (modes for conference, discussion or collaboration for small private groups).

The virtual class appears as a set of tools offering an alternative for remote written exchanges and their relative cumbersomeness (in time and in communication effort). It proposes, thanks to the multimodal video/audio/written channel, the necessary conditions for close exchanges of authentic communications in person. The relational dimension, consolidating actions of sociability, seems to be richer in VC than in PR, with more empathy, variety and ease of exchange [FER 15]. Marcoccia [MAR 11] thus asserts that the spatial context (i.e. the home) influences the familiarity of exchanges with more references to personal subjects. The analysis of speaking turns in VC [COD 12, KER 11], nevertheless, reveals more frequent interruptions and overlaps than in in-person conversations. These technical problems can compromise exchanges in VC [MAC 09] and will have a direct effect on the difficulty of interactions and the participants' anxiety [DEV 08], MAR 05].

4.3.3. *Training and support for learning in virtual classes*

Synchronous video collaboration offers, according to Develotte, Kern and Lamy [DEV 11], perspectives that support "remote face-to-face" exchanges. It fosters the feeling of belonging to a learning community. The multimodality of exchanges in virtual classes also enriches pedagogical communication, didactic strategies and the modalities of the interactive management of learning [DEV 08]. VCs complement meetings in PR during hybrid training and foster "quality support" [SAV 13] centered on support for learning. The multimodal VC system enriches effective support through the modalities of "presence at a distance" [JÉZ 10, PAQ 11, WEI 99] which are likely to favorably influence professional learning.

4.3.4. *Professional knowledge*

4.3.4.1. *Training for professional teachers*

The different kinds of knowledge that make up professional knowledge seem to have a close relationship that largely surpasses their simple juxtaposition or their sum [RAI 93]. They are "connected by a dialogic relationship" [GRA 11, p. 145]. Precisely circumscribing knowledge despite its interrelationship appears to be a condition inherent to the modeling of a logical professional training system.

According to Buysse and Vanhulle [BUY 09], professional knowledge is made up of referential knowledge (theoretical knowledge about training and institutional, contextual and normative knowledge) and experiential knowledge (constructed by students through their experiences in the field and connected to their ideas and values). Baslev, Vanhulle and Tominska define them "as statements that the students formalize through valid discourse with respect to reference knowledge connected to social, academic, and institutional expectations, and which they imbue with meaning connected to their training experiences through reflexive and conceptual approaches" [BAL 10, p. 1]. With regard to the complexity of such a process of elaboration, we can examine the potential of the VC artifact for sustaining the expression of professional experience and scientific knowledge.

4.3.4.2. *Construction of professional knowledge*

According to the Vygotskian concept of learning [VYG 97], referential knowledge, initially external, is internalized thanks to the understanding stemming from the discourse produced by the student during his practice. More precisely, knowledge of research proposed during training transforms experiential knowledge (everyday knowledge) into professional knowledge (scientific concepts), thanks to reflexive and interactional processes, and thus contributes to the restructuring of mental functions [BUY 09, BUY 10, BUY 11a, BUY 11b]. The "potential for improvement through collaboration with someone with a superior intellectual level" [VYG 97, p. 353] plays a primary role in learning that goes hand in hand with its social dimension.

Reflexivity favors detachment from initial concepts and distancing from the object of learning. This objectification allows, through the dynamic of the co-construction of meaning between peers, for the interiorization of referential and experiential knowledge. The production of professional knowledge by students can therefore engender a real subjectification of knowledge, which then becomes a tool for thinking and acting. We can therefore ask how relational mediation, mediatized by the VC, attains the status of facilitator of learning.

Furthermore, if "the activity of constructing professional knowledge endowed with meaning is a discursive activity" [VAN 09a], then it is still necessary to consider that, in exchanges with peers, it is accompanied by the construction of their professional ethos [JOR 09]. This double elaboration is not without destabilization for students, thus leading to revisit their initial ideas while protecting their self-image [GOF 73].

4.4. Hypotheses and research questions

Does the VC call into question or preserve the student's image during interchanges in online collaboration situations? Generally resistant when faced with theoretical input and unresponsive to immediate problems of their practice, some students also express reticence to digital technologies. Does the use of this technical tool constitute an additional impediment, engendered by the stress linked to the adoption of ICT, or, on the contrary, does it generate, by its innovation, the motivation and investment of students? Our hypotheses are, on the one hand, based on remarks by this group of students with regard to the stress generated by technical difficulties linked to the use of this virtual class tool: the weakness of the connection and the fear of not being able to participate in a course or not being heard/being able to hear because of technical problems. On the other hand, some of these students offer a certain amount of resistance to the use of the VC to the extent that, according to them, human relationships are impeded by the technology. Finally, collaboration regularly takes place in person in most of the training classes; students are familiar with this social form of work and perceive it positively. We think, on the one hand, that the technical constraints of the VC and the anxiety it generates can limit the quality of collaborative analysis. On the other hand, because of its separation from the institutional training context, the spatial context (at home) risks orienting the level of mutual commentary in the VC towards exchanges of experiential knowledge. We expect, on the other hand, that interactions in PR, within the training institution, integrate referential knowledge in a richer way. These hypotheses lead us to formulate the following initial question: what is the contribution of the virtual class to the construction of professional knowledge? The specific research question can therefore be expressed as follows: "what knowledge does the student leverage during situation analysis in VC/in PR?"

4.5. Methodology

The population of this study includes eight students, aged 27–40, in two training programs: secondary education master I and the diploma for secondary education I-II[2]. Each of the two groups studied was composed of four people, including two women. The displacement time from their home to the institution was between 70 and 140 minutes. These students teach (60 to 80%) math and science. Beyond their disciplinary affinity, their bi-weekly sessions in disciplinary didactics (math and science) as well as

---

2 The secondary education master I leads to a professional accreditation for teaching in schools of secondary education I (schools for the last 3 years of obligatory education, from 12 to 15 years). The diploma for secondary education I-II leads to a professional accreditation for teaching in schools of secondary education I and in schools of secondary education II (schools for post-obligatory education: professional schools, general education schools, business schools and high schools).

the specific problems of teaching in these disciplines contribute to forging their connections.

Nevertheless, their personal profiles differ: four students (identified here by the letters AVC, BVC, EP and FP) were married heads of household and had one or two children, and the other four are single.

Their student profiles are characterized as follows:

– three participants in PR (EP, FP, HP) and two in VC (BVC, DVC) engaged in a very dynamic and motivated way in their training;

– three participants, one in PR (GP) and the others in VC (AVC, CVC) only expressed their resistance to the theoretical contribution to training;

– three participants, one in PR (FP) and the others in VC (AVC, CVC) managed the three poles with difficulty: training/employment/private life (family, multiple engagements, leisure activities, etc.).

These students participated in a course in the second-year program entitled: "Teaching in heterogeneous classes: pedagogical differentiation". They were required to register, in small groups, for a session, in their choice of either PR or VC, whose objective is to regulate learning. The formation of groups by affinities led to grouping by discipline.

The duration of the activity (55 minutes) and the instructions were identical for the two groups. Each designed a system for pedagogical differentiation, tried it out in class and submitted it to his or her peers. Then, using an evaluation criteria grid integrating the course concepts, the proofreader responsible for the presentation of a text and the proofreading peers discussed the quality, relevance and consistency. The author of the system responded to the comments made in the group. Following this activity, the students reworked their projects and uploaded them with their reflexive texts to the learning platform.

The materials on which our analysis is founded are composed of the recording and transcription of the exchanges in the two groups of four different students, one in VC and the other in PR.

Interaction discourse analysis [KER 05] allows us, first, to note the number of interventions, the management of speaking turns and the specificities of language acts, according to the virtual or in-person context.

The content analysis of our corpus aims, then, to delineate the professional concepts harnessed and their frequency during group situation analysis. It therefore adopts the categories of professional knowledge stemming from the TALES research group[3] [BAL 10, BAL 11, BUY 09, BUY 11a, BUY 11b, VAN 09a, VAN 09b]. Four dimensions, coming from different sources, constitute professional knowledge:

1) theoretical and scientific knowledge, stemming from education research and offered, in the training institution, to students as scientific references for understanding and designing their profession;

2) institutional and prescriptive knowledge, stemming from texts that are prescriptive, referential, rules-based and program-based, offered as an orientation for acting based on the expectations of society, the establishment and the employer;

3) practical knowledge, stemming from teachers who receive trainees in their classes, proposed to students as relevant or effective practices;

4) experiential knowledge, more subjective and internal, that is often implicit and unconscious. This knowledge is associated with experiences in their own right, imbued with values and beliefs forged through family, academic and social history, and through contact with specific work contexts and situations.

Thus, theoretical and scientific knowledge is situated in the formulation of concepts such as self-evaluation, meta-cognition, simultaneous differentiation, coordinated training evaluation and self-management of learning.

Institutional and prescriptive knowledge is revealed through institutionally prescribed statements such as: "This is the problem with physics, the Swiss study design (SSD) clearly requires it to be quantitative", "According to the program, they are supposed to have already seen this in the third and fourth grades" and "That is because of the teaching method we use".

---

3 The TALES (*Théorie, Action, Langage Et Savoirs*) research group of the Faculty of Psychology and Education Sciences at the University of Geneva is led by Sabine Vanhulle and Kristine Baslev. It is particularly interested in the development of professional knowledge by teachers in training. On this subject, see https://www.unige.ch/fapse/tales/.

Practical knowledge is identified from language acts, clarifying the source of practical knowledge emanating from establishments and trainers in the field who receive interns, such as: "When I had the meeting with my training supervisor, I saw a group rotation with such and such a theme, and I thought that was great", "It was my training supervisor who defined the objectives" and "It was my training supervisor who advised me to set the objectives they would have for review".

Experiential knowledge arises from contributions specifying the subject's preliminary experiences, values and ideas, such as:

"These groups aren't something I like doing, you see, but well, after all it's a question of taste."

"I often have the impression that sometimes the students like it at the beginning because well 'they are interested in me' and at the end of the year its 'ugh it's that thing again'"

"This sequence, I know it well, there aren't fifty ways to do it, you can't do it in a thousand different forms"

"I had done an activity, like a yokel, that I picked up on the web, and that organized the concrete examples online. And well, yeah, it was nice!"

Three proofreaders cross-checked their transcription analysis. Disagreements became the object of clarification and discussion. The categorization was modified or removed as a result.

4.6. Results and analysis

First, we show the general results relative to the structure and the number of speech acts in the exchanges depending on whether the context is mediatized or not. Second, we will present the results relative to the types of knowledge occurring in both virtual and in-person interactions.

4.6.1. *Interactions in virtual classes/in person*

The breakdown in interactions – in VC as in PR – should occur according to the four analyzed situations. However, if the four students in VC each analyze the four situations, those in PR begin with an organizational sequence and only analyze three situations. Interactive work is structured based on the object to be taught and learned in each situation.

	Teaching object in the analyzed situations	
	In VC	**In PR**
Org		Organizational sequence
S.1	Sustainable development	Flat geometric shapes
S.2	Reproduction	Geometric shapes (median and mediating)
S.3	Conversions (mass, capacity, volume)	Relative numbers (4 operations)
S.4	Electricity	

Table 4.1. *Teaching object in analyzed situations*

Group work lasted 55 minutes and 34 seconds in VC and 53 minutes and 35 seconds in PR. Despite the similar time periods, the number of total speech acts was considerably different depending on the context: 338 speech acts in VC compared to 606 in PR. Among these speech acts, 65 signs of agreement were made in VC, compared to 25 in PR. It should also be mentioned that 42 specific speech acts in the VC concerned technical problems related to the connection and use of the VC.

Interactions in VC began *in medias res* with the announcement of the beginning of the exchanges and the assignment of speaking to a peer: "Well then let's get going! This is CVC talking about myself!" On the contrary, the beginning of the PR took place with 47 speech acts related to the organization of the exchanges.

The following tables conclude this section dedicated to quantitative data about interactions. They summarize the number of speech acts per participant, for each of the situations, as well as the duration of analysis of each situation, in VC and in PR.

	1	**2**	**3**	**4**	**Total**
AVC	23	21	35	11	90
BVC	20	39	20	14	93
CVC	5	47	18	15	85
DVC	17	9	34	10	70
Total	65	116	107	50	338
Duration	8 min 06 sec	17 min 09 sec	20 min 01 sec	10 min 08 sec	55 min 34 sec

Table 4.2. *Number of interventions per participant and situation in VCs*

	Beginning	**1**	**2**	**3**	**Total**
EP	14	87	36	47	184
FP	18	39	83	45	185
GP	12	53	46	67	178
HP	3	13	21	22	59
Total	47	192	186	181	606
Duration	3 min 40 sec	16 min 09 sec	18 min 18 sec	15 min 19 sec	53 min 35 sec

Table 4.3. *Number of interventions per participant and situation in PR*

4.6.2. *Measurement of incorporated knowledge*

Let us linger, in this section, on the results of the identification of the types of knowledge used by students in their mutual analyses of situations.

References to theoretical concepts in the education sciences were distributed in a differentiated way: 143 in virtual class, compared to 90 in person. Experiential knowledge arose unequally in the two groups: 49 in virtual class, compared to 132 in person. Institutional knowledge and knowledge stemming from practice weakly appear in both the virtual class (18 and 12) and in person (11 and 13). The following graphs (Figures 4.1 and 4.2) illustrate these overall references and present the evolution of each of the analyses.

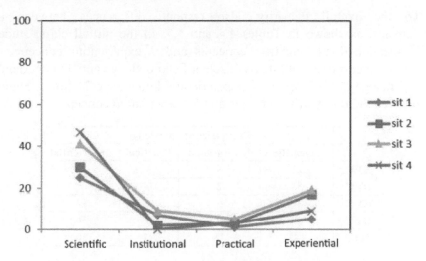

Figure 4.1. *Knowledge mentioned per situation during analyses in VCs*

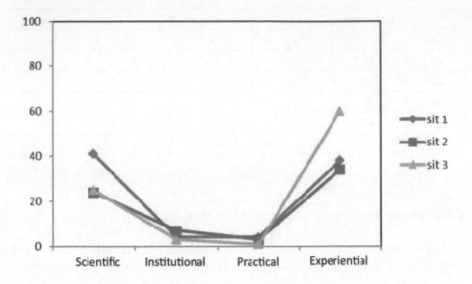

Figure 4.2. *Knowledge mentioned per situation during analyses in PR*

It is apparent that the references to scientific knowledge progressively increase with each situation analysis in the virtual class. While experiential knowledge in the last situation analysis decreased to 9 occurrences in the virtual class, it exploded in person and increased to 60 occurrences.

To the overall disparity, also respond differences between the participants, as shown in Tables 4.4 and 4.5. In the virtual class, student BCV mentioned 54 scientific concepts and 7 experiential concepts. In person, EP incorporated 40 items of scientific knowledge and 47 experiential ones, although HP only expressed experiential knowledge 21 times. Student FP referred to 30 scientific concepts and 50 experiential concepts.

	Categories of knowledge			
	Scientific	Institutional	Practical	Experiential
AVC	25	9	3	20
BVC	54	2	0	7
CVC	31	3	4	14
DVC	33	4	5	9
Total	143	18	12	50

Table 4.4. *Knowledge mentioned by participant during interactions in VCs*

| | Categories of knowledge | | | |
	Scientific	Institutional	Practical	Experiential
EP	35	2	3	47
FP	24	9	1	50
GP	31	3	4	14
HP	0	0	0	21
Total	90	14	8	132

Table 4.5. *Knowledge mentioned by participant during interactions in PR*

4.7. Discussion of interactions in virtual classes and in person

Following the presentation of the results, we are ready to contradict – carefully, given the exploratory character of our research – our initial hypotheses and to respond to our research question. Students refer more often to scientific knowledge in the virtual class and to experiential knowledge in person. Our results are certainly not generalizable and only concern the activity of two different groups of students in a specific context. Despite this limitation, they deserve clarification through a more detailed analysis of the contents of interactions.

4.7.1. *Progressive interpenetration of theoretical knowledge in virtual classes*

4.7.1.1. Beginning in virtual classes

The artifact's functionalities are immediately revealed in this beginning by the choice of document sharing on screen and the confirmation of its readability. Instrumentalization operates in this way from the beginning and indicates an appropriation of the artifact for the purpose of exchange [RAB 95].

> DVC: Wait because apparently we can ummm we can share the document on this thing! ... Here, this is good! You see?

> AVC, BVC, CVC: Yes yes, it's good.

Taking notes is also done in the module integrated into the virtual space.

> AVC: Then I'll take a few notes in the notes space and I'll transfer them to you afterwards.

4.7.1.2. *Review of knowledge*

The student discussant, DVC, briefly presents the first situation to AVC about sustainable development. BVC questions the validity of the implemented system: does this connect more to a varied pedagogy, without preliminary training evaluation, or to a system centered on self-management of learning. Confronted with a lack of comprehension ("Huh! How's that?") and with resistance from his interlocutor, AVC ("Me, theory!... Can you translate, please?"), BVC reformulates and explains some theoretical concepts and indicates their relevance to practice.

A possible turnaround, emblematic of exchanges in VC, took place during the last exchanges in this discursive sequence. Student AVC wanted to return to the preceding comments made by BVC and proposed an interpretation of his differentiation system by having, in turn, recourse to the concepts of education sciences.

> AVC: To revisit the kind of differentiation you were speaking about before, BVC, it's true that it's rather successive, but, ummm... For me it's not as divided as that. It's not because I vary the means and tasks that I don't take account of the students' objectives. It's precisely then that I can identify their problems, enter into interaction with them, and orient them. Follow-up can also be simultaneous, if you see what I mean.

Subsequently, DVC's discourse, which had previously only been filled with experiential knowledge, transformed to explicit references to theoretical knowledge:

> DVC: As BVC said, you didn't give a task that was differentiated based on the specific objectives for managing learning.

4.7.1.3. *Translator, knowledge smuggler*

The second situation concerns a simultaneous differentiation in preparation for the final evaluation of a sequence about reproduction. The analysis was the object of comments from BVC, primarily covering scientific concepts. He regularly reformulated his peers' experiential discourse into scientific language.

> CVC: It was an exercise, in fact, that makes you manipulate this information for gametes, and that, concretely, they each had a sheet and they could work in pairs or trios. Afterwards, they could join groups around a table ummm and then work umm with me on... some themes.

> BVC: O.K., and umm, it's a choice of differentiation by homogeneous groups with specific groups of needs?

Subsequently, AVC and CVC, who had previously only focused on experiential knowledge, responded to him using the same level of professional language. This translation of experiential discourse into scientific language reorients the subsequent debates towards a generalized use of theoretical knowledge in the group. As in the first situation, a shift of interactions into a scientific register occurs.

Like AVC, DVC also regularly used scientific references. Their shared reflection about the understanding of different course concepts and their transfer into practice, moreover, concludes this analysis and caps the orientation given to the choice of scientific reference concepts.

During the analysis of the third situation, using mathematical conventions, DVC responded to peer questions with scientific references. He focused the illumination of the objects of analysis – reversing the choice of class, risk of student stigmatization, *a priori* analysis of the teaching object, groups of needs, etc. – on the contribution of didactic theory.

The analysis of the fourth situation by BVC about electricity showed a rich theoretical knowledge, which the preceding sequences did not offer: gaps between use of professional language and everyday language, by participants, faded. During CVC's interventions, this progression, illustrated in Figure 4.1, is particularly notable. The analysis in the VC concluded with a perspective about system management.

DVC: Thanks for your comments, I am going to revisit my system with a differentiated work plan that integrates learning strategies, which is very interesting.

Beginning with BVC's analysis of self-management, an internal consistency was established in the interactions in the VC. The language shifted from a familiar to an elevated register. Meaning emerged from the dynamic of exchanges and seemed to give rise to understanding. We see here an illustration of the role of scientific knowledge as an instrument of thought and action [BUY 09, VAN 14, VYG 97]. It fosters detachment and contributes subsequently to a restructuring of knowledge and perspectives for managing practice [BUY 09, VAN 14].

4.7.2. *Scientific knowledge inoperative in person*

4.7.2.1. *Organizational sequence*

Student EP begins the interaction in PR with a reformulation of the instructions:

"... we are going to reconsider the analytical criteria based on the components of differentiation, diagnostic evaluation, ummm, the theoretical framework of the system for simultaneous differentiation, etc."

FP adds to this:

"Well ummm for diagnostic evaluation: there are objectives, data collection, error analysis, the students' underlying obstacles, and the differentiation system."

The conceptual framework having been precisely recalled, exchanges follow about the necessity of reading the criteria for analysis again, alternating speaking turns and document access. Finally, the decision is made unanimously that each author will present his work. This modification of the instructions can explain, in part, a weaker detachment in the face of the situations presented and the lack of reflexivity of the analyses in PR.

4.7.2.2. *Application of theoretical knowledge*

During the analysis of the first situation by EP, on geometric figures, both EP and FP made regular use of scientific concepts. Despite numerous theoretical references, EP's discourse analysis reveals a certain degree of confusion:

> "And then, ummm, in fact, ummm, I wanted to categorize specific objectives, so what is, what are the points in relation to the sequence, for these, these concepts and then the criteria, ummm, for success. So I didn't know if they were criteria or ummm indicators, we got in each others' way a bit, but ummm..."

It was more a question of a reproduction than of a real integration of scientific concepts. Student EP appended, without explanation, scientific concepts acquired about the experiential knowledge of his peers. These ideas were not the object of questions and were not reformulated by the other students. This process characterized interactions in PR that developed in a familiar register, despite the use of scientific concepts.

> GP: I believe I had, that I had placed with help, with ummm I had placed several people around, that implies either a classmate or a prof...
>
> EP: Ha yeah, peer guidance or something like that.
>
> GP: Yeah, so I had put a fourth column, I don't know anymore, "I tried to", I think, to know or to check the box.

Following the interactions, EP continued to relate to the theoretical concepts in the experiential discourse of his peers. Then, little by little, he was influenced by his peers and continued in the category of knowledge to which his interlocutor referred.

> GP: But okay, what would be interesting would be maybe to give them something right at the beginning.
>
> EP: Something to check?

GP: No, once, at the beginning of the themes, well here's what you should know.

EP: Ha - specific objectives, yeah.

GP: Yeah the objectives, you see, very detailed, maybe.

EP: Well aside from that I always make worksheets at the beginning with the themes, I don't know if you've already seen my worksheets.

HP: Yeah that's good.

These examples, representative of interactions in PR, do not lead to a reconfiguration of knowledge used by the subject in light of instructions to act professionally. The simple restoration of theoretical knowledge, without internal consistency in the discourse, does not proceed from connections to practice; management is subsequently explored at the level (technical) of developed tools [BUY 09].

4.7.2.3. *"Tips" for practice*

FP presented the second situation, about geometric figures, with precise scientific discourse. A turnaround occurred following FP's question: "Does anyone have any improvements to suggest, I don't know, ideas or tips for my practice?" Subsequently, the students formulated responses stemming from their experience. Then, FP presented the website from which he downloaded exercises to facilitate the elaboration of the material for differentiation. The sequence about the site's multiple features for practice took up more than 8 minutes and generated 66 speech acts. It was concluded with a time reminder from GP, and FP's excuses: "Sorry, we were talking about other things". In the end, the examination of multiple resources in the online space supplanted mutual evaluation of the peer differentiation systems.

GP imbued the presentation and the analysis of the third situation concerning relative numbers with an experiential dimension. This sequence of 12 minutes included 181 speech acts, during which the students formulated their experiences and designs with regard to the object to be taught. EP reproduced the four scientific concepts, without links or re-explanation, so well that the experiential nature of the exchanges was not reconfigured.

FP: Yeah there where I had trouble, that was with relative numbers.

GP: Yeah in any case, there are those for whom it's hard ummm eh, it's a brain-teaser.

EP: They understood ummm the bars. I, they have trouble.

FP: I am going to see how they are going to ummm handle addition for the first time.

The destabilization produced by preoccupations in the field (pragmatic obstacles) contributes, according to Vanhulle [VAN 14], to the construction of professional knowledge, thanks to the illumination and detachment of the experience that scientific knowledge can foster. However, this reference knowledge can generate strong resistance from students (epistemic obstacles). Now, the search for practical solutions without theoretical illumination does not allow for awareness or re-explanation of the experience that is the result. The discourse is characterized by a succession of interactions, and numerous interruptions of speech, without the perspective of system management. "The urgency of acting" [PER 96] reduces the reflexive capacity to the benefit of an intense reactivity. The handful of theoretical reference knowledge, appended to discourse, remains, by its very exteriority, inoperant in the re-explanation of the experience [VAN 14].

The fourth situation, area and perimeters, from HP was never analyzed for lack of time. This explains, in part, the smaller number of HP's interventions.

4.7.3. Mediatized/non-mediatized interactions

The flow of exchanges is incessant and as abundant in the VC as in PR. Speech was easy in both modalities, despite several additional overlaps caused by some audio latency in the VC. The three interruptions in activity are due to technical problems in VC (jerky and low-volume sound, frozen image and high-pitched whistle (Larsen effect)), generating 41 interventions and lasting 2 minutes in total. This assessment allows for the technical limits foregrounded by the literature to be put into perspective in the framework of our small sample (e.g. [COD 12, DEV 11, MAC 09, MAR 05, WAL 12]).

Despite several technical weaknesses, nevertheless not to be underestimated, the VC artifact allows for remote collaborative work and seems to generate exchanges that are more focused on the prescribed task.

Consistent with the research conclusions (e.g. [FER 15, JÉZ 10, MAR 03, MAR 11]), our analysis reveals socio-affective acts [PER 03] that are richer in the VC. The formulation of these personal ideas seems more explicit there, in conformance with the results from Marcoccia [MAR 11]; this is still narrowly argued and interwoven with theoretical knowledge. Does the filter of the screen produce a disinhibiting effect?

While an intense focus on the prescribed task occurred in the virtual class, in person, the sharing of practices and resources replaced the expected critical analysis. The exchanges, at first marked by concern for following the instructions and a list of criteria, moved towards a re-explanation of the instructions. The interactions centered on experiential knowledge of teaching/learning relative numbers seemed to stem from a redefinition of the task. As for the presentation of the site with teaching resources, it can be seen as a reorientation towards prescriptive methods and discourses, while the goal sought a connection to theoretical knowledge.

If the interactions are half as frequent in the virtual class as in person, contrary to Ferone and Lavenka's results [FER 15], it is important to underline that technical flaws play a small part. The analyses are characterized by their richness and their density: to formulate, reformulate, debate and deepen theoretical knowledge and to show the meaning, formulate the rules of its practice and so on. They are not necessarily formulated at the same rate as the description of practice in common language. Situation analyses in virtual classes have also demonstrated the appearance of real professional controversies.

In person, experiential knowledge prevails, with reframing with theoretical illumination sometimes being elaborated in a stammering fashion. The sharing of practices is substituted little by little by mutual evaluation. Now, the reflexive discourses produced through the sharing of experience-based resources is concentrated on a technical level: methods used, experiences, behaviors, contents and so on [BUY 11a]. They do not lead to any formulation of ways to manage pedagogical differentiation systems elaborated and implemented in classes.

4.7.4. *An orchestration of instruments*

Students bring their own technological equipment to class. Subsequently, references to ICT appear, as much in person as in the virtual class, along with the concern of each presenter to indicate how to access the reference document in the digital repository.

It is necessary to point out that, during debates about theoretical concepts, students in the virtual class referred to online course resources. They invited their peers to become familiar with certain film lessons stored on the course platform, presented transpositions and interpretations, put the class concepts into dialogue with each other, referred to concepts to clarify the situation, reinterpreted the produced experience in light of theory, formulated improvements to a peer's practice and seemed to provoke understanding; moreover, indicators of management appeared.

Far from being subjected to the artifact, the participants inscribe it with effective, efficient and meaningful use. Material objects thus give way to the status of what Rabardel [RAB 95] has called "instruments," that is, a technical artifact and the social schemes for its use. These instruments, or cognitive tools, are addressed as much to the exterior object as to the subject and generate new knowledge about external objects, transformations of the subject itself and others. Within this orchestration of instruments, students become not only actors in their training, but also actors in the system that they contribute to modifying and reconfiguring.

4.8. Conclusion

We have shown that a hybrid professional training system supported by a telepresence tool, the virtual class, not only integrates the foundational stakes of professional training, but also enlarges the field of possibilities by fostering a digital culture, an illumination of practice enriched by technologies and the analysis of practices, collaboration, detachment and reflexivity.

The process of instrumentalization [RAB 95], during which the subject assimilates the artifact's different functions little by little and identifies the relevant characteristics for the task, seems inescapable and is an integral part of learning mediated by technology. Even though the technical flaws are not as great as expected, the technical problems in the virtual class are sufficiently anxiety-producing to impede some students. Subsequently, technical support, not only at the beginning of training but also remotely, is worth rethinking, so that the virtual class really participates in the development of the subject and the resources in the long term, which Rabadel [RAB 95] defines as a constructive activity.

Our exploratory analysis reveals, in the very narrow framework of the observed sample, a contrasting use of the appropriation of knowledge in student exchanges depending on the mediatization or the absence of mediatization through the virtual class. Exchanges in person in a group of four students largely privileges experiential knowledge stemming from "their urgent professional action". The use of scientific concepts in discursive and interactive analyses in the virtual class seems to have played a real catalytic role and to offer a broad possibility of understanding and internal management of students [BUY 09, BUY 10, MAU 11, VAN 14]. Our research highlights that, during the interactional activity of four students in the virtual class, the cognitive tools seem largely favorable for the construction of professional knowledge. The digital artifact constitutes a vector of multiple mediations: epistemological, praxiological, relational and reflexive [PER 08].

A next step stands out following this first exploration. Our results and analyses deserve to be expanded to the set of students in training with a comparison of interactive work by similar groups of students, in both the virtual class and in PR. They will be enriched by the analysis of interviews and reflexive texts written by the students following each session.

Our study examines the engineering of professional teacher training for more than one qualification. It reveals, on the one hand, a reconfiguration of the instructions and a transformation of the task by the group members in person. This phenomenon can be connected to the parameters of the communications used in the situation: since the participants are in person, this facilitates (re)negotiations concerning what is to be done (the task), or even how to do it (the activities). If this hypothesis can be validated, it would suggest that approaches to training of "open problem" type will be more effective in person. Meanwhile, tasks whose expected activities are more prescribed will find an adequate environment in VCs.

On the other hand, our analysis highlights that the mediations offered in training seem to need to be rethought and readjusted, endlessly, in light of the excess of pragmatic and epistemic imbalances. How can students be brought to perceive theoretical contribution as a real instrument for acting and thinking about his practice in an appropriate and effective way? How can we foster the mobilization of this knowledge, considered to be vague or even ineffective, by students struggling with preoccupations in the field?

At the end of this research, other questions arise. Does this system stimulate, precisely because of the detachment from space-time in the training environment, the back and forth between objectification and subjectification of knowledge? Does the virtual class favor a detachment from the part to be preserved? What else is in play compared to in person? Since "pseudo-face-to-face" [KER 11] only restores a truncated image of peers, doesn't it therefore constitute precisely the strength of the virtual environment, allowing the student to speak to himself in an eminently singular discourse and to thus gain access to self-reflection and understanding?

4.9. References

[ALT 15] ALTET M., "Les compétences de l'enseignant-professionel : entre savoirs, schèmes d'action et adaptation, le savoir-analyser", in PAQUAY L., ALTET M., CHARLIER E. *et al.* (eds), *Former des enseignants professionnels. Quelles stratégies ? Quelles compétences ?*, pp. 43–57, 4th edition, De Boeck, Brussels, 2015.

[BAL 10] BALSLEV K., VANHULLE S., TOMINSKA E., "Tracer la construction des savoirs professionnels dans les interactions entre les formateurs et enseignants en formations", *Actes du Colloque International Spécificités et diversité des interactions didactiques : disciplines, finalités, contextes*, Lyon, France, 24–26 June 2010, accessed March 2017 at: https://halshs.archives-ouvertes.fr/hal -00534603/fr/.

[BAL 11] BALSLEV K., TOMINSKA E., VANHULLE S., "'Le jour où je serai dans ma classe, ce sera différent'. Entretiens de stage et construction de savoirs professionnels", *Les Sciences de l'éducation – Pour l'Ère nouvelle*, vol. 44, no. 2, pp. 85–102, 2011.

[BAR 87] BARTH B.-M., *L'apprentissage de l'abstraction*, Retz, Paris, 1987.

[BUR 11] BURTON R., BORRUAT S., CHARLIER B. *et al.*, "Vers une typologie des dispositifs hybrides de formation en enseignement supérieur", *Distances et savoirs*, vol. 9, no. 1, pp. 69–96, 2011.

[BUY 09] BUYSSE A., VANHULLE S., "Écriture réflexive et développement professionnel : quels indicateurs ?", *Questions vives*, vol. 5, no. 11, 2009.

[BUY 10] BUYSSE A., VANHULLE S., "Le portfolio : une médiation contrôlante et structurante des savoirs professionnels", *Revue suisse des sciences de l'éducation*, vol. 32, no. 1, pp. 87–104, 2010, accessed January 2018 at: http://www.rsse.ch/past-issues/32-1-2010-forschung-uber-die-lehrerinnen-und -lehrerbildung-ansichten-und-aussichten/?page_id=2467.

[BUY 11a] BUYSSE A., "Une modélisation des régulations et de la médiation dans la construction des savoirs professionnels des enseignants", in MAUBANT P., MARTINEAU S. (eds), *Fondements des pratiques professionnelles des enseignants : pour une lecture compréhensive des fondements des savoirs professionnels des enseignants*, pp. 243–284, PUO, Ottawa, 2011.

[BUY 11b] BUYSSE A., "Les mécanismes inductifs et déductifs dans la genèse des savoirs des enseignants en formation", in MAUBANT P., CLENET J., LENOIR Y. (eds), *Débats sur la professionnalisation des enseignants*, pp. 267–307, PUO, Ottawa, 2011.

[CHA 06] CHARLIER B., DESCHRYVER N., PERAYA D., "Apprendre en présence et à distance : une définition des dispositifs hybrides", *Distances et savoirs*, vol. 4, no. 4, pp. 469–946, 2006.

[COD 12] CODREANU T., COMBE CELIK C., "La médiation de l'interaction pédagogique sur une plateforme de visioconférence poste à poste", *Alsic*, vol. 15, no. 3, 2012, accessed April 2013 at: http://alsic.revues.org/2572.

[DEV 08] DEVELOTTE C., GUICHON N., KERN R., "'Allo Berkeley ? Ici Lyon… Vous nous voyez bien ?'. Étude d'un dispositif de formation en ligne synchrone franco-américain à travers les discours de ses usagers", *Alsic*, vol. 11, no. 2, 2008, accessed April 2013 at: http://journals.openedition.org/alsic/892.

[DEV 11] DEVELOTTE C., KERN R., LAMY M.-N. (eds), *Décrire la conversation en ligne : le face à face distanciel*, ENS Éditions, Lyon, 2011.

[FER 15] FERONE G., LAVENKA A., "La CV, quels effets sur la pratique de l'enseignant ?", *Distances et médiations des savoirs*, vol. 10, 2015, accessed June 2016 at: http://dms.revues.org/1047.

[GOF 73] GOFFMAN E., *La présentation de soi*, Éditions de Minuit, Paris, 1973.

[GRA 11] GRANGEAT M., "Des savoirs enseignants : des savoirs-processus en prise avec les acteurs, les dispositifs et les théories", in MAUBANT P., MARTINEAU S. (eds), *Fondements des pratiques professionnelles des enseignants : pour une lecture compréhensive des fondements des savoirs professionnels des enseignants*, pp. 143–164, PUO, Ottawa, 2011.

[JÉZ 10] JÉZÉGOU A., "Créer de la présence à distance en *e-learning*. Cadre théorique, définition, et dimensions clés", *Distances et savoirs*, vol. 8, no. 2, pp. 257–274, 2010.

[JOR 09] JORRO A., "La construction de l'éthos professionnel en formation alternée", *Travail et apprentissage*, vol. 3, pp. 13–25, 2009.

[KER 05] KERBRAT-ORECCHIONI C., *Discours en interaction*, Armand Colin, Paris, 2005.

[KER 11] KERBRAT-ORRECHIONI C., "Conversations en PR et conversations en ligne", in DEVELOTTE C., KERN R., LAMY M.-N. (eds), *Décrire la conversation en ligne : le face à face distanciel*, pp. 173–196, ENS Éditions, 2011.

[LAM 08] LAMEUL G., "Les effets de l'usage des technologies d'information et de communication en formation d'enseignants, sur la construction des postures professionnelles", *Savoirs*, vol. 17, no. 2, pp. 71–94, 2008.

[MAC 09] MACEDO-ROUET M., "La visioconférence dans l'enseignement, ses usages et effets sur la distance de transaction", *Distances et savoirs*, vol. 7, no. 1, pp. 65–91, 2009.

[MAR 03] MARQUET P., NISSEN E., "La distance en formation aux langues par visioconférence : dimensions, mesures, conséquences", *Alsic*, vol. 6, no. 2, pp. 3–19, 2003, accessed January 2018 at: http://journals.openedition.org/alsic/2205.

[MAR 05] MARCELLI A., GAVEAU D. TOKIWA R., "Utilisation de la visioconférence dans un programme de FLE : tâches communicatives et interactions orales. Apprentissage des Langues et Systèmes d'Information et de Communication", *Alsic*, vol. 8, no. 3, pp. 185–203, 2005, available at: http://alsic.u-strasbg.fr/v08/marcelli/alsic_v08_18-pra2.htm.

[MAR 11] MARCOCCIA M., "T'es où maintenant ? : les espaces de la conversation visiophonique en ligne", in DEVELOTTE C., KERN R., LAMY M.-N. (eds), *Décrire la conversation en ligne : le face à face distanciel*, pp. 95–115, ENS Éditions, Lyon, 2011.

[MAU 11] MAUBANT P., MARTINEAU S., "Introduction", in MAUBANT P., MARTINEAU S. (eds), *Fondements des pratiques professionnelles des enseignants*, pp. 23–31, PUO, Ottawa, 2011.

[PAQ 11] PAQUELIN D., "La distance : questions de proximités", *Distances et savoirs*, vol. 9, no. 4, pp. 565–590, 2011, accessed January 2018 at: http://www.cairn.info/revue-distances-et-savoirs-2011-4-page-565.htm.

[PAQ 15] PAQUAY L., ALTET M., CHARLIER E. *et al.*, *Former des enseignants professionnels. Quelles stratégies ? Quelles compétences ?*, 4th edition, De Boeck, Brussels, 2015.

[PER 96] PERRENOUD P., *Enseigner : agir dans l'urgence, décider dans l'incertitude. Savoirs et compétences dans un métier complexe*, ESF Éditeur, Montrouge, 1996.

[PER 03] PERAYA D., DUMONT P., "Interagir dans une classe virtuelle : analyse des interactions verbales médiatisées dans un environnement synchrone", *Revue française de pédagogie*, vol. 145, pp. 51–61, 2003.

[PER 08] PERAYA D., "Un regard critique sur les concepts de médiatisation et médiation. Nouvelles pratiques, nouvelle modélisation", *Le déploiement des Tics dans l'enseignement supérieur : évidences et tendances*, Grenoble, France, 9–12 September 2008, accessed January 2010 at: http://w3.u-grenoble3.fr /les_enjeux/2008-supplement/Peraya/index.php.

[RAB 95] RABARDEL P., *Les Hommes et les technologies : une approche cognitive des instruments contemporains*, Armand Colin, Paris, 1995.

[RAI 93] RAISKY C., "Problème du sens des savoirs professionnels agricoles, préalable à une didactique", in JONNAERT P., LENOIR Y. (eds), *Didactique du sens et sens des didactiques*, pp. 101–121, Éditions du CRP, Sherbrooke, 1993.

[ROG 11] ROGER L., "La situation : pour une meilleure compréhension du processus d'apprentissage professionnel dans la formation des maîtres", in MAUBANT P., MARTINEAU S. (eds), *Fondements des pratiques professionnelles des enseignants : pour une lecture compréhensive des fondements des savoirs professionnels des enseignants*, pp. 213–218, PUO, Ottawa, 2011.

[SAV 13] SAVARIEAU B., DAGUET H., "L'introduction des « classes virtuelles » synchrones, un moyen de renforcer la qualité de l'accompagnement en formation d'adultes ?", *Frantice,* no. 6, 2013, accessed November 2014 at: http:// www.frantice.net/document.php?id=710.

[SCH 09] SCHNEUWLY B., "Le travail enseignant", in SCHNEUWLY B., DOLZ J. (eds), *Des objets enseignés en classe de français*, pp. 29–43, PUR, Rennes, 2009.

[TAR 15] TARDIF M., GAUTHIER C., "L'enseignant comme acteur rationnel : quelles rationalité, quel savoir, quel jugement ?", in PAQUAY L., ALTET M., CHARLIER E. *et al.* (eds), *Former des enseignants professionnels. Quelles stratégies ? quelles compétences ?*, pp. 239–270, 4th edition, De Boeck, Brussels, 2015.

[VAN 08] VANHULLE S., "Au coeur de la didactique professionnelle, la subjectivation des savoirs", in PASTRE P., LENOIR Y. (eds), *Didactique professionnelle, didactique des savoirs professionnels*, pp. 227–254, Octarès, Toulouse, 2008.

[VAN 09a] VANHULLE S., "Savoirs professionnels et construction sociodiscoursive de l'agir", *Bulletin VALS-ASLA (Association suisse de linguistique appliquée)*, vol. 90, pp. 167–188, 2009.

[VAN 09b] VANHULLE S., "Dire les savoirs professionnels : savoirs de référence et logiques d'action", in HOFSTETTER R., SCHNEUWLY B. (eds), *Savoirs en (trans)formation. Au cœur des professions de l'enseignement et de la formation*, pp. 245–263, De Boeck, Brussels, 2009.

[VAN 09c] VANHULLE S., *Des savoirs en jeu au savoir en "je". Cheminements réflexifs et subjectivation des savoirs chez de jeunes enseignants en formation*, Peter Lang, Bern, 2009.

[VAN 14] VANHULLE S., "Comprendre le développement professionnel par l'analyse des discours", *Forumlecture.ch*, vol. 1, 2014, accessed March 2017 at: http://www.forumlecture.ch/myUploadData/files/2014_1_Vanhulle.pdf.

[VYG 97] VYGOTSKI L., *Pensée et Langage*, La Dispute, Paris, 1997.

[WAL 12] WALLET J., "De la synchronie médiatisée en formation à distance", *Sticef*, vol. 19, 2012, accessed September 2016 at: http://sticef.univ-lemans.fr /num/vol2012/14r-wallet/sticef_2012_wallet_14rp.pdf.

[WEI 99] WEISSBERG J.-M., *Présences à distance*, L'Harmattan, Paris, 1999.

Support for Work through Telepresence: Teachers' Feelings of Self-Efficacy and Strategies for Self-Management

5.1. Introduction

Telepresence has been integrated into teaching activities primarily in the framework of university training. At the level of teacher education schools in Switzerland, the use of telepresence has not yet been widely implemented. Some systems have appeared because of teacher motivation. Bourdeau [BOU 02] underlines, in this regard, that there is a lack of knowledge about the design of pedagogical events using telepresence. Teachers also find themselves confronted with the creation of new systems. The transition to innovation is sometimes experienced with difficulty, and it is important to understand the stakes of innovative practice and the strategies implemented to resolve them.

From these assessments, we first present a study undertaken by teachers in teacher education schools to evaluate the place occupied by telepresence for support, collaborative work (frequency, uses, contributions and limits of interchange), general perception and the feeling of self-efficacy among teachers in this practice [BAN 86, BAN 88, BAN 93]. Second, we look at the implementation of telepresence systems in work support activities in order to better understand self-management strategies implemented by teachers.

Chapter written by Stéphanie BOÉCHAT-HEER.

The study took place in the 2016–2017 academic year with all of the professors in the teacher education schools in the cantons of Berne, Jura and Neuchâtel (HEP-BEJUNE), in Switzerland. In this establishment, the professors who use telepresence do so voluntarily. They are motivated to innovate in their teaching and to produce isolated practices. Work support using telepresence is achieved in a hybrid manner, by alternating presence and distance. This practice is accomplished through synchronous videoconference (Skype) or e-mail, to deepen exchanges without a simultaneous connection. No system is currently proposed to foster the use of telepresence. This context is even more interesting to analyze since it allows for the discovery of perceptions and strategies implemented by teachers motivated to launch themselves into innovation and for a response to the following questions: what are the perceptions of teachers with regard to the use of telepresence in the training of teachers? What is the feeling of self-efficacy among professors in the support of work through telepresence? What are the self-management strategies that have been implemented?

To respond to these questions, our study was conducted in two phases. First, a questionnaire was sent to all of the teachers in training for elementary, secondary, continuous and postgraduate education. Second, we interviewed six teachers who were practicing support with telepresence in training, to deepen and to allow for the cross-verification of the data.

5.2. Conceptual framework

5.2.1. *Social interactions in telepresence and the feeling of presence*

The support of activities in telepresence raises questions about social interactions and the feeling of presence. According to Jézégou, "technology offers the opportunity to experience collective communication that resembles in-person experiences, particularly during collaborative remote activities, through the shared manipulation of virtual objects or through the use of avatars" [JEZ 10b, p. 258]. Jacquinot considers that exchanges in telepresence allow for "the taming of distance, at least of spatio-temporal distance, thanks to the use of synchronous and asynchronous modes of communication supported by web tools, most often integrated with dedicated pedagogical platforms [...]. They thus contribute to suppressing the absence that was so dreaded during the previous decades" [JAC 93, p. 257]. The notion of presence relies on interactions that mobilize the body as much as verbal language [WEI 00]. According to Wallet [WAL 07] or Annoot and Bodergat [ANN 16], the in-person experience, even when extremely limited, plays a major role in the establishment and the dynamics of the pedagogical relationship, particularly through the eye of the beholder. According to Jézégou [JEZ 10a], three dimensions allow for the characterization of presence in e-learning: cognitive presence, socio-affective presence and pedagogical presence. Cognitive presence is based on the operations carried out by students during the resolution of problematic situations. These latter are social interactions concerning points of view, mutual adjustments, negotiations and deliberations. Socio-affective presence results from social interactions favoring symmetrical relationships and a favorable socio-affective climate. Pedagogical presence unfolds from social interactions that the teacher puts in place with students to maintain cognitive and socio-affective presences. The support of different kinds of presences is accomplished through testing strategies that the teacher calls on. On this subject, Verquin-Savarieau and Daguet [VER 16] assert that testing at a distance is an important element that cements the results of training. Testing can manifest through the following activities: "Respecting fixed schedules; directly facing potential dysfunctions; maintaining pedagogical objectives all while reacting in real time to all kinds of questions" [VER 16, p. 52].

5.2.2. The pedagogical system and the organization of interaction between participants

To accomplish support in telepresence activities, the pedagogical system and the organization of interactions between participants play an important role. According to Peraya, "a system is an instance, a place for social interaction and cooperation possessing intentions, its symbolic and physical operation, in sum, its own modes of interaction" [PER 99, p. 153]. Lameul [LAM 08] considers that the system is a set of human and hardware tools constructed to achieve an objective. In the development of a remote collaborative dynamic, several authors [CHA 02, DIL 03, HEN 03, DAE 06] are of the opinion that it is important to be attentive to others, to express disagreement with others' points of view without being aggressive, to be empathic with respect to others, to encourage each other and to help each other. Jacquinot defends the idea that "putting distance at the heart of the teacher/learner process brings along a certain number of changes that are equally 'provocations' with regard to the classical mode of teaching face-to-face and the system in which it is integrated" [JAC 10, p. 153]. Rabardel and Samurçay [RAB 01] refer to support modalities to better understand and analyze four kinds of instrumental mediations: epistemic mediation, oriented towards knowledge of the object; praxiological mediation, oriented towards action; reflexive mediation, oriented towards the subject himself and relational mediation, which occurs between subjects. Mediation in the educational and training context consists of "relating one or more learners to knowledge and skills in order to construct their own knowledge" [RIN 15, p. 1].

5.2.3. *The feeling of self-efficacy in the implementation of pedagogical design*

We know how reticent teachers are to take the plunge into the exploration of new tools for fear of finding themselves confronted with technical problems or tools that often do not immediately meet their needs. Numerous studies show the connection between the feeling of self-efficacy and the acceptance of innovative practices [ABB 07, BOÉ 12, CAR 02, DEA 02]. Guskey [GUS 88] shows the connection between the feeling of elevated competence and positive attitudes with regard to new practices. Teachers who feel competent will be more motivated to take the plunge into new activities with their students.

According to Bandura [BAN 97], the feeling of personal efficacy is a fundamental and immediate determinant of the engagement and performance of the subject during the task. Judgments of personal self-efficacy are constructed from four sources of learning [BAN 77, BAN 97]: lived experience (success, failure); vicarious experience (social learning); verbal persuasion and physiological state (damp palms, dry throat, etc.). He also asserts that the person is proactive, capable of self-organization, self-reflection and self-management.

In Zimmerman's model of self-regulated learning [ZIM 00], self-management is exercised in three cyclic phases: planning, supervised execution and self-reflection (see Table 5.1). Planning corresponds to the beliefs that precede learning. Supervised execution corresponds to the process that occurs during learning and that has an influence on concentration and on the results. Self-reflection is a process that occurs after learning. This model insists, therefore, on two indissociable facets of self-regulation: a proactive self-regulation that creates goals and plans of action and a reactive self-regulation intended to overcome the obstacles preventing the achievement of the goal.

Cyclical phase		
Planning	**Executive control**	**Self-management**
Task analysis: – goal setting; – strategic planning	Self-testing: – self-instruction; – imagery; – centering of attention; – strategies connected to the task	Self-adjustment: – self-evaluations; – causal attributions
Self-motivating beliefs: – self-efficacy; – expectation of results; – intrinsic interest/value	Self-observation: – self-rating; – self-testing	Self-reaction: – self-satisfaction/affectivity; – adaptive inferences

Table 5.1. *Structure of the phases and sub-processes of self-regulation [ZIM 00]*

Being an agent, creating intentions and following them through to the end require one to possess beliefs that push one to act; this is the role of the feeling of self-efficacy. Numerous studies have shown that a feeling of elevated personal efficacy favors the use of effective cognitive strategies, engagement in more difficult activities, the level of effort and the time spent studying. It seems to be an essential determinant of self-regulatory behaviors. According to Zimmerman, learners skilled in self-management have goals oriented towards learning, a feeling of elevated self-efficacy, and show intrinsic motivation.

5.3. Methodological approach

5.3.1. *Objectives and research questions*

The general objective of this study is to understand the place occupied by telepresence with regard to support in teacher training, as well as the stakes of its implementation. More specifically, we hope to obtain, first, information about the general perception of teachers on the subject of the use of telepresence (type of use, frequency, advantages and inconveniences).

Second, we will analyze in more detail the feeling of self-efficacy and the self-regulatory strategies put in place by teachers during their telepresence meetings. We propose to respond to the following research questions: What are the perceptions of teachers on the subject of the use of telepresence in teacher training? What is the feeling of self-efficacy among teachers in the support of work through telepresence? What are the self-management strategies that have been implemented?

5.3.2. *Research type and method*

This study relies on a comprehensive approach linked to different dimensions of the process of integration and the feeling of self-efficacy among teachers when using telepresence. In the framework of our investigation and for data collection, we have called on two instruments: questionnaire and interview. It is through the connection of these two sources of data that this study tries to bring out the perceptions of teachers with regard to the use of telepresence and the feeling of self-efficacy and self-management strategies that develop from it.

Numerous studies [BUR 04, CRE 07] prove the interest in the use of mixed methods to show not only the complexity but also the richness of collected data. In our approach, mixed methods will be used as a combination of two types of sources (quantitative and qualitative), notably using the rationale of triangulation across methods [THU 08].

5.3.3. *Overview of research, participants and instruments*

The study was conducted in two phases in the 2016–2017 academic year. First, a questionnaire was sent to all of the teachers in the BEJUNE teacher training school, including those in training for elementary, secondary, continuous and postgraduate education. A total of 46 teachers out of 105 responded to the questionnaire, resulting in a rate of approximately 44%. Second, we interviewed six teachers who were practicing support with telepresence in training, to deepen and to allow for the cross-verification of the data. The teachers who were interviewed were randomly chosen from the list of teachers who agreed to participate in an interview following the questionnaire.

We were inspired by the scale for measuring the perception and feeling of self-efficacy of learners with regard to video-communication by Giroux and Lachance [GIR 08] to construct our questionnaire. Based on Bandura's socio-cognitive theory, this scale allows for the evaluation of two dimensions: the general perception of video-communication and of the individual's own level of competence in this context. We chose 17 items on a four-level, Likert-type scale running from "strongly disagree" to "strongly agree" and added two questions related to the type of use (class, thesis support, collaborative work, sessions, internships) and the frequency of use. We voluntarily separated the teachers using telepresence from those who never use it.

For semi-directed interviews, we separated the questions into three dimensions: planning (motivation, feeling of self-efficacy, establishment of strategic goals); uses connected to the implemented system (types of practice, frequency, strategies connected to the task, self-control) and self-reflection (self-evaluation and self-satisfaction).

5.3.4. *Data analysis*

For data collected via questionnaire, we proceeded to a descriptive analysis by calculating the frequencies and percentages for all of the available items. Then, we calculated the measures of association with the variables on an ordinal scale (chi-squared). The data collected via interview was processed through a transversal analysis and multi-case comparison in order to bring out the distinctive characteristics. This type of analysis consists of the discovery of convergences. We use content analysis as a method to achieve a thematic study.

5.4. Analysis of the results and discussion

5.4.1. *Contrasting opinions depending on the level of the teachers' practice in telepresence*

We hope to begin our analysis of the results by specifically focusing on the perceptions of teachers with respect to the use of telepresence. Through the data resulting from the questionnaires, we observe a significant difference ($p = 0.0255 < 0.05$) between teachers who have practiced telepresence and those who have never used it. By regrouping the results by factors, we realized that the teachers obtain the same grade concerning the reasons that motivate them to use telepresence. They have the same perception concerning the fact that telepresence is an excellent means to augment access to information, that it allows for durable learning, that the exchanges are motivating and that it makes it possible to notably decrease the time and resources attributed to travel. We observe, on the contrary, a significant difference between teachers who have practiced telepresence and those who have not with regard to cognitive dimensions, the feeling of self-efficacy and communication. It turns out that teachers who have already used telepresence have a more positive perception in relation to learning: "The classes given in telepresence are favorable for learning"; to memory: "I have trouble remembering exchanges in the telepresence environment"; to the development of strategies: "I have developed strategies allowing me to succeed in telepresence exchanges" and to concentration: "I manage to remain focused in telepresence courses". The teacher-users have a greater feeling of self-efficacy when conducting a presentation or a demonstration in telepresence: "I was comfortable when I had to do a presentation or a demonstration in telepresence", and feel capable of explaining the general operation of telepresence. At the level of communication, the teacher-users are more of the opinion that telepresence allows for clear and effective communication despite the distance and that it is a reliable method.

5.4.2. Teachers' feelings of self-efficacy and their self-management strategies

We analyzed the data from the interviews by taking inspiration from Zimmerman's self-regulatory model [ZIM 00]. This model is composed of three phases: planning, supervised execution and reflection. We first analyze the aspects connected to planning. It consists, for the teacher, of setting goals, planning his actions strategically, focusing on the intrinsic interest of the activity and persuading himself that he can succeed.

5.4.2.1. Planning before support in telepresence

5.4.2.1.1. Teachers' feelings of self-efficacy: between resourcefulness and problem-solving strategies

As far as self-motivation beliefs are concerned, the data from the interviews shows that professors have an intrinsic interest in the savings in time and travel. They consider that telepresence allows them to avoid unnecessary travel and to save time: "Very practical, for prosaic questions of time management and space" (E1); "It's for feasibility, that is to say, it allows one to avoid useless travel and then to streamline time to the utmost" (E3); "It allows one to save travel time" (E5).

Concerning teachers' feelings of self-efficacy, the results show that they feel competent and that they have developed problem-solving strategies. When they feel confronted by a problem, they have acquired strategies allowing them to find solutions. They all mention their capacity to throw themselves in, to try, "to tinker", "to rummage around" and to address the challenges that appear on the way: "I feel competent with these two tools (Skype, Google Drive)" (E1); "I am what one calls a tinkerer, so I try things" (E2); "I feel relatively competent because I want to rummage around, I want to try, there is that element of challenge, of curiosity, as soon as I try something" (E2); "I always find some solution" (E6).

When teachers anticipate the task, they say they feel little apprehension: "No, I didn't have any apprehension... I wasn't scared. I told myself, if there's a bug, it's not that bad, we can meet up another time" (E4); "I'm not scared of computers, I try, and then it's probably by trying that I have refined certain knowledge, certain little ways of working" (E2). For them, practice allows them to increase their competence, to develop gestures, to improve relations with the student and to become quicker in problem-solving: "I know how to explore and I'll be able to do it faster next time" (E2); "With time, you also develop skills, like in real teaching, that you improve your attitude, your presence, and then that also allows you to have a better quality relationship and contents" (E3); "It is by doing that you say to yourself, you have to do it like this, I have to do it like that in order for it to work well" (E6). The results show that teachers are confident in their practice of telepresence and are not scared of taking the plunge into new activities because they know that regular practice allows them to improve and to acquire problem-solving strategies. They feel sufficiently capable of succeeding.

5.4.2.1.2. More preparation and anticipation

The teachers agree that support in telepresence requires more preparation. They are preparing to be confronted by possible technical problems: "I should take into account that maybe the student doesn't necessarily know this application" (E1). Telepresence activities require more reflection about organization, to write down more things on paper to remember the elements to develop: "I prepare more if it's through Skype, I notice more things" (E4); "It requires more thought about the object on which one wants to work, to think about what organization should be put in place" (E1). Exchanges in telepresence are more formalized: "It requires me to anticipate that moment in advance and maybe to put it in a more formal way" (E1).

5.4.2.1.3. First meetings in person to establish the framework and the relationship

The teachers all mentioned the need for a first in-person meeting to establish a framework: "It's good to create a framework, you see, where we can, all things considered, we can get to know each other reciprocally and then, basically, to create this format. This common format that can be reactivated later" (E3); "I like to see them once for real" (E4); "In general, I try to have meetings in person, because first meetings are more pleasant in person, there are details that can be shared in person" (E1).

The in-person meeting allows the teacher to create a connection, a format for mutual communication, to begin with a trusting relationship and to provide the desire to work together: "To see a bit if I can trust the student" (E1); "I always start work in person to establish some conditions but also, basically, to become aware of who the person is, how she thinks, how she reasons, and then also to create a sort of connection that, afterward, can be maintained, but you have to start in person" (E3). This beginning is important for teachers because it allows them to establish milestones for lasting communication, which can later be remotely reactivated: "Well because we created, all things considered, a mutual communication format and then it's reactivated, what I wanted to say is that it's reactivated once we're in telepresence. If we did not create this format, then what is this format? It's sometimes non-verbal, it's empathy, all things considered, it's the desire to work together" (E3).

These observations connect with those of Wallet [WAL 07] (cited by Annoot and Bodergat), who highlights that "the in-person experience, even when extremely limited, plays a major role in the establishment and the dynamic of the pedagogical relationship, in particular through the eye of the beholder" [ANN 16, p. 10]. To create pedagogical presence, defined by Jézégou [JEZ 10a], teachers need to build a socio-affective presence in person; this is part of a need that is inherent to practice in telepresence.

	Sub-process	Dimension stemming from interviews
Planning	Belief in self-motivation	Intrinsic interest: the savings in time and travel
		Teachers' elevated feeling of efficacy: - elevated competence in problem-solving (resourcefulness and self-training) - little apprehension, little fear of plunging in - positive experience (practice allows for an increase in their competencies)
	Task analysis	Establishment of goals and strategic planning: - more preparation and anticipation - first meeting in person to establish the framework.

Table 5.2. *Dimensions of planning and support in telepresence*

5.4.2.2. *Executive control during support in telepresence*

We are interested here in the teacher's performance during the practice of telepresence. More precisely, it is a question of presenting the results linked to the conduct of the chosen strategy, to the use of self-guiding strategies, to the verification of intermediate results (debugging, research assistance), to the attention brought to the task and to self-observation.

5.4.2.2.1. Strategies connected to the task

Among the strategies employed, the importance emerges of the availability of a document in front of one's eyes that one can hold onto: "Each time, I asked them if they could send me a document before a meeting. Afterward I examine the document and we can read it and comment on it together" (E1); "I always have a sheet with keywords or key sentences in front of me" (E4). The teachers said they used this support in order to not forget the important points: "Not seeing the person who has these documents, or something like that, suddenly I'm afraid I'll forget to talk about certain things" (E4).

It is also important for professors to see the student in person again to verify the learning they have undergone in telepresence: "I always prefer, afterward, seeing the student again in person to, sort of to finish, to finally close the loop... To see them again in the halls, that allows for closure...

A sort of a receipt" (E5); "So we need to meet again, at a given time, for real, as if a little bit was lacking, effectively" (E5); "I may have a greater tendency to take stock. That is to say, to verify that what we said the last time was okay. Although it's true that I realize now as I'm saying it that I don't do this when I've seen them in person. As if, because of the distance, I needed to verify that everything was understood" (E4).

The results show, in a recurring way, the need to check and verify the comprehension of what has been said: "I try to evaluate, at that time, if there is a need to reorient certain things" (E1). The teachers need to obtain feedback and evidence that allow for agreement and verification that the student has understood. The fact of not having direct contact can imperil communication, which can sometimes lead to a lack of understanding: "I would have I think a lot more trouble getting a sort of implicit feedback from students" (E1); "because we didn't have direct contact, and then we don't see the little details that mean the person is becoming bored or that he would like to react" (E3); "we don't have enough indications that show that it is necessary, basically, to stop and then maybe to ask for a reformulation or an explanation" (E3).

5.4.2.2.2. The teacher's self-observation

The teacher adapts to these changes by being more supervisory, by explaining more and by frequently verifying comprehension for reassurance: "By using this tool, I tend to be more supervisory in fact" (E4); "to prepare more, to verify that everything's okay. To come back to it afterward, although it's true that, in person, I think I leave more implicit. Bizarrely, I tend to explain more remotely. Because I don't have that physical impression of saying to myself, yes, everything's okay" (E4); "as if I need to reassure myself: did what was said actually go over well?" (E5). Teachers emphasize the need to check the student's level of comprehension. This observation connects with the results obtained by Verquin-Savarieau and Daguet [VER 16], which show that verification is an important element in training interactions, as are the respect for fixed schedules, facing potential dysfunctions and holding onto one's pedagogical objectives by reacting in real time to all kinds of questions.

	Sub-process	Dimension stemming from interview
Executive control	Self-control	Strategies connected to the task: - verify the student's comprehension - need for feedback and evidence - need to see the student again in person
	Self-observation	Self-rating: - more supervisory - need to be reassured - more explanation - having a document on hand

Table 5.3. *Dimensions present in the teacher's executive control during support in telepresence*

5.4.2.3. *Reflection about actions after support in telepresence*

We focus on the aspects connected to practice and to the professor's personal evaluation. It is a question of the perceptions connected to the evaluation of the way in which the task was accomplished, self-evaluation of one's degree of satisfaction and the assessment of adaptations to be made in the procedure.

5.4.2.3.1. Non-verbal is lacking, difficulty with staying focused and loss of control

We are interested in how the teacher asks himself about the obstacles that negatively affect the task and how he thinks about remediation strategies to overcome them. The results show that the teachers agree that non-verbal communication is weaker during exchanges in telepresence: "It's really the act of showing the end of the path, in fact, we detect less of the non-verbal" (E4); "I am going to see them but there will be less of the little actions or things" (E1); "but Skype, suddenly, I always saw comments in writing if I ever wanted a certain passage to really be discussed and then orally, I came back to it, you see, in the document, I marked it in yellow, the really physical aspect" (E4).

The results show that teachers think that it is very difficult to remain focused on a task in telepresence. They reported being distracted by external elements connected to the system (windows, technical interruptions, etc.): "You get the impression that the communication is not complete, with respect to the image. And then you're caught up by other things" (E5); "we weren't always at our best because communication was repeatedly hampered, and then, to conclude, we didn't even know where we were anymore" (E3); "the eyes, I think, shift from the person with whom we're talking, to that little window, and it's difficult to control yourself in this regard, and to only focus on the largest image, and I think that it influences the conversation, I think" (E5). The teachers connect this difficulty of remaining focused to technical problems that arise: "a connection problem can be bothersome" (E1); "problems when the video and sound become out of sync. It can also cut out at any time" (E3); "the problem is that it's a showstopper, a frozen image" (E5); "it's disturbing because the image is slowed in relation to the sound and, in relation to non-verbal communication about what's happening, it becomes problematic, but it didn't prevent us from, from continuing to talk" (E4).

5.4.2.3.2. More focused on the task and the feeling of elevated presence

Interview extracts show that teachers are more focused on the task and on the cognitive aspects of telepresence: "I have more of an impression of working on the object in question and that, together, we point toward the same object of reflection than of trying to agree about something" (E1); "I think we're more focused on the cognitive aspects, sometimes, than on aspects of communication, or in any case of relations, of the student relationship, even if these terms are a bit intertwined" (E1). This allows the teacher to be more focused on the important points and to emphasize the elements to be worked on more directly: "Sometimes it can make work easier because you're really focused on a concept, on work, and therefore telepresence allows, in the end, sometimes, to remove what you'd call 'sensoriality'. Basically, it allows one to work a bit more rationally, and then, basically, to be more focused on the important things" (E3); "to improve the information a bit, that is to say, to go more directly at what's important, at what has to be done, to talk in order to really give pertinent information" (E3); "to be a bit more rational, to go more rapidly through acquisition, competencies, and developments" (E3).

They also mention the fact of being more present for students and more invested in the task: "I found that I was more present, and they were more invested" (E2); "when I put myself in front of the screen, I had the impression of being with him, which is a very strange feeling" (E2); "that is to say that, at the moment when you're communicating with the student, you're sure you're communicating with his brain and not with an image, because the connection is direct" (E3).

Finally, they think that telepresence sessions are more organized and effective: "it's more organized" (E6); "the intervention is programmed, less spontaneous" (E4); "it's much more mechanical, there are less interruptions, people respect the presentation and then ask questions... This organized side... We're maybe more effective than if we were in person because we're clear" (E4); "there's an obligation to be present, so we maybe invest more sometimes when in telepresence and therefore we also get really good results with that" (E3). Interview excerpts foreground that telepresence makes it possible to accomplish several tasks at the same time: "We interacted on Google Doc" (E2); "this Google Drive tool that is exactly what makes that incredible sharing possible" (E5); "we can simultaneously talk, work, draft, write, and read at the same time with Google Doc" (E1).

The results show that teachers above all focus on the cognitive presence described by Jézégou [JEZ 10b], which consists of social interactions that involve confrontations of points of view, mutual adjustments, negotiations and deliberations. As for the socio-affective presence, it is constructed first in person and then by alternating between distance and presence. Teachers need to verify in person that students have clearly understood the message delivered in telepresence.

	Sub-process	Dimension stemming from interviews
Self-reflection	Self-adjustment	Self-evaluations: - the non-verbal is lacking - difficult to stay focused - loss of control/destabilization - more focus on the task/significant feeling of presence
	Self-reaction	Self-satisfaction: - the possibility of accomplishing several activities at the same time

Table 5.4. *Dimensions connected to professors' self-reflection during support in telepresence*

5.5. Conclusion

The results of this study show that the passage from in person to telepresence, in activities of support in teacher training, requires adjustments on the teachers' part. Their way of being and of conceiving their meeting changes requires adjusting to each new experience. The fact of practicing telepresence brings a consolidation, a confidence in its use and a willingness to continue the process. These observations prompt us to ask ourselves about the importance of motivating teachers to take the plunge, daring them to try and supporting them through the process so they can be up to date with innovation.

Through the interview extracts, certain aspects of users linked to their self-management strategies emerge. The teachers are not afraid to take a risk, to rise to the challenge, to do it over and to find solutions when problems arise. They also have an intrinsic interest in the task and an elevated degree of motivation and feeling of self-efficacy. These observations connect with the results of Zimmerman [ZIM 00], who stipulated that learners skilled in self-management have goals oriented towards learning, have an elevated feeling of self-efficacy and show intrinsic motivation.

As the extracts show, professors adapt their self-management strategies to the distinctive procedures of telepresence throughout the process. These strategies refer to the following dimensions: more preparation and anticipation; a need to arrange a first meeting in person to establish the framework; a need to see the student in person again and a need to check and verify the student's understanding. The teachers claim to be in a more supervisory situation that involves more explanation and that they need to be reassured. The non-verbal communication is lacking, and teachers say they have difficulty in focusing, but are more focused on the task and can accomplish several tasks at a time. What emerges from these aforementioned strategies is the professor's need for verification, as if distance raised questions about the relationship and destabilized it.

The strategies we have discovered through the interviews allow us to understand more about the dimensions in play in the situation of support in telepresence and to be able thus to better reply to the need for training and supervision for teachers. These results contribute to enriching knowledge relative to the feeling of self-efficacy and to teachers' self-management strategies in a telepresence activity, but show a certain number of limitations that lead to directions for future research. Even though quantitative and qualitative cross-tabulation allow for the expansion of the range of the results, it remains difficult to envisage a generalization. These results have the advantage of contributing interesting information that provides suggestions for following up these analyses with other teachers. Besides, it will be pertinent to engage with professors who are reticent to engage in telepresence and to observe if there is a difference at the level of perception and the feeling of self-efficacy. It will also be interesting to accompany several teachers who have never used telepresence during their first experience and to document the potential changes in perceptions.

5.6. References

[ABB 07] ABBITT J.T., KLETT M.D., "Identifying influences on attitudes and self-efficacy beliefs towards technology integration among pre-service educators", *Electronic Journal for the Integration of Technology in Education*, vol. 6, pp. 28–42, 2007.

[ANN 16] ANNOOT E., BODERGAT J.-Y., "Diriger les mémoires à distance à l'université : un levier pour la compréhension d'une dimension du métier d'universitaire ?", *Distances et médiations des savoirs*, vol. 13, p. 1–16, 2016, accessed November 2017 at: http://dms.revues.org/1329.

[BAN 77] BANDURA A., "Self-efficacy: Toward a unifying theory of behavioral change", *Psychological Review*, vol. 84, pp. 191–215, 1977.

[BAN 86] BANDURA A., *Social Foundations of Thought and Action: A Social Cognitive Theory*, Prentice Hall, Upper Saddle River, 1986.

[BAN 88] BANDURA A., "Self-regulation of motivation and action through goal systems", in HAMILTON V., BOWER G.H., FRIJDA N.M. (eds), *Cognitive Perspectives on Emotion and Motivation*, pp. 37–61, Kluwer Academic Publishers, Dordrecht, 1988.

[BAN 93] BANDURA A., "Perceived self-efficacy in cognitive development and functioning", *Educational Psychologist*, vol. 28, no. 2, pp. 117–148, 1993.

[BAN 97] BANDURA A., *Self-efficacy: The Exercise of Control*, W.H. Freeman and Company, New York, 1997.

[BOÉ 12] BOÉCHAT-HEER S., "Évaluation d'une formation aux TICE : développe-ment de compétences et sentiment d'auto-efficacité", in BOÉCHAT-HEER S., WENTZEL B. (eds), *Génération connectée : quels enjeux pour l'école ?*, pp. 151–166, Éditions BEJUNE, Bienne, 2012.

[BOU 02] BOURDEAU J., "Vers une intégration pédagogique de la vidéocommunication dans la formation des maîtres", *Revue des sciences de l'éducation*, vol. 28, no. 2, pp. 289–304, 2002.

[BUR 04] BURKE R.J., ONWUEGBUZIE A.J., "Mixed methods research: A research paradigm whose time has come", *Educational Researcher*, vol. 33, no. 7, pp. 14–26, 2004.

[CAR 02] CARUGATI F., TOMASETTO C., "Le corps enseignant face aux technologies de l'information et de la communication dans les pratiques d'enseignement", *Revue des sciences de l'éducation*, vol. 28, no. 2, pp. 305–324, 2002.

[CHA 02] CHARLIER B., DESCHRYVER N., DAELE A., "Apprendre en collaborant à distance : ouvrons la boîte noire", in GUIR R. (ed.), *TIC et formation des enseignants*, De Boeck, Brussels, 2002.

[CRE 07] CRESWELL J.W., PLANO CLARK V.L., *Designing and Conducting Mixed Methods Research*, Thousand Oaks, Sage, 2007.

[DAE 06] DAELE A., CHARLIER B. (ed.), *Comprendre les communautés virtuelles d'enseignants : pratiques et recherches*, L'Harmattan, Paris, 2006.

[DEA 02] DEAUDELIN C., DUSSAULT M., BRODEUR M., "Impact d'une stratégie d'intégration des TIC sur le sentiment d'auto-efficacité d'enseignants du primaire et leur processus d'adoption d'une innovation", *Revue des sciences de l'éducation*, vol. 28, no. 2, pp. 391–410, 2002.

[DIL 03] DILLENBOURG P., POIRIER C., CARLES L., "Communautés virtuelles d'apprentissage : e-jargon ou nouveau paradigme ?", in TAURISSON A., SENTINI A. (eds), *Pédagogie.net,* PUQ, Quebec, 2003.

[GIR 08] GIROUX P., LACHANCE L., "Élaboration et validation de l'échelle de la perception et du sentiment d'auto-efficacité en vidéocommunication", *Revue internationale des technologies en pédagogie universitaire*, vol. 52, pp. 6–20, 2008.

[GUS 88] GUSKEY T.R., "Teacher efficacy, self concept, and attitudes towards the implementation of instructional innovation", *Teaching and Teacher Education*, vol. 4, no. 1, pp. 63–69, 1988.

[HEN 03] HENRI F., LUNDGREN-CAYROL K., *Apprentissage collaboratif à distance*, PUQ, Quebec, 2003.

[JAC 93] JACQUINOT G., "Apprivoiser la distance et supprimer l'absence ? ou les défis de la formation à distance", *Revue française de pédagogie*, vol. 102, pp. 55–67, 1993.

[JAC 10] JACQUINOT G., "Entre présence et absence. La FAD comme principe de provocation", *Distances et savoirs*, vol. 2, no. 8, pp. 153–166, 2010.

[JÉZ 10a] JÉZÉGOU A., "Créer de la présence à distance en e-learning : cadre théorique, définition et dimensions clés", *Distances et savoirs*, vol. 2, no. 8, pp. 257–274, 2010.

[JÉZ 10b] JÉZÉGOU A., "*Community of Inquiry* en *e-learning* : à propos du modèle de Garrison et d'Anderson", *Journal of Distance Education/Revue de l'Éducation à Distance*, vol. 24, no. 2, pp. 1–18, 2010.

[LAM 08] LAMEUL G., "Les effets de l'usage des technologies d'information et de communication en formation d'enseignants, sur la construction des postures professionnelles", *Savoirs*, vol. 2, no. 17, pp. 71–94, 2008.

[PER 99] PERAYA D., "Médiation et médiatisation : le campus virtuel. Vers les campus virtuels", *Hermès*, vol. 25, pp. 153–167, 1999.

[RAB 01] RABARDEL P., SAMURÇAY R., "From artifact to instrument-mediated learning", *Symposium on New Challenges to Research on Learning*, Helsinki, Finland, March 2001.

[RIN 15] RINAUDO J.-L., "Médiation numérique en éducation", *Distances et médiations des savoirs*, no. 12, 2015, accessed November 2017 at: http://dms.revues.org/1190.

[THU 08] THURSTON W.E., COVE L., MEADOWS L.M., "Methodological congruence in complex and collaborative mixed method studies", *International Journal of Multiple Research Approaches*, vol. 2, no. 1, pp. 2–14, 2008.

[VER 16] VERQUIN SAVARIEAU B., DAGUET H., "La classe virtuelle synchrone une substitution médiatique de l'enseignant pour renforcer la présence en formation à distance ?", *Revue STICEF*, vol. 23, no. 1, 2016, accessed May 2017 at: http://sticef.univ-lemans.fr/num/vol2016/04-savarieau-ensaccapp/sticef_2016_NS_savarieau_04p.pdf.

[WAL 07] WALLET J. (ed), *Le Campus numérique FORSE : analyses et témoignages*, PURH, Saint-Aignan, 2007.

[WEI 00] WEISSBERG J.-L., "Entre présence et absence. Outils de communication et présence humaine", *Actes des deuxièmes rencontres Réseaux Technologiques/ Réseaux humains*, Poitiers, France, June 2000, accessed November 2017 at: http://rhrt.edel.univ-poitiers.fr/document.php ?id=429.

[ZIM 00] ZIMMERMAN B.J., "Attaining self-regulation: A social cognitive perspective", in BOECKAERTS M., PINTRICH P.R., ZEIDNER M. (eds), *Handbook of Self-regulation*, pp. 13–39, Academic Press, San Diego, 2000.

Part 3

Telepresence Robots

Effect of a Telepresence Robot on Remote Students' Bodily Impressions: Extended or Mended Body

6.1. Introduction

With the framework law of July 8, 2013, the French national education minister (NEM) renewed his encouragement to include all students in classes, including students with special needs. Thus, the question of the inclusion of students with disabilities is a real concern for universities that are trying to find permanent solutions. The emergence of robotics in numerous sectors of society, and particularly in education, provides a real possibility of enabling the inclusion of students with physical disabilities. In particular, telepresence robots allow students with mobility problems to be "present at a distance" when attending their university classes. It is therefore interesting to examine this new form of presence at a distance. In particular, in an academic culture, where the form of presence considered as "full" is that of integrated presence, that is, actualized by the physical body, we examine here the new ontophany brought about by the telepresence robot.

We consider ontophany to be the means by which "something shows itself to us" [VIA 13, p. 110]. According to Vial, "the technique can thus be defined as a master ontophany, that is to say a general perceptual structure that conditions *a priori* how beings appear" [VIA 13, p. 111]. Thus, thanks to robots, the user is present because he appears to others and can see others through a screen. A previous study [FUR 16] made it possible to

Chapter written by Françoise POYET.

highlight that this new form of presence could lead to differences between the perceptions of remote students and their peers. Besides, we have discovered that "the analogies produced between the human and technological functions seem to signify that the disabled student proceeds with a symbolic transfer of his real body to a technological body" [FUR 16, p. 164].

In an extension of this work, we wanted to delve into the perceptual differences of remote students and to analyze in more detail the nature of the relationships that can be established between human and technology. Notably, we want to know how the robot allows for an "augmentation" and/or a "reduction" of the body's physical potential, in terms of mobility and sensoriality, and the repercussions for the user in perceptual terms.

6.2. A new ontophany engendered by the telepresence robot

According to Vial, the arrival of digital technologies not only constitutes a historical event that is encompassed by technical history, but is also really a "phenomenological revolution" [VIA 13, p. 96] to the extent that these technologies affect our perceptual culture, that is, they affect "the set of ways of feeling about and representing the world, as much as they depend on customs or aptitudes learned by man as a member of a society" [LÉV 69]. The fact that our environment is hybrid by nature, both digital and non-digital, leads to changes in our perceptual habits by thwarting them. The very notion of reality is thus called into question and seems to provide a new way of perceiving beings and things, that is, a new ontophany. Subsequently, each individual is led to carry out phenomenological work that is both physical and social in order to understand the world in which he evolves and to reinterpret it so that it seems comprehensible to him.

In the case of the use of a telepresence robot, this double perceptual and social renegotiation is necessary because the user is physically present in his home and virtually present in class. His physical reality can be considered hybrid, both non-digital (material and embodied at home) and digital (via the robot in class). On the social front, the perception of a user who is present at a distance also calls the traditional framework for social interactions for himself and his peers into question once more. In effect, he simultaneously belongs to two traditionally separate social spaces: that of the family (home) and of work (university). We will here examine this dissociation between matter and presence: how do we come to psychically understand the fact of moving in two different places and perceiving via a robot? To try to answer this question, we will analyze the sensory motor and/or operating schemes connected to the use of a robot and their impact on the student's bodily schema. However, first, we will recall several essential definitions concerning the concepts of scheme and bodily schema.

6.3. Sensory motor and bodily schema: towards an augmented body?

From the perspective of a coordinated origin, according to Rabardel [RAB 95], the appropriation of an artifact relies on the construction of use schemes in service of human activity. The notion of a scheme as first defined by Piaget and Inhelder as "the structure or the organization of actions such that they transfer or generalize during repetition of this action in similar or analogous circumstances" [PIA 66, p. 11] allows us to approach the appropriation of a telepresence robot in light of the construction of sensory motor and operating schemes that are more or less complex. For example, the use of a computing interface requires the construction of schemes that allow the robot to orient and steer in the classroom. These schemes can be simple (mouse prehension) or complex, and behavioral (movement) or cognitive (location in space). Continuing with Piaget's theory, the construction of these different schemes relies on varied experiences that the subject acquires in his environment from his earliest years. Thus, it is by experimenting and successive trial-and-error method that the child learns about the world around him, as well as about himself. These experiences, which are initially sensory and locomotive, privilege different areas of the body according to age and contribute to the development of the individual's bodily schema.

The notion of bodily schema, which refers to the representation of the body, was used as early as 1911 by Head and Holmes to refer to an internalized model of the body [HEA 11]. According to them, the subject accumulates a stock of impressions about his body, which reach his consciousness in the form of images. These thus form organized models of the subject himself, which their authors call "schemas". In this sense, the bodily schema is a kind of postural standard to which the subject refers permanently. This knowledge of his own body thus allows the individual to coordinate his gestures and to orient himself in the environment in which he finds himself, along three axes: top-bottom, left-right and front-back.

Although this notion is ambiguous because it is historically strongly connected to the notion of "muscular feeling" or "bodily feeling," underscoring that bodily knowledge depends exclusively on feelings born from movement, according to Jeannerod, it also allows them to be reconciled within the same theoretical framework of more or less complex disorders extending beyond the level of the body itself and arising from the achievement of a "self-image" [JEA 10, p. 187]. At present, scientific literature seems to refer more to the notion of a "bodily image", which integrates the tools and objects associated with bodily experiences and which is not therefore limited to the body's perspective aspects.

In our research, we use the notion of bodily schema in the same sense as "bodily image", considering that experiences with tools or associated objects also participate in the development of this schema, which is constructed through the cross-checking of multimodal sensory indicators, including particularly sight, hearing (for balance) and touch (for resistance of the medium of touch and movement). For example, the attribution of the properties of "high" and "low" seem directly connected to motor experiences relative to different bodily positions to reach the relevant positions. These positions are equally connected with the individual's subjective experience: what can appear to be "low" for some can seem "high" for others. Thus, the bodily schema represents a real instrument for measuring and positioning in space. In sum, this schema is constructed through the projection of experiences lived through the individual's physical body, to which tools and objects can be associated.

In our case, when a new physicality intervenes, that of the telepresence robot, for example, the user's relationship to the body can be disrupted on several levels and undoubtedly to different degrees: construction of user schemes connected to the body and/or modification of the bodily schema to allow for an adjustment of the physical body. Specifically, the handling of the robot seems to require the construction of new sensory-motor schemes and the accommodation of old schemes (sensory motor and/or operational) to be able to manipulate the artifact (the robot) and to transform it into an instrument (extension of the user's body).

Furthermore, the perception of his presence at a distance can modify his subjective relationship to the robot, whose physical entity can become an extension of the student's body. For example, the fact that the robot moves in a remote place on the student's initiative can "augment" his perceptual possibilities on the visual, auditory and kinesthetic levels. Finally, the student's bodily schema can be temporarily altered because of modified spatial and temporal landmarks and the new ontophany generated by the robot. This is what we will explore in the discussion of our results.

6.4. Methodology

Note that this study proceeds in the framework of a call for proposals from the Université du numérique en Région Rhône-Alpes (UNR-RA, 2015), which includes the École centrale de Lyon, the École supérieure du professorat et de l'enseignement (ESPE) de Lyon and the École du management Business School (EM Lyon).

The technical system is made up of robot hardware (see Figure 6.1) situated in a remote location (the classroom) and a navigation interface downloaded to the user's computer. The latter allows the robot to be moved remotely thanks to the Wi-Fi network, a visualization of the remote environment and synchronous communication. The robot, which is about 1.6 meters tall, moves on wheels steered remotely by the user through the control interface.

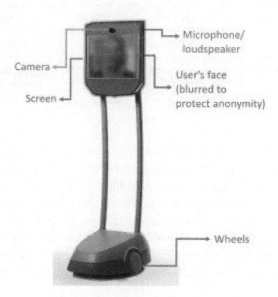

Figure 6.1. *The telepresence robot*

The experiment was conducted from 2015 to 2017, allowing students with a disability to pursue their teaching master's degrees remotely. The students submitted by the Disabled Service at Université Lyon 1 were randomly selected based on two criteria: availability of a computer with Internet access and use of a robot for academic activities. The sample comprised 10 users. Given the limited size of our sample, our study is currently exploratory; it should be supplemented in the future by other experiments.

	Name	Institution	Age	Status
1	Claire	EM	20–25	Student
2	Paul	École centrale	20–25	Student
3	Jeanne	EM	20–25	Student
4	Florence	ESPE	20–25	Student
5	Constance	ESPE	20–25	Student
6	Philippe	ESPE	20–25	Student
7	Yolande	École centrale	25–30	Student
8	Caroline	ENS IFE	25–30	Student
9	Alexis	École centrale	20–25	Student
10	Olivier	École centrale	20–25	Student

Table 6.1. *Surveyed population*

At the end of each experiment (which varied between two and eight months, depending on the case), semi-directed interviews that lasted approximately 1.5–2 hours were conducted. The interviews were all transcribed and, by analyzing the contents of these transcripts, we were able to collate the parts of the responses related to our research question. Different experimental situations with the robot were also video-recorded, which allowed us to confirm certain observable and described elements during the interviews. For details about the methodology, refer to our article [FUR 16].

6.5. Discussion

The results presented in the following paragraphs recap the major themes addressed during the interviews, namely:

– the technical appropriation of the robot connected to the students' sensory-motor schemes;

– the student's perceptual modifications with respect to the robot, which lays the foundation for a new ontophany;

– the impact of the robot with regard to the student's bodily representation and bodily schema;

– the status of the robot in the human–computer relationship: extended or mended body?;

– the physical location of the robot and the interpersonal distance within the class;

– the repercussions of the use of the robot in the learning process.

We will thus see that the use of a telepresence robot alters or augments, depending on circumstances, the students' sensory perceptions and that the latter can be subjected to perceptual illusions. Our observations will therefore favor a new ontophany.

6.5.1. *Technical appropriation of the robot facilitated by the transfer of old sensory-motor schemes*

The steering can be controlled using directional arrows or the mouse. In fact, most users use the directional arrows, except in Alexis' case, whose disability did not allow him to use the arrows manually; the robot is therefore controlled occipitally: "It's just when I press on the headrest [...] (he shows the movement with his head against the headrest) it's really like a joystick (he presses on the headrest and the chair makes a clicking noise), I press left and it goes left, I press right, and it goes right."

In all cases, the robots' users have already developed competencies for using a joystick or arrows through video games, for movement, or during the use of a word processor to move from one word to the next. Consequently, learning the fundamental movement controls is almost intuitive, which is not the case for navigation between the different visuo-spatial spaces to which the user has access: the classroom, the visualization of the user above his computer and the robot's wheels. Constance explained the development of her thoughts as she constructed new operational schemes with the robot: "I didn't understand at the beginning (laugh) and after I understood that I had to move in the thing (she indicates the corresponding image on the video feedback from the robot's upper camera) and, in the beginning, I moved with that and I told myself but it's not possible it zooms out each time so that annoyed me a bit (laugh) and it's afterward that I understood that you could move with the mouse on the screen and that was much better."

It was through progressive experimentation that Constance managed to master the navigation controls for moving, for attending the class session and for sometimes looking at the classroom and other times at the blackboard (with the projection of presentations in most cases). This was also true for the surveyed users, who selected some functions more than others and adapted the environment to their convenience.

Other analogous transfers were made from experiences with video games or on-board cameras: "I didn't have vertigo because it's like with on-board cameras, I've already experienced these perceptions and also with video games when I was little," Constance said. Philippe also relied on previous situations to describe his experience with the robot: "This first experience was very good, well, very fluid I'd say, because we were on the premises and the Internet worked very well [...] and it's true that, when we moved, there was no lag[1], it felt like driving a video game."

6.5.2. *Modified perceptions, a new way to perceive and understand ubiquity as an ordinary phenomenon*

Visual and auditory perceptions were limited in comparison to the traditional situation. This is what Jeanne said: "My vision was constrained, which was limiting to me. Likewise, with regard to sound, I never really knew who was speaking and where the sounds were coming from, if they came from the left or right, in front or behind." The sensory perceptions via the robot were limited, particularly with regard to sound. The user therefore had to make adjustments. Some perceptions were therefore dependent on

---

1 A lag designates a computer's slowness during start-up or during a task, according to the online dictionary, Merriam-Webster available at: https://www.merriam-webster.com /dictionary/lag (consulted in August 2018).

sensory compensations, particularly with regard to sound, by visual information. This is what Constance explained: "Since I couldn't hear, I had to orient myself to see the person who was speaking because of interference." Constance therefore proceeded to rotate the robot to position herself facing the speaker or a student who was taking the floor. In addition, the users noted a feeling of disorientation: "I lost my sense of orientation even though it was a place I knew," explained Paul. Claire had the same perception: "I didn't know where I was, and I had lost my orientation landmarks, so I couldn't go back myself."

On the other hand, kinesthetic feelings connected to bodily movements were "augmented" (Claire) by the ability to move in two different places: "I felt my body was there where it was located physically but at the same time I perceived it during the robot's movement as if it was doing something again," specified Claire. Jeanne also described this contradiction, which led her to perceive her own presence differently: "[...] physically I'm not there and yet I'm present physically, it's stupid but I'm in two places at once and I have a real environment and an unreal environment where I'm driving and it's really disconcerting; suddenly I have trouble getting into it, and as soon as I hear interference it brings me back to reality and it's difficult and then you have your eyes focused on the screen the whole time." Jeanne's remark makes us to realize that the use of the robot required her to construct a new way of perceiving, linked to the feeling of ubiquity. This construction required a real psychological effort to make it mentally possible to move in two different places.

Moreover, the robot engenders perceptual differences. What surprised Philippe "was this distinction between a 2D face that is moving around in the space while the movement is actually in 3D", after having externally captured images with the robot. Jeanne evoked a "loss of temporal markers, [she had] the feeling that time was passing more quickly."

Furthermore, this situation leads to disruptions depending on the connection quality, the amount of downtime or slowdowns during image transmission, which required adaptation on the part of users. According to Alexis, "the vision, the actions, are too slow, so when I talk, I slow down my delivery rate as if I were speaking to foreigners or on Skype." Like Alexis, Olivier adapted his way of communicating while taking into account the delays caused by remote transmission by relying on communication experiences with foreign students: "I think it's more connected to habits, in fact I simply transposed habits I engaged in with foreign students in French language class in terms of the pace of my speech and my diction [...] it didn't bother me because it's something I've already done [...] therefore without knowing what the feedback from the other side was... [...] I don't know if it was better or worse."

Finally, the collection of information about the class was significantly reduced: "I missed out on certain perceptions, such as the class ambiance, whether it was warm and pleasant, and it was harder for me to initiate interactions with my classmates," declared Paul.

6.5.3. *Constructing a new representation of one's body and adapting one's bodily schema*

The users did not necessarily see the remote robot; furthermore, it was neither always the size they pictured nor the one they saw on the screen (17 inches). This represented an additional difficulty for evaluating the distance between the robot and objects in the remote environment when the robot moved. Caroline expressed it in this way: "I thought the robot wasn't going to be able to get between the chairs and tables, I had never seen it physically, which would have helped me get an idea of its proportions." It seemed necessary for Caroline to redefine the contours of a kind of "extended corporeality", in order to adjust her movements when the robot moved; she thereby carried out a sort of actualization of her appearance and her own body: "When I saw myself in the robot, I had a strange, bizarre impression, as if I were wearing a disguise [...] There's an image I have of my body in motion and real images with the robot and there was a delay between them. [...] When I moved, I had the impression that my body was moving. I superseded the robot; it was my own perception that moved, but it wasn't the object." The robot therefore seemed to fade in the student's representation when she used it.

When she moved, it was the student herself who had the feeling of being in motion. The robot therefore allowed the student's body to be "extended" beyond the walls. Caroline concluded by insisting on the artifact's transparency: "I didn't have the impression that it was my body in the object; for me, the robot didn't exist; it was my body that dominated the robot. It's an extension that allowed me to move around." Her perception was the same with or without the robot: "My perception was unchanged, whether it was with the robot or in a real situation." Moreover, her classmates also made the same observation, because Caroline had been able to come to class physically in the afternoon: "They said to me, it's weird, two seconds ago you were rolling, and now you're walking. [...] Although, for me, I didn't have the same impression because I had the feeling I had spent the morning with them in class, as if I had been physically present."

Florence's position echoes Caroline's: "I had the feeling that it temporarily modified my perceptions, because I had the feeling that it was really me who was in the classroom." Jeanne also explained, "we raced, we started to dance in the hallway, and honestly, when my classmate turned me around, I turned on my bed." Given that the robot seems to be involved in the extension of Jeanne's physical body, it seems that there was not much of a gap with the student's bodily schema: "I didn't feel that I had problems with spatiality, because the robot extended my body."

6.5.4. *An open window to the class: from an extended to a mended body?*

As we have just shown, the robot is not perceived as a physical entity by the user, but rather as an open window onto other places. According to Florence, "The robot is a window onto something else, so I didn't have the same perception as the students who saw me through the window." Florence thus escaped from her living space because the robot allowed her to leave her home: "I wanted to be there because leaving my house was my oxygen, so I didn't have many moments when I slipped away." The robot thus allowed her to push back on her own body's limits regarding localization and, furthermore, it seemed to act as a temporary "prosthesis", offsetting her disability by allowing her to experience lost feelings of mobility.

This was also Alexis' opinion, whose physical disability is extreme: "I lost a lot of mobility, so now, to be able to be part of this thing, even if it was still a robot, wasn't bad, [...] there was the fact of turning towards someone and towards another person and moving toward the table, I don't know, it added a dynamic that was generally positive." For Alexis, his "extended" body, thanks to the robot, gave him the feeling of being able to live a normal life and to temporarily have a "mended body": "I had the feeling that I had an additional use. I was happy to be able to move around, to lead a normal life, since it had been several months since I had been able to do so." We were really seeing a form of temporary compensation for a physical disability. This is also what Yolande said: "I was really there because I was captivated by what was happening and I also wanted to do what we had been asked to do, so yes, it was good for me to get back into that context, to get back into all that and to get away from doctors, treatments, so there, at least, I was talking about something else. Even if someone asked me how I was, it was nice, but at least I was talking about things other than health."

6.5.5. *A location, an interpersonal distance and redefined social behaviors*

All users expressed a certain degree of difficulty in positioning themselves spatially with the robot in the class. The robot could very quickly come to seem like an encumbrance and to be an annoyance for the people there in person. Very quickly, a location was assigned to him after a short negotiation with the participants. According to Florence: "Since I didn't need a desk, it was rather the teacher who said to me: 'Well, put yourself over there,' so then, I knew where I had to go, to what place." In general, the location assigned to the robot was at the entrance to the room and a bit to the side, so as not to make it hard to read the board. Few students allowed themselves to move to avoid creating a disturbance, because their unintentional movements often surprised the face-to-face students, who jumped in response to the sound of the drive motor. It was most often a question of remaining unnoticed because their presence was inherently different. This is what Paul explained: "I waited to be told because it was the teacher who put me there directly, and he then asked me if I could see clearly, if I felt alright, and if not, he pushed me, or I moved, but I looked at the class first to see." Furthermore, Paul concluded: "You don't ask people how they feel in the same way; for example, I was asked if the technical components were working."

Moreover, this extended body, simultaneously human and object, was sometimes moved by others, which caused discomfort because his personal space was affected. This is what Yolande said: "It's still a bit intimate (laugh), in the end, I don't know, but I'd rather move myself, as if I was in class [...] rather than having someone push me [...], I preferred being asked: 'Can you move a bit?' rather than someone saying to me, 'Okay I'm going to move you aside for a minute'; that, no, I didn't like that." For Claire: "Personal space was sometimes more limited in person, but even when I was very close to someone I felt safe because it wasn't completely me." This new ontophany therefore leads us to reconsider interpersonal distances between the robot and others. Carrying the robot and moving it are gestures that can be anodyne for in-person actors, while, for remote students, these "contacts" take place in their personal space and modify the proxemics [HAL 71] connected to the body's absence and physical presence.

6.5.6. Repercussions on learning styles: a focus on attention and a change in strategy

Students also adapted to the different modes offered by the robot. Notably, it is not possible to write and to see what is happening in the classroom simultaneously because the interface is exclusively used to extend the field of vision as much as possible. All of the students' attention is thus dedicated to listening and watching presentation slides. This is what Constance said, who indicated she had to make an extra effort of concentration and memorization because she could not take notes, given that the interface did not allow it: "When I remembered the slides in class and when I saw them again, it made me think of the contents, because I only had the slides. After, when I looked at them again, it helped me remember the class."

Given that the robot limited the user's ability to process information by taking notes, one part of the attention normally reserved for this task is harnessed to memorize the slides and the teacher's remarks. This visual information is then reprocessed when the supporting material is consulted after the meeting. This is what Olivier's comments confirmed. To the question "Do you remember the teacher's explanations?" he replied: "Yes I remembered because, when I listen hard, I remember more, especially when I have classes where I'm not learning new things, but it's more about reflection, comprehension, implementation, so there weren't too many things."

6.6. Conclusion

As with all new technology, the use of a telepresence robot raises the question of its acceptance by users. Like Brangier, Dufresne and Hammes-Adelé [BRA 09], we think that the question of acceptance is no longer concerned with the fact of accepting or rejecting this technology, but rather with knowing how the user lives with and adapts to it. Thus, our study has tried to shed some light on the way the user integrates and lives with or "through" a telepresence robot in an academic context. The student and the robot therefore appear to be linked by strong mutual dependence or even by a strong symbiotic connection [BRA 09], for the reason we cite below.

We have highlighted that remote movement procures for the user a feeling of having an "extended" or even a "mended" body, in cases where the student has a serious physical disability. We therefore have confirmed our hypothesis, according to which the proprioceptive appropriation of the robot by the user directly affects the perception of his real body and, beyond that, his own bodily schema. As a digital prosthesis, the robot thus allows for a partial compensation of the user's disability, but generates, on the other hand, sensory restrictions. Moreover, some of these restrictions are spontaneously compensated for by each other (particularly, the sound by the visual). For example, the user made the robot turn so that he could see the person who was speaking, in order to better understand where the sound was coming from.

Consequently, the telepresence robot is not a training artifact that fits in line with a certain tradition of digital practice (as is the case for videoconferencing, for example), because it introduces fundamental changes in perception for its user. Given that it places the user in a symbiotic relationship, teacher support for its use appears unavoidable. This support can rely on the user's personal experience of using the robot, so that teachers can themselves experience these perceptual changes as users.

Finally, this study allows us to see very interesting possibilities with respect to the pedagogical use of telepresence robots in university, on the condition of taking into account the contributions and limits of this system with regard to perception, during teacher support for its use.

6.7. Acknowledgments

We convey our sincere thanks to Dorothée Furnon, a doctoral student in education sciences who contributed to data collection and the transcription of the interviews for this study; these data are also part of her thesis. We also thank all of the students involved in this experiment.

6.8. References

[BRA 09] BRANGIER E., DUFRESNE A., HAMMES-ADELE S., "Approche symbiotique de la relation humain-technologie : perspectives pour l'ergonomie informatique", *Le travail humain*, vol. 72, no. 4, pp. 333–353, 2009.

[FUR 16] FURNON D., POYET F., "Étudiants en situation de handicap physique et robotique", *Revue Diversité*, vol. 185, pp. 160–165, 2016.

[HAL 71] HALL E.-T., *La Dimension cachée* (translated from English by A. Petita, postface by F. Choay), Le Seuil, Paris, 1971.

[HEA 11] HEAD H., HOLMES G., "Sensory disturbances from cerebral lesions", *Brain*, vol. 34, nos 2–3, pp. 102–254, 1911.

[JEA 10] JEANNEROD M., "De l'image du corps à l'image de soi", *Revue de neuropsychologie*, vol. 2, no. 3, pp. 185–194, 2010.

[LÉV 69] LÉVI-STRAUSS C., *Entretiens avec Georges Charbonnier*, 10/18, Paris, 1969.

[PIA 66] PIAGET J., INHELDER B., *La psychologie de l'enfant*, PUF, Paris, 1966.

[RAB 95] RABARDEL P., *Les hommes et les technologies, une approche cognitive des instruments contemporains*, Armand Colin, Paris, 1995.

[VIA 13] VIAL S., *L'être et l'écran*, PUF, Paris, 2013.

Co-construction of Tangible, Dispersed and Multi-semiotic Spaces through the Use of a Telepresence Robot

7.1. A new phenomenological experience

Since 2014, we have been experimenting and assisting with the development of the use of telepresence robots in secondary and postsecondary education. These robots are primarily earmarked for students whose handicaps, illnesses or hospitalization makes it difficult or impossible to travel and/or to participate in academic and university life. This form of presence via a telepresence robot raises the potential for producing pedagogical and learning acts by robot users during interactions with their environment (social, symbolic, material, etc.). This interrogation of these individuals' capacities for action results from the perception of their agency [BAN 97, BUT 02], which, during interactions mediated by a telepresence system, becomes involved in the mobilization of bodily and technological resources, sometimes raising questions about the source of so-called actions and bringing up questions that we will summarize here: who is acting? Is it the student or the robot? What remains of the bodily faculties of the student using the robot? Furthermore, the digital introduces new modalities of action that are subject to spatio-temporal constraints, which lead, at the same time, to the development of new ways of translating these acts in an innovative relationship with space, social relations and the physical [CAS 09].

Chapter written by Dorothée FURNON.

The results obtained during the exploratory phase preceding this study indicate that the use of a robot both influences the user's perception and proprioception and effects social relations between actors (the student-user, the other students and the teachers), from the point of view of identity and alterity. In effect, the driving interface and the robot-object constrain the student-driver's perceptions to the technology's functional limits. Subsequently, interactions mediated by the robot constitute a new perceptual experience, but which comes, all the same, to refer to a previous perceptual culture, that of telephone and video conference. The evolution of the real ontophany [VIA 13] is situated in the driver's autonomous movement. Being seen and heard, seeing and hearing, moving in a location that is remote from one's biological body, creates a new phenomenological experience within a new perceptive, proprioceptive and intersubjective experience.

This phenomenological experience is unprecedented not only for the robot's user, but also for his social environment; this can generate, as we have previously suggested, doubts on the part of pedagogical teams as to the student's capacities for action using the robot. During our experiences in the field, we encountered this kind of rejection from teachers of the student's participation during the class including activities of practical application and implicating the student's physical locomotion. We have chosen to empirically address the effects of this sometimes suspect agency in order to understand the way in which actions are intersubjectively co-constructed in a modified corporeality during the use of a robot.

We choose to take into account the effects of this kind of presence in a pedagogical format that proposes practical implementation during which students engage in problem-solving group work or in the implementation of a project during practical work. This activity, analogous to a real professional situation, requires student mobility and encourages socio-cognitive conflict in social relations with peers.

Our reflections and questions come first of all from our professional practice as project manager and then as director of the robotics project at the *École centrale de Lyon*. Our experiences in the field led us to support the integration of robots into academic and university institutions. In this way, our approach is first of all inductive and ethnographic, and it is during encounters with users, their families, teachers and classmates that our questions emerged concerning perception and physical spaces. This work is conducted in the framework of a thesis in education sciences underway at *Université Lyon-2*.

First, we will present our scientific and theoretical position, from which our central question will emerge. Then, we will describe the scope of our study as well as the data collection method used. Finally, we will propose two primary results, which we will analyze in light of selected theoretical concepts.

7.2. Understanding physical experience from a systemic perspective

We situate our study in an interdisciplinary approach combining education sciences, phenomenology and psychology. These perspectives are, from our point of view, fundamental to understanding this new perceptual experience in an educational context. We propose to articulate an intrasubjective dimension with a systemic approach to activity. In this way, we are interested in interactions between the different environmental aspects that compose the system, according to the theory of activity described by Engeström [ENG 87]. The activity of the student using the robot to participate in a remote lab session incorporates actions that are collective and integrates contextual elements that will interact with the entirety of the system, namely the subject, rules, community, division of labor, instruments and goal [ENG 87]. These elements thus constitute mediatization acting on the activity and that interact with other systems of activity.

In relation to this theory of activity, we consider the subject as the agent of a given activity at a given time; the instrument refers to the artifact transformed by the participant and his intentionality [HUS 85, RAB 95]; the community refers to the groups to which the subject belongs and that govern this particular class; the division of labor relates both to the distribution of tasks in the group and also to the organization of each person's roles. The system of the subject's activity equally interacts with that of other subjects, particularly when the goal to be achieved is mutual. In this chapter, we focus on the system of activity by the student using the robot, which includes the student-driver, the entire telepresence system, the participants, the rules managed by the community, the object of the activity and the way in which the latter interacts with other systems of activity.

From an intrasubjective perspective, we consider the subject through his history, his previous experiences, his individual self and his perceptions. The mediatized actions will be studied using a phenomenological approach to perception [MER 45]. This approach considers perception from the physical perspective. Thus, perception and action develop in relation to the world and to objects, which are always an embodied experience of the world. This physical relationship to the world extends beyond the limits of the body itself and extends the bodily schema to potentially tangible spaces situated outside the physical body. This concept of the bodily schema, described by Merleau-Ponty [MER 45] and then by Berthoz [BER 97], refers to the experience of the body in a given space-time, constituting a positional system that is both current and open to other orientations.

For this work, we take into account different aspects of the robot, that is, the driving interface with the set of icons, the robot object, its screens, microphone and loudspeakers, as potential spaces for perception made available for action. This phenomenological consideration views the bodily space as a perspective on the world from an extended perception that can go beyond the body itself [MER 45]. This conception of the bodily schema refers to the bodily experience in a perceptual projection of the individual, a felt body that cannot correspond to the biological reality of bodily limits. Thus, this perceptual experience can extend to the object, which has become an instrument, when the latter stops being an object in itself and transforms into a tangible zone of locomotive meaning: "The habit shows the power that we have for expanding our being in the world or for modifying our existence by annexing new instruments" [MER 45, p. 168]. This embodied relationship to objects occurs in the mode of instrumentality [HEI 53], with a perception of the object that is not neutral, but which appears to the individual through its purpose and its meaning in a given space-time and for a given individual. In this way, Heidegger connects the technique to the prosthesis, "that is to say, the tool that is integrated physically with its carrier, which therefore determines the form in return" [HEI 53, p. 79]. In return, the technique transforms the individual by modifying his relationship to the world and by constructing new competencies [RAB 95] not only to produce actions in his environment, but also to bring out his environment [VAR 93]. Thus, action cannot be understood in a strictly individual dimension, but must be considered as a co-construction between the person and his environment (social, material, symbolic, etc.). In effect, perception that is intrinsically connected to action [BER 97] replaces a subjective projection of the world that is never exactly the same from one person to another. In this way, co-construction of an action between two or more individuals underpins the negotiation of a perceptual consensus that renders action intelligible to the participants and occurs, in part, by reciprocal bodily adjustment [COS 97, GOO 07]. Thus, the participants will place their bodies so they can be perceived by the other and, thus, facilitate non-verbal and gestural communication. This adjustment is implicated in the creation of a common space of intelligibility, and therefore in the construction of meaning that allows for interaction [GOO 07]. This common space of intelligibility corresponds to this zone, this gap, situated between the participants or, to be more precise, between their perceptions. It is therefore a question of a space in which each participant can share and accede to others' perspectives and, thus, arrive at a consensus about the meaning of the information they perceive in their environment. The impossibility of an individual to accede to another's point of view, to put oneself "in another's place", leads to a common incomprehension of the situation.

All aims of human action are subjected, in part, to the constraints of social life in which the individuals are situated. School, in a wider sense, is subjected to a set of rules and traditions whose existence precedes and persists beyond the existence of these actors, who themselves experience it and participate in its evolution and its application [WOO 90]. The social rules are more dependent on the location in which they occur, namely in the classroom. We are witnessing, with the development of the use of the digital in teaching, an evolution of the relationship to space-time, which is kept at a distance and which comes to renew, through transformation, the common space of interaction between students and their educational environment [JÉZ 10]. Individuals also participate in social facts that influence the meanings they formulate from situations. Between subjectivism and objectivism, Giddens [GID 84] proposed a consensus by taking the path of duality, which makes it possible to understand human practices in their reflexive character and understand them also as being situated in a pre-existing social world. This theory accepts the historicity of action and the structure of social systems that allow us to consider students' collective activities through their recursive character. This perspective thus allows for the appearance of changes in ethnomethods and emphasizes routines, negotiations, misunderstandings or even conflicts. These elements are made even more salient when sources of disturbance appear in the current system, which arise during new situations. In effect, classroom life assumes mastery of one's own social competencies, which arise from the rules of interaction or the use of places according to their role and activity. The contributions of

Giddens' theory of structure [GID 84] allow us to consider the failures, rule breaking or even confusion that arise during actions mediated by the robot, as indicators of the sources of disturbance provoking areas of uncertainty for the actors.

7.3. Intersubjective negotiation for the construction of tangible spaces

The use of a telepresence robot by a student, in the framework of his participation in a lesson through lab work that requires mobility, raises questions about its ability to construct learning actions in relation to his social, material, symbolic and technological environment. The theoretical contributions described above add to a clear understanding of the mobilization of the body as the foundation of action. This embodied relationship to the world locates the emergence of meaning in an available space of meanings that can be positioned beyond the body itself. This space is not only situated but also contextualized and mediatized by aspects that intervened in the educational context in which we conducted our observations. The students and teachers we accompanied were used to participating in their education with a degree of presence that we would call "immediate". Throughout their careers as students and teachers, these actors have developed action schemes whose positive recursivity constitutes, according to Giddens, a structured system [GID 84]. The latter tend towards self-management and seek stability during encounters with the events that occur and cause disruption. The use of a robot by a student engaged in a learning activity induces perturbations in perceptual activity. In effect, the presence of a student mediated by this technology affects, or even destroys, the perception of the environment, namely vision, hearing, touch, smell and proprioception. Thanks to this study, we hope to understand the way in which the actions of students and their instructor are negotiated and co-constructed intersubjectively, in a relationship mediated by a telepresence robot, through pedagogical activities during which the student's locomotion is more mobilized than during lecture-based training. Through this question, we also examine the possibility for the subjects who, caught up in systems of activity, manage to transform the available spaces into tangible zones in which the subjects will be able to project their meanings and thus to construct a feeling about the situation, through an expansion of the physical space.

7.4. Field study and data collection methods

As expressed above, we will privilege an inductive research approach, in order to emphasize surprises and questions that arise in the field. Nevertheless, we have been confronted with recurring refusals to participate from student-users of the robot during education that is considered "practical" for well-founded reasons, according to our own analysis, of cognitive biases connected to a lack of knowledge about the robot and the possibilities for learning and pedagogical acts mediated by this technology. The understanding of possibilities of learning acts on the student's part and pedagogical possibilities on the teacher's part, as well as the construction of knowledge about the use of the robot by a student, incited us to change our position and to adopt a less ecological approach, and in a certain way, a more experimental approach by provoking situations for robot use. We conducted our experiments with the robot at the *École centrale de Lyon*, which is a general engineering school. We worked in collaboration with the physics-chemistry team, who agreed to try the robot during their practical work (PW) in chemistry in the chromatology specialty. This chemistry PW includes 24 students divided into three subgroups, based on the specialty in which they were registered. The students worked in pairs in a room equipped with chromatographs and injection systems. Their required activity was to remove chemical components using a syringe, inject them into the injection machine, and then analyze their evolution using the chromatograph. The process then became the subject of a written report. The teacher watched over the students' work and their involvement, intervening when necessary and replying to their questions. We opted for this lesson because, on the one hand, it provided the opportunity for interactions between students and the teacher and, on the other hand, the configuration of the class allowed for collective activities that can generate socio-cognitive conflicts, negotiations and exchanges between actors as well as practical work and experiments with tools. In order to simplify interpretation, we called the student using the robot the "student-driver" and, when it was a question of a team activity with another student, we called the latter the "team-student".

This study is based on a mixed methodological approach in first and third person, formulated from our own observations during our time in the classroom, video recordings, and a post-activity, self-confrontation style interview.

We observed six lab sessions in chemistry-chromatography. A volunteer student used the robot to participate in the session from a remote building. The one-and-a-half-hour-long lab session was recorded using a camera and a lapel microphone located either on the teacher or on the team-student. The student-driver's computer screen was also recorded. This data supplied contextual and also behavioral elements that were obvious to the observer. They were subsequently used as a memory aid during post-activity interviews. For this reason, we conducted 15 individual, self-confrontation style interviews with each actor (student-drivers, students in teams and teachers). The self-confrontation style interview leads the actor to recollect, relying on the video recording, which provides a memory aid. The researcher led the interviewed actor to spell out the key points of his activity on a conscious level that was pre-reflexive [THE 10]. The object of this interview is thus to obtain information regarding subjective experiences with conscious and communicable awareness relative to the construction of meaning for the action. The progress of the self-confrontation style interview is first based on a communication contract established between the researcher and the interviewee, indicating the use that will be made of the data as well as each person's position. The interviewee agrees to recall the context and to make his activity explicit, without undertaking an analysis. The researcher leads the interviewee to describe his activity using reminder techniques and through active listening. Our interviews were focused on the actor's perceptual experiences and therefore, in connection with the self-confrontation style interview, which respects the principle of intrinsic precedence, we are interested in seeing which experiences were significant to the actor.

7.5. Illustrations of perceptual adjustments during mediatized interactions

For this work, we propose observation and analysis of two perceptual modalities that were significant for the actors during data collection (vocal and proprioceptive/visual). The first analysis came from observations conducted for all of the experiments, as well as interviews with six students who drove the robot and four team-students. The second analysis came from the observation of the first session and the interview of the relevant student-driver and the teacher.

7.5.1. *Transformation of a cursor into an instrument of vocal proprioception*

Vocal proprioception corresponds to the awareness that the subject has of his own vocal production, that is, the actions that he produces with his voice to adapt to the context in which he finds himself. It is a question, subsequently, of a proprioceptive experience during which the student reproduces the existing schemes applied *in situ*, therefore in context. In a classroom, the student's speech must be sufficiently intelligible to the participants and must conform to a set of social interaction rules in effect in the class group to which he belongs and about which he also knows the norms and the rules appropriate for this particular context of lab work. Effectively, this configuration leads to verbal exchanges and to movement in the room, which naturally increases the number of decibels compared to a lecture situation. In this context, the competencies and methods of interaction developed by the student during his time with the group and with the academic system form a recursivity for adapting the volume of his voice, disrupted by the new proprioceptive experience [GID 84]. This obstacle to the proprioceptive sense during use of the robot requires the student-driver to verify the volume of his voice with other participants, primarily with his classmates. When he participates in the class via the robot, the source of the sound broadcasting his words is no longer the student's, but instead is located in the robot's loudspeakers, which are only adjustable by the student-driver. The latter therefore cannot check the volume of the robot's speakers with his own hearing, but he must still manage the sound volume.

On the interface there is a microphone symbol that, when selected, displays a cursor with a nominal scale from 0 to 100, where 0 indicating no sound and 100 indicating the microphone's maximum volume. Furthermore, a graphical illustration of the change in the sound volume, captured by the student-driver's computer's microphones and analyzed by the driving software, is located on the bottom right of the interface near the webcam feedback window. This illustration is presented in the form of a vertical line divided into five segments that light up blue in a crescendo from the first to the fourth segment, according to the intensity, then in red for the last segment. Red indicates a volume above the one expected for "normal conversation". These indications provided by the designer were intended to give the user visual indicators of the volume picked up by the robot's speakers. Nevertheless, this visual signal does not provide immediate meaning, allowing for the interpretation of the intensity level experienced by the participants, who perceive the sound through the robot's speakers. Furthermore, this indicator does not take into account the relationship to the decibels emitted in the classroom, which will require a contextual adjustment of the participants' vocal activity.

During our observations, we systematically noted that each connection to the robot by a student was followed either by a request for volume adjustment by the participants, or by a check by the student-driver with someone else. This manifested through requests such as: "Am I speaking too loudly? Because I have no idea", "Can you turn down your microphone's volume because you're speaking too loudly", or even "Can you increase the volume? Because there's noise around and I can't hear you anymore". Jean, a first-year student in engineering school, said to us in this regard: "After a moment, I managed to figure out that 3 wasn't loud at all and that 15 was pretty loud except when there was noise in the room [...] but I didn't really realize in fact and sometimes they said to me that I was speaking too loudly because there was no noise, but I didn't know that".

This data indicates that the student-driver must accommodate new schemes in his interaction with the social and digital environment. He adjusts the microphone volume based on the participants' perception, who tell him what they think about his voice volume. For his part, the student-driver constructs meanings in this new relationship to objects (sound and "microphone" cursor). None of the interviewed students indicated to us that they had used the vertical line indicating the volume level. Nevertheless, the "microphone" cursor became a tool because the student constructed meaning from it. In effect, the numbers presented on the cursor had no meaning in and of themselves, that is, no independent existence. It was during the encounter between the student, the object, his environment, and therefore the experience he had of it, that meaning was created for the student-driver: "I came to understand that 3 wasn't very loud at all and that 10 was pretty loud except when there was noise in the room". It was through use that the student transformed the tool into an instrument, all while transforming himself in return. Thus, he developed a new form of proprioceptive experience in a system that included the student-driver, the digital interface, the social environment, the group's rules and the goal they sought to attain. These aspects compose a system of plurisemiotic meaning, which is simultaneously technical, technological and human.

7.5.2. *Perceptual adjustment in the co-construction of a statement within the pedagogical relationship*

We selected a sequence from our corpus in which the teacher gave a description to the student-driver of the injection machine located in the PW room, as well as its functionality. The video data, as well as the interview with the teacher, indicate to us that the latter uses the robot's main camera feedback window to construct knowledge about the view his student has of the teacher's current environment. In effect, the latter could not use the student's gaze to infer the visual direction or the orientation of his attention. In this situation of mediated interactions, the reciprocal physical adjustment necessary for intercomprehension between the teacher and the student is not immediately made available by environmental conditions because of the visual constraints experienced by the student, on the one hand, and the difficulty for the teacher in accessing the student's perceptual point of view, on the other hand. Thus, the teacher designated the spatial landmarks through deictic gestures to locate the machine's functions, that is, gestures that he associates with statement about their function. In a "natural" face-to-face situation, the speaker uses these gestures to direct the listener's attention by physically adjusting himself to the latter. Subsequently, the teacher explained to us that he adjusted his gestures based on what he saw in the feedback window, that is, to the perception he had of what his student was perceiving in the situation. To this effect, the teacher told us, during the interview: "At a given moment, he [the student] was too close to his machine, and since he was too close, he was partially hiding the screen and I couldn't see the little screen on the bottom [...], and so I couldn't see if he could see what I was showing or not, and I said to myself that, in my opinion, he couldn't see anything I was showing him, which was located above the machine even if he used the zoom [...], so it's true that I may have provided more explanations in case he couldn't see what I was showing." The teacher used the camera feedback window with the goal of perceptual adjustment because of the meaning of the image he perceived. This meaning led to his activity, relative here to the explanation of the functions of the injection machine, which he co-constructed in interaction with the student, the robot screen and the injection machine. The teacher said concerning this: "I had to ask him if he could see clearly [...] he said to me that yes, but I wasn't really sure but well..." This pedagogical situation caused the student-driver and the teacher to interact, and also the injection machine, the robot, the two robot screens and the student's digital interface: the explanations given by the teacher were therefore co-constructed in this network of human-digital and technical interactions. This multimodal interaction also raises the question of the agency of the student-driver and the perception that the teacher has of it: what are the student's perceptual faculties? What aspects does he master and how will he use the tool to produce his actions? The teacher used this camera window to obtain information about the student's agency and, while this image was hidden, the teacher relied on the interpretation he had based on the student-driver's linguistic feedback: "[...] he said to me that yes, but I wasn't really sure." The absence of validation on the teacher's part points to a difficulty in negotiating a common space of interpretation between him and the student. In return, the teacher must modify his explanatory modality by giving more verbal explanations and less demonstration [GOO 07].

7.6. Creation of multiple spaces for the appearance of the self and the other through an expansion of physical spaces

The observations we have made show the phases of adaptation for the face-to-face actors in the environment, and also of the environment, which take place during the encounter with the sources of disruption in the system's structure. We observed these adjustment processes primarily during the early uses of the robot, and they tended to reduce with time. This form of habituation proceeds through incorporating the environment into the relationship to the robot through the construction of driven input of its functions.

We have presented and analyzed two situations during which sources of disturbance cause a change in perceptual and proprioceptive acts, and which were significant for the actors who made up the system at an activity time T. In effect, we analyzed the actors (student-drivers, teachers and other students in the class) as subjects in a system and/or members of a community to which we refer for analysis, but we also analyzed the constitutive elements including the systems of activities, the driver's computer with the driving interface and his immediate physical environment, the robot and its component parts (the cameras, screens, microphone, speakers), as well as the physical class environment, the distribution of tasks and the social rules [ENG 87]. In the two situations presented, the telepresence robot and its system were experienced by the actors as an obstacle to reciprocal physical adjustment [GOO 07] and therefore as an obstacle to the correct operation of expected interactions. The disruptions changed the perceptual experience of the relevant students and teachers and made salient a form of recursivity in the system's structure, such as the communication rules in a class group or in the pedagogical relationship, which is modified via renewal in a particular context of interaction mediated by the robot. The search for solutions by the actors shows systems that interact and that tend towards self-management through a process of stabilization. They co-constructed a common space of intelligibility situated between the participants and a zone (or several zones) of the robot (and its system), transforming it/them into a space of meaning of and for action. In the second situation, the teacher adapted his gestures and speech to what he saw in the camera window and to the meaning he created about what the student perceived. The zone of the window became a tool for interpretation for the teacher, allowing him to physically adjust to the student's point of view. At the same time, in the first situation, the student-driver co-constructed with the team-student a meaning for the microphone cursor, which became a tool for vocal proprioception to adapt the intensity of his voice to the classroom environment and its social rules. The co-construction of these common spaces is based on the incorporation of digital spaces: these different digital zones are integrated into the individuals' physical spaces to construct a perceptual system in an embodied relationship with objects. This relationship to the object is tested therefore in the mode of instrumentality [HEI 53], which is then found to be a reciprocal relationship: the individual transforms his relationship to the object by developing techniques for perceiving the environment and transforms himself [RAB 95] by transforming his presence in the world.

The relationship between the actors and the telepresence robot (and its components) becomes a distributed and interconnected perceptual experience that functions in a circuit of networks of meanings. Thus, the different spaces available to the robot at the time T of the action are instrumentalized in shattered, fragmented and plurisemiotic tangible zones (human and technological), and experienced as an extension of the participants' bodily schemas.

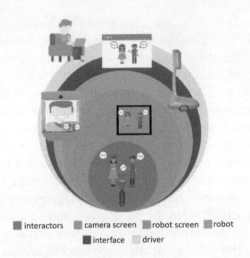

interactors   camera screen   robot screen   robot
interface   driver

Figure 7.1. *Representation of different tangible spaces. For a color version of this figure, see www.iste.co.uk/rinaudo/telepresence.zip*

In Figure 7.1, we represent the robot's different spaces that were meaningful for the actors we observed and accompanied throughout our research. Different points of view appear there, experienced as extensions of the bodily schema and taken as a positioning system that provides information for interaction: "I see what the driver sees of me and my direct environment, so I can see myself from his point of view and put myself in his place to give him information." Thus, the multiple spaces in which the self and the other appear are physical spaces, therefore points of view on the world.

7.7. The biases and limits of provoked absence in a study based on a systemic approach

We wanted to observe and analyze the processes of the co-construction of a learning activity during teaching that requires manipulations through *a priori* direct physical access to pedagogical objects. Hence, we favored a lab session during which knowledge is co-constructed through interaction with a team-student, a teacher and pedagogical objects to be manipulated. The students we accompanied could not have access to these pedagogical modalities, and therefore we chose to provoke the voluntary absence of students to experiment with the robot. This simulation engendered several effects in the situation and constituted a limit to understanding in our results.

In effect, the teachers accepted this experimentation under the condition that the volunteer students participate in part of the course in person so they could take part in the manipulations in the classroom. During interviews, all of the interviewed students explained that they had put in less effort to engage in the class via the robot, knowing that they would come back later in-person. This limit also related to the student's motivation for using the robot and therefore his intentionality and his goal. In effect, his story, his personal and psychological situation, and also his relationship to the group and to the teacher, will influence the meaning he constructs about the robot, the situation, and therefore the use he will make of it. Reciprocally, and always from a systemic point of view, these aspects and the interpretation that others construct about the situation also influence the use they make of the robot. These aspects are to be integrated into the analysis of their use. Finally, a simulated situation must be interpreted with care.

7.8. Conclusion and recommendations

The first use of the robot in an educational context constitutes a new phenomenological experience [VIA 13] in relation to a world where the perceptual implementation is disturbed. Our observations indicate that, during interactions mediated by the robot, individuals tend to act with a certain recursivity in their actions that cannot be actualized in reality because of technological and technical constraints. This is the case, as we have seen, for the two students who wanted to have a discussion in the classroom, but for whom the absence of the driver's verbal proprioception made it difficult to know whether his voice volume was audible, on the one hand, and whether he was respecting social rules, on the other hand. In effect, in contrast to a classical video conference context, where the listener who cannot hear the speaker clearly can increase the volume of his own loudspeakers without necessarily informing the speaker, in the context of the use of a telepresence robot, the listener (i.e. the person in front of the robot) has no technical way to adjust the volume of the robot's speaker because it can only be managed by the driver who, on the contrary, has no information relative to the propagation of his voice. This paradoxical situation necessarily induces a phase of adjustment each time the driver's voice volume is too low in relation to the social rules in effect. This situation often provokes discomfort to the driver and is experienced as wasting time by participants. If the objective for these technologies is to make interaction as natural as possible, it would then be helpful to provide the student-driver with functionality, allowing him to either be informed of the volume in the classroom and his own volume broadcast by the robot, and to adjust his microphone based on the social rules that he has already mastered, or to provide functionality allowing for the volume level in the room to be measured and for the speaker's volume to be automatically adjusted.

These constraints are similar to the situation in which the teacher and the student-driver cannot physically adjust themselves so that the teacher can see where the student's gaze is directed during a pedagogical explanation. The participants are therefore led to co-construct new perceptual spaces in order to reconstruct a common space and to thus constitute a new technique for interaction, which involves the incorporation of the available functions for the robot and the actor in a given space-time. The analysis of these observations shows that the actors possess perceptual capabilities that mitigate the absence of sharing a direct common space that prevents them from putting themselves in the other's place to understand his perception of the situation, at least when the robot's properties allow for it. In effect, access for the teacher and the other students to a window that shows the student-driver's perception is crucial for the mutual adjustment process, to be thus able to arrive at a common comprehension in the situation. Nevertheless, it is important to underline that the robot's front feedback window, shown on the robot's screen, is not really what the student sees, being merely a video stream captured by the robot's camera. It therefore does not correspond to the image shown on the student's computer screen, whose quality can be influenced by other factors linked to this technical environment. Furthermore, the access to another's point of view is also limited to a single sense, that of vision. However, greater access to the student-driver's direct environment must, above all, carefully take into account its ethical aspect with regard to respect for privacy because, above and beyond the lab work experiment that we have described in this chapter, the students use the robot either from home or from their hospital room. However, this question must eventually be confronted by the legitimacy of the teacher's ability to access what his student is doing during class, as well as perceiving information about the student's physical and perceptual capabilities within the pedagogical relationship: as much to be able to adjust to the student during pedagogical explanations as to establish his authority as a teacher, which he thought immutable before the arrival of telepresence robots in education. Nevertheless, this study shows that participants should arrive at a process of perceptual negotiation, that is, a perceptual consensus between them: these spaces having been created as tangible spaces through a process that transforms an object into a tangible tool through the intentionality bias, which gives it another existence. This space becomes an extension of the tangible zone of activity. In the case of an activity that involves two or more actors, this transformation must lead to consensus between the actors.

7.9. References

[BAN 97] BANDURA A., *Self-efficacity: The Exercise of Control*, W.H. Freeman, New York, 1997.

[BER 97] BERTHOZ A., *Le sens du mouvement*, Odile Jacob, Paris, 1997.

[BUT 02] BUTLER J., *La vie psychique du pouvoir : l'assujettissement en théories*, Éditions Léo Scheer, Paris, 2002.

[CAS 09] CASILLI A., "Introduction. Culture numérique : l'adieu au corps n'a jamais eu lieu", *Esprit*, no. 3, pp. 151–153, 2009.

[COS 97] COSNIER J., VAYSSE J., "Sémiotique des gestes communicatifs", *Nouveaux Actes Sémiotiques*, nos 52–54, pp. 7–28, 1997.

[ENG 87] ENGESTRÖM Y., *Learning by expanding: An activity-theoretical approach to developmental research*, Orienta-Kosultit Oy, Helsinki, 1987.

[GID 84] GIDDENS A., *The Constitution of Society: Outline of a Theory of Structuration*, University of California Press, Berkley, 1984.

[GOO 07] GOODWIN C., "Participation, stance and affect in the organization of activities", *Discourse Society*, vol. 18, pp. 53–73, 2007.

[HEI 53] HEIDEGGER M., *Essais et conférences. La question de la technique*, Gallimard, Paris, 1953.

[HUS 85] HUSSERL E., *Idées directrices pour une phénoménologie*, Gallimard, Paris, 1985.

[JÉZ 10] JÉZÉGOU A., "Créer de la présence à distance en *e-learning*", *Distances et savoirs*, vol. 8, no. 2, pp. 257–274, 2010.

[MER 45] MERLEAU-PONTY M., *Phénoménologie de la perception*, Gallimard, Paris, 1945.

[NIZ 10] NIZET J., *La sociologie d'Anthony Giddens*, La Découverte, Paris, 2010.

[RAB 95] RABARDEL P., *Les hommes et les technologies. Approche cognitive des instruments contemporains*, Armand Colin, Paris, 1995.

[THE 10] THEUREAU J., "Les entretiens d'autoconfrontation et de remise en situation par les traces matérielles et le programme de recherche 'cours d'action'", *Revue d'anthropologie des connaissances*, vol. 4, no. 2, pp. 287–322, 2010.

[VAR 93] VARELA F., THOMPSON E., ROSCH E., *L'inscription corporelle de l'esprit*, Le Seuil, Paris, 1993.

[VIA 13] VIAL S., *L'être et l'écran : comment le numérique change la perception*, PUF, Paris, 2013.

[WOO 90] WOODS P., *L'ethnographie de l'école*, Armand Colin, Paris, 1990.

8

The Telepresence Robot in Universities: Between Subjectification and Unlinking

8.1. Introduction

What today is commonly called the digital, and which was until recently still referred to as information and communication technologies, activates for everyone, whether it is the user or not, representations, fantasies and psychological processes. We can organize the latter into two broad categories: on the one hand, processes of unlinking and, on the other hand, processes of subjectification [RIN 11], although this classification is very schematic and we can think about one of these processes without referring to the other. The advent of telepresence robots in educational situations probably leads students who benefit from it, as well as their teachers, peers, friends and family, etc. to subscribe to psychological experiences of the same type.

This chapter aims to analyze the psychological reality, in the Freudian sense, experienced by students who benefit from the telepresence system to overcome their inability to get to class, which may be temporary but lasting for several weeks.

Chapter written by Jean-Luc RINAUDO.

First, we discuss two details: one concerning the telepresence system, and the other about the scientific approach used. Then, we will present a brief review of the scientific literature concerning the approach to psychoanalytical orientation towards robots in our societies. In the following section, we will present a relatively traditional methodology, followed by the results concerning subjectification that is related to unlinking, and finally a discussion.

8.2. A telepresence system

Some students on the campus of Mont-Saint-Aignan, at the University of Rouen-Normandie, were unable to attend their regular classes for a long time because of an accident, an illness or a disability. We therefore suggested that, despite their impediment, they attend class through a telepresence system.

The technical part of this system consists of a screen mounted on rods with casters. Through an interface installed on a connected communication device (e.g. computer, tablet, smartphone), the telepresent student sees and hears what is happening in the classroom, is seen and heard by those there in person, and has, furthermore, the opportunity to move the robot. A photo of the robot is provided by Françoise Poyet in Chapter 6 (Figure 6.1).

It is a "slave" robot [TIS 15] without autonomous capabilities; that is, it does not choose its own actions and therefore is part of the teleoperation category [DEV 17]: it only does what it is told to do by the user, except to indicate the level of charge for its batteries. As an alternative to the term "robot", which the designer uses, we prefer that of "avatar", so much does it seem to us that the machine represents the incapacitated student, in a form of extension or duplication of the self [TUR 11]. However, in keeping with the chapters in this third part of the book, we will keep the word "robot" in this chapter.

Moreover, above and beyond the technical aspects, we consider that we are in the presence of a real system because, in addition to the relevant student, several actors with multiple functions are involved: the student's peers who are responsible for setting up and storing the robot, which is not able to open doors or to push elevator buttons; the teachers who teach in the presence of a remote student; the instructional supervisors or the departments that relay information; the computer specialists who manage the maintenance of the machines and help the students install software and become familiar with the tools; and finally the team of researchers who study the effects of pedagogical mediation mediatized by telepresence robots. This study has benefited from financing from the University of Rouen-Normandie.

Finally, this system of telepresence robots at the university is also subject to certain procedures for reservations, allocations of rights of connection and use, software installation and storage.

We can make Daniel Peraya's proposition ours with regard to the system: "an instance, a place for social interaction and cooperation possessing intentions, its symbolic and physical operation, in sum, its own modes of interaction" [PER 99, p. 153].

8.3. The psychoanalytical clinical approach

The expression "psychological reality" refers to a psychoanalytical clinical approach. This scientific approach relies on three fundamental pillars.

The first pillar comprises the theoretical corpus of psychoanalysis to which the clinical researcher refers to giving meaning to the situations he/she studies. This corpus is not only the result of psychoanalytical treatment but, equally and essentially, for those concerned, of what Stijn Vanheule [VAN 02] calls "extra-clinical data": artwork, writing and especially manifestations of the unconscious in daily life such as lapses, oversights and witticisms. However, if we limited ourselves to this aspect of recourse to theory, we would probably find ourselves in an approach that applies psychoanalysis to the educational field, in which educators who were contemporaries of Freud such as Oskar Pfister, Hans Zulliger or Auguste Aichhorn, engaged in Austria or Switzerland [CIF 85, CIF 98, MIL 07, MOL 89, OHA 09], or even in France [OHA 06].

The second pillar consists of the whole essence of he or she who encounters the researcher. It is not a question of imposing tests or experiences nor of a point of view that orients his/her speech or action, but to consider him/her fully as a subject constructed from his/her personal and family history, his/her social, institutional and group affiliations, his/her relationship to knowledge, his/her pleasures and his/her suffering. Moreover, as indicated by Emmanuelle Brossais in the introduction to an issue of the journal *Les sciences de l'éducation pour l'ère nouvelle*: "As researchers referring to psychoanalysis, the contributors consider individuals to be subjects whose practices and actions are in part determined by their unconscious" [BRO 16, p. 10]. This line allows us to contribute an important detail to studies about the digital. The recourse to the psychoanalytical clinical approach requires an in-depth interest in subjective situations and configurations. The emphasis is therefore rather placed on the practices mediatized by the digital, inasmuch as that implies the actors' subjectivity, rather than on the uses that arise more from the collective [RIN 12]. Using the notion of practice necessarily leads to taking into account not only observable acts, actions and reactions, but also the implementation processes for the activity in a given situation, for making choices and decisions [ALT 02]. Leveraging the notion of practice implies work following the double aspects that Jacky Beillerot [BEI 96] described particularly well: on the one hand, gestures, behaviors, speech patterns and ways of doing things, and on the other hand, rules, beliefs, ideologies, representations and previous personal experiences, including unconscious ones. Thus, the practices are not only conscious and formalized, but also they partly elude their actors.

Finally, the last pillar of the approach in order of presentation, but just as important as the two preceding pillars, consists of considering that the researcher himself/herself is also a subject, constructing knowledge that cannot be independent of his/her culture, speech, and a personal and professional experience. By choosing this approach to subjectivity, the researcher makes himself/herself more attentive to movements of transference to the work for the person or the group he/she encounters, as for himself/herself, in all the stages of research. We therefore understand why, in keeping with this research method, it is important for the researcher to "present his/her colors".

In an interview for the journal *Distances et médiations des savoirs*, I indicated that it is crucial for a student conducting research about the digital in education and training to identify the distance between himself/herself and the object of investigation, from the greatest degree of exteriority to total involvement [RIN 16]. Of course, this statement is valid for all researchers and not only for the students we accompany. Following the invitation from Georges Devereux [DEV 80], it is therefore important for me to present from whence I am speaking, from where I am trying to construct knowledge about telepresence systems.

I discovered telepresence robots during a seminar from the Multimodal Interactions group by ÉCran (IMPEC), during which Christine Develotte invited me to propose a conference [RIN 15a] (for details about this seminar and the use of telepresence tools in a research group, the reader may refer to Chapter 9). I was immediately enticed. These machines probably coincided with my interests, for more than 30 years, in research about information and communication technologies in the field of education and training [RIN 02, RIN 11]. They also intersect with my pedagogical experience [RIN 96]. Furthermore, while my health has allowed me to not have to live through the everyday experiences of ill or injured students, these telepresence robots resonate with part of my current everyday experience. Given that my family home is located some 350 kilometers from my university, I found myself confronted four to six days a week by the desire and the need to be simultaneously here and there, between my family home and my administrative home, as is indicated in teacher-researchers' request forms.

8.4. Psychoanalytical approach to robots

Research that focuses on the social practices mediatized by robots is, of course, diverse, depending on the researchers' epistemological perspective, their disciplinary domain and their methodological orientations, as for all scientific research. That said, what makes research on robots more complex is the fact that this generic appellation brings together a diversity of objects, from domestic "robots" (e.g. vacuum cleaners or lawnmowers) through training simulators [COU 13], to games or programmable machines [NIJ 15] or social robots [DUM 16, TUR 11]. Some robots are programmed to "learn" to respond to their interlocutor in order to give the impression that their capacities can evolve, while others are programmed by their designers once and for all. It is not here a question of carrying out an exhaustive review of the scientific literature about social practices mediatized by robots, although we limit ourselves to the field of education and training, but to identify what the psychoanalytical clinical orientation can contribute to these questions.

The development of information and communication technologies, and perhaps more so the advent of robots, not only in industries for difficult or dangerous tasks, but equally in the spheres of education, training, care and social services, are based on social representations or old fantasies [DEV 17, RIN 15b]: the robot will take the work and the place of the human [GEL 17];

the machines will lead us to a world with disaffected relationships; or robots will take control of all aspects of society and will escape their creators in the image of Doctor Frankenstein's creature [SHE 18] or the robot HAL in *2001: A Space Odyssey*. The title of a recent work by Pascal Picq, a paleoanthropologist at the *Collège de France*, seems representative of these beliefs: *Who Will Take Control? The Great Apes, the Politicians, or the Robots?* [PIC 17]. Frédéric Tordo even talks about robophobia, in pathological situations where the subject overinvests, in part unconsciously, in the persecutory side of the machine to the detriment of the fascinating side [TOR 16]. Sylvain Missonnier recalls that humanoid robots reflect a double transgression: the robot revolt that overturns the master–slave relationship, on the one hand, and "the transgressivity of the human who defies God by usurping his supreme creative power", on the other hand [MIS 17, p. 24].

A few years ago, Sherry Turkle considered digital technologies as spaces for projection of the user's unconscious psychic life. She compared computing to a Rorschach test. According to this researcher from the Massachusetts Institute of Technology (MIT) in Boston, the computer was an evocative object, which the English title of the work *The Second Self* describes more directly than its French translation, *Les enfants de l'ordinateur* (*Children of the Computer*) [TUR 84]. Today, she considers that we are emotionally and philosophically ready to welcome robots as social companions and assistants, not only at work, but also in schools, at the hospital, in retirement homes or at home. We will be in a situation what she calls "the robotic moment", which will cause us to leave the projection in order to orient ourselves towards engagement in the relationship [TUR 11]. Serge Tisseron extended this idea by identifying that the robots' processing power will allow them to simulate reality as closely as possible, a conversation with humans "with impressions and gestures capable of generating the illusion that they understand the human's affective states and that they are 'sensitive' to them" [TIS 15, p. 31], and thus to generate empathy towards robots, which he calls "artificial empathy". Frédéric Tordo pursues this line of thought and evokes robotic self-empathy. This researcher indicated that an "empathic relationship toward the part of ourselves that is externalized in our avatar" [TOR 16, p. 181] is constructed from the externalization of actions by robot users as well as from their personality.

8.5. Methodology

As soon as it is presented to them, the students who benefit from the telepresence system engage in a form of reciprocation through an encounter with a researcher from the team. This section relies on the analysis of four non-directive research interviews conducted with students in a "license" or Master of Education Sciences degree program in 2016 and 2017. The introductory instructions, the only element of the interview really formalized in advance, were as follows: "You have benefited from a telepresence robot during your absence from university, lasting X weeks. Can you tell me how you personally experienced it, what you felt, the advantages and disadvantages, as it comes to you?" The duration of the interviews varied from 35 to 50 minutes. They took place, in most cases, remotely (we can almost say that the research interviews were conducted in telepresence), recorded and then transcribed. The first names in the text were, of course, changed for confidentiality.

8.6. A surprising opportunity

Generally, the tone of the interviewed students' discourse was very positive. They asserted that they experienced this system as a quasi-miraculous opportunity that solved a problem they had thought insoluble, because how could one continue attending class while incapacitated and stuck at home for health reasons? "I didn't expect to be offered this." Sophie said, for example.

The benefits mentioned most quickly during the interviews concerned the pedagogical aspects. The comments from one of the students perfectly synthesize all of the students' comments: "I was out of work for eight weeks and I was able to attend class and complete my semester" (Corine).

Furthermore, comments were made fairly quickly that one could through context analysis classify as personal aspects, particularly those relative to mobility. For example: "I was completely dependent on a lot of things to get around so then to be able to in a university 200 kilometers away like that was fantastic, frankly, it's a little taste of freedom that you don't have any more when you're stuck at home [...] it opens doors [...] it's good for you" (Sophie) or this: "It wasn't just for attending classes, it was moving around the room" (Virginie).

The interviewed students' comments make an important implication: "I really had the impression of being united with everyone [...] I didn't feel separate even if I was in my living room" (Virginie). This subject implied the potential for maintaining or even reinforcing social connections, despite a form of isolation connected to immobility: "I could even go to the coffee break with my friends [...] so that was great" (Virginie). We are therefore in the presence of a form of emancipation through this telepresence robot, in a system for augmenting the subject, which extends the incapacitated students' capabilities [LER 64], not only on the physical level with the robot's movements, but also on the level of maintaining social connections. On this last point, our findings show what researchers at the University of California have previously demonstrated in the youngest students [NEW 16].

Beyond opportunity and mobility, what is particularly remarkable is the fact that, in a very large proportion of the interviewed students' comments, the machine was referred to using first-person singular pronouns. For example: "My movements took place so I could understand who was talking"; or, for another student: "Umm, also something sometimes without meaning to since it was pretty high I blocked others' vision in fact [...] they told me because I put myself [...] I didn't realize that eventually I was blocking the board [...] or sometimes I saw two hands on my robot and I found myself moved" (Corine), and for a third, discussing the potential for moving the robot during the class: "It's true I didn't move" (Lydia). This use of the first person for the robot goes along with referring to the machine by other students or teachers with the name of the represented person. To exist as a subject, it must be possible to be the author of one's words and, at the same time, to be able to be recognized as a subject. Intersubjectivity, inter-I, in the sense proposed by René Roussillon, that is, for "thinking about the question of an encounter with a subject animated by impulses and an unconscious psychic life, with an object, which is also an other-subject, and which is itself also animated by an impulsive life, part of which is unconscious" [ROU 08, p. 2], is essential for the potential of thinking about oneself as a subject.

We also noted the personalization of the robot: "They even dressed me. They dressed the robot with a little scarf" (Virginie). We could see in this gesture only a form of amusement, but it seems to me that we are here in the presence of a form of reassurance for this student's peers, which allows them to consider that the student is not only a machine. This feeling of confusion between machine and human being described by Searles [SEA 60] may be further implicated in situations of incapacity related to illness or accident. Everything occurs as if a small piece of colored fabric had the symbolic function of allowing for interplay, indispensable for a real meeting with a subject beyond the machine that it represents, to make it so that the remote student will be considered and think of himself in return as a subject and, at the same time, for the face-to-face students to feel they are equally subjects.

This referring to the robot in the first person, this extension of the incapacitated body and, furthermore, this process of the extended subject does not lead, in students who benefit from the system, to a feeling of confusion between themselves and the robot. Consequently, they do not experience this as a process of desubjectification. This is undoubtedly reinforced by the fact that, during the class, the F2F students and the teachers refer to the robot using the incapacitated student's name. In other words, they are not addressing a robot but the present-absent student through the robot. Only computer specialists associated with the research felt the need to name the robots for the purpose of maintenance and installation of software for controlling the robot. We can here assert that the telepresent students feel that the teachers at the university are paying attention to them, taking care of them, considering them, and therefore they are led to only have positive feelings for this system proposed by teachers that did them "so much good". We find here the characteristics that Eugène Enriquez had foregrounded in a gallery of teacher portraits [ENR 81]. The interviewed students' capability of feeling surrounded and present is probably a source of these views dominated by an extremely positive tone, just as it constitutes a foundation for the production of a quality educational relationship.

We can assert that the response offered by the system probably strongly offsets what these students sometimes mention as a form of collapse and that, as a result, they can only consider it on the positive side and thus to live in a better reality, if not on the physical level, at least on the psychological level. It is as if the robot was experienced as a form of deliverance or of emancipation from the injured, sick, immobile body as a mobile extension of self. We also understand here that the use of telepresence robots has offshoots that largely surpass the pedagogical framework.

8.7. Other considerations

Beyond these positive words, a few negative elements stand out, infrequently in the context of the full set of discourse. They first concern aspects related to technology. In the first place, the difficulty of adjusting the sound level because of the distance of the robot from the person who is speaking: "Also, sometimes I had the impression that I wasn't being heard [...] it was a technical problem [...] the sound was too loud during the first session [...] it was annoying" (Corine). To these perceptual adjustments, we here make a connection to Dorothée Furnon's analyses (see Chapter 7). In addition, the impossibility of controlling the camera on the vertical axis, the inevitable connection problems, or even the need to return to the charging station were of concern: "The only thing was that it ran down pretty quickly apparently and so then I kept an eye on it and so as soon as I saw that I was running out I put myself back on the charger that was installed specifically in the classroom and also in the conference room [...] on the other hand I didn't move after that I stayed on the base" (Lydia). These technical difficulties mentioned by the students did not seem to me to be concerned specifically with the telepresence system, but were elements that can be found in every study that collects user experiences, informed or not, of systems of digital tools in the field of education and training.

In contrast, some elements are notable for their less laudatory character. Thus, a student mentioned the confusion of spaces when the remote came close and became worrisome:

Virginie: But then all of a sudden there was a big screen [...] I could be seen clearly [...] everyone came to my house then.

Researcher: Everyone visited your house then?

Virginie: No but they could see my house then behind me [...] it's not important, but I think that they [the students present in the class] saw me very very well in close-up.

Work with digital machines fosters these fears and phantasms of confusion and depersonalization. Yet, if it was too worrisome, the subjective work of unlinking would occur instead of the work of subjectification.

Another student mentioned the discomfort of seeing his own image while interacting with his fellow students or with the teachers. She added the concern that she said she had generated in the other F2F students because, she thought, of the machine's noise or the room taken up by the robot in the classroom: "I knew the image I projected [...] you couldn't really see my hands [...] you couldn't see [...] it was uncomfortable to see myself [...] and then the fear of bothering others when I moved the robot I don't know maybe because it made noise it was annoying [...] my classmates turned their heads, laughing [...] I wasn't a major bother [...] rather that's how I felt" (Corine). Another student expressed the same discomfort: "I was really uncomfortable making it move among everyone [...] sometimes I couldn't manage to see the whole board, but it was because I didn't dare move anymore [...] I know everyone was looking at the little robot as soon as I moved so I didn't want to" (Lydia).

These elements of speech can be interpreted as signs of worrisome strangeness, based on the proposition that Freud had formulated [FRE 02], when the familiar becomes strange, landmarks fail and feelings of concern about the world dominate. We must recall that this notion was referred to by Masahiro Mori, concerning robots, as the "uncanny valley" [MOR 70].

8.8. The psycho(patho)logy of the virtual everyday: a presence in the absence

My research work takes part in the analysis of the psycho(patho)logy of the virtual everyday [MIS 06], in the field of education and training. I maintain that the practices of mediated teaching and learning through information and communication technologies are ordinarily constructed in an articulation between two polarities at the level of the unconscious psyche: a work of subjectification, on the one hand, and a work of unlinking, on the other hand [RIN 11].

Because they occur in response to a situation that can be psychically experienced as a breakdown, the experience lived through this system offers possibilities of (re)construction through an intersubjective process that allows students to engage in the work of subjectification. However, at the same time, because they make presence possible in absence and ubiquity, these same systems generate for students a feeling of worrisome strangeness linked to an impression of confusion of spaces and limitations, giving the impression of a fluid world [BAU 13] and, in this way, provoking the psychological work of unlinking.

The telepresence robot system transforms the presence/absence dichotomy. Geneviève Jacquinot drew our attention to the fact that we should try harder to consider that "the modification that can lead to the use of these technologies requires us or allows us to imagine a presence, the 'benefit of a presence'" [JAC 00]. In a telepresence robot system, where a student attends classes through the intermediary of a robot he/she controls, it is impossible to clearly define what stems from presence and what stems from absence. It seems to me here that the experience of students asked about these questions of distance and presence cannot be thought about in a divided way, but rather in an articulation between them. They are both at home and in class, here and there, in a form of ubiquity that telepresence allows. This comparison between presence and distance indicates, it seems to me, two paths. On the one hand, this comparison between presence and distance opens a gap, a transitional space [WIN 71], a play area, in the mechanical sense of play, that is, where things do not dovetail as planned in the arrangement of the gears so dear to Seymour Papert [PAP 81], where intersubjectivity is constructed first and foremost by the recognition of the self and the other as subjects. The other path is that of the confusion of spaces: the distant becomes close, the intimate mixes with the professional and becomes worrisome, provoking a psychological act of unlinking. This work of ordinary unlinking, that is, that does not stem from pathology but from normal functioning [CAN 66], occurs when, on the one hand, the feelings and emotions experienced through the system are too dangerous for the integrity of the self and require the creation of defense mechanisms such as projective identification or denial, and on the other hand, when these psychological, persecutory experiences have not encountered the capacity for dreaming [BIO 62], that is, a receptacle that is favorable to their transformation towards connective work. These are, for example, the feelings of solitude and dependence that are visible through the students' comments: "And once the day was over I was put back into the closet [...] in the morning I could turn it on [...] I was in the closet [...] I was waiting for someone to come get me" (Lydia) or also "the first day I felt very frustrated [...] I saw everyone leave and the door close [...] I stayed alone in the empty classroom" (Corine).

The essential point is probably a form of presence-absence that can simultaneously bring about a feeling of worrisome strangeness [FRE 02] or a feeling of being alone in the presence of another kind person [WIN 58]. We therefore must probably orient our studies beginning from the feeling of the presence of different participants (teachers, present-absent students, present peers); a feeling of presence that Lise Haddouk [HAD 16] reminds us is formulated by the emotional intensity of the experience of interaction that the subject engages in with other human participants.

8.9. References

[ALT 02] ALTET M., "Une démarche de recherche sur la pratique enseignante : l'analyse plurielle", *Revue française de pédagogie*, vol. 138, pp. 85–93, 2002.

[BAU 13] BAUMAN Z., *La vie liquide*, Pluriel, Paris, 2013.

[BEI 96] BEILLEROT J., "L'analyse des pratiques professionnelles : pourquoi cette expression ?", *Cahiers pédagogiques*, vol. 416, pp. 12–13, 1996.

[BIO 62] BION W.R., *Learning from Experience*, William Heinemann, London, 1962.

[BLA 05] BLANCHARD-LAVILLE C., CHAUSSECOURTE P., HATCHUEL F. *et al.*, "Recherches cliniques d'orientation psychanalytique dans le champ de l'éducation et de la formation", *Revue française de pédagogie*, vol. 151, pp. 111–162, 2005.

[BLA 99] BLANCHARD-LAVILLE C., "L'approche clinique d'orientation psychanalytique : enjeux théoriques et méthodologiques", *Revue française de pédagogie*, vol. 127, pp. 9–22, 1999.

[BRO 16] BROSSAIS E., "Introduction", *Les sciences de l'éducation pour l'ère nouvelle*, vol. 49, no. 2, pp. 7–18, 2016.

[CAN 66] CANGUILHEM G., *Le normal et le pathologique*, PUF, Paris, 1966.

[CIF 85] CIFALI M., MOLL J., *Pédagogie et psychanalyse*, Dunod, Paris, 1985.

[CIF 98] CIFALI M., IMBERT F., *Freud et la pédagogie*, PUF, Paris, 1998.

[COU 13] COURTIN V., JEAN A., "Recherches et formations en maïeutique à l'aide des sciences de l'éducation : quelle(s) approche(s) pour une analyse du travail des enseignants sages-femmes face à un simulateur d'accouchement interactif ?", *Recherche en soins infirmiers*, vol. 114, pp. 68–74, 2013.

[DEV 17] DEVILLERS L., *Des robots et des hommes. Mythes, fantasmes et réalité*, Plon, Paris, 2017.

[DEV 80] DEVEREUX G., *De l'angoisse à la méthode dans les sciences du comportement*, Flammarion, Paris, 1980.

[DUM 16] DUMOUCHEL P., DAMIANO L., *Vivre avec les robots. Essai sur l'empathie artificielle*, Le Seuil, Paris, 2016.

[ENR 81] ENRIQUEZ E., "Petite galerie de formateurs en mal de modèle", *Connexions*, vol. 33, pp. 93–109, 1981.

[FRE 02] FREUD S., "L'inquiétant", *Œuvres complètes*, vol. XV, pp. 147–188, PUF, Paris, 2002.

[GEL 17] GELIN R., "Les robots et l'intranquillité", in FRYDMAN R., FLIS-TREVES M. (eds), *L'intranquillité. Déni ou réalité ?*, pp. 103–107, PUF, Paris, 2017.

[HAD 16] HADDOUK L., *L'entretien clinique à distance*, Éditions Érès, Toulouse, 2016.

[JAC 00] JACQUINOT G., "Le sentiment de présence", *Actes des deuxièmes rencontres Réseaux Humains/Réseaux Technologiques*, Poitiers, France, 24 June 2000, pp. 183–191, accessed June 2017 at: http://edel.univ-poitiers.fr/rhrt/document773.php.

[JAC 10] JACQUINOT G., "Entre présence et absence", *Distances et savoirs*, vol. 8, no. 2, pp. 153–165, 2010.

[JAC 93] JACQUINOT G., "Apprivoiser la distance et supprimer l'absence ? Ou les défis de la formation à distance", *Revue française de pédagogie*, vol. 102, pp. 55–67, 1993.

[JUN 15] JUNG J., *Le sujet et son double. La construction transitionnelle de l'identité*, Dunod, Paris, 2015.

[LER 64] LEROY-GOURHAN A., *Le geste et la parole*, Albin Michel, Paris, 1964.

[MIL 07] MILHAUD-CAPPE D., *Freud et le mouvement de pédagogie psychanalytique 1908–1937*, Vrin, Paris, 2007.

[MIS 06] MISSONNIER S., "Psycho(patho)logie psychanalytique du virtuel quotidien", in TISSERON S., MISSONNIER S., STORA M. (eds), *L'enfant au risque du virtuel*, pp. 39–85, Dunod, Paris, 2006.

[MIS 17] MISSONNIER S., "Pourquoi les robots humanoïdes désirent-ils devenir méta-humains ?", *Le Carnet Psy*, vol. 204, pp. 21–27, 2017.

[MOL 89] MOLL J., *La pédagogie psychanalytique*, Dunod, Paris, 1989.

[MOR 70] MORI M., "La vallée de l'étrange", *Gradhiva*, vol. 15, pp. 26–33, 2012, 1970.

[NEW 16] NEWHART V.A., WARSCHAUER M., SENDER L.S., "Virtual inclusion via telepresence robots in the classroom: An exploratory case study", *The International Journal of Technologies in Learning*, vol. 23, no. 4, pp. 21–27, 2016.

[NIJ 15] NIJIMBÈRE C., BOULC'H L., BARON G.L., "Apprendre l'informatique par la programmation des robots. Cas de Logo Mindstorms", in BARRON G.L., BRUILLARD E., DROT-DELANGE B. (eds), *Informatique en éducation. Perspectives curriculaires et didactiques*, pp. 265–277, PUBP, Clermont-Ferrand, 2015.

[OHA 06] OHAYON A., "Psychanalyse, éducation nouvelle et éducation morale dans les années 1930 en France", in HOFSTETTER R., SCHNEUWLY B. (eds), *Passion, fusion, tension. Éducation nouvelle et sciences de l'éducation*, pp. 325–339, Peter Lang, Bern, 2006.

[OHA 09] OHAYON A., "Psychanalyse et éducation : une histoire d'amour et de désamour. 1908–1968", *Cliopsy*, vol. 1, pp. 25 40, 2009.

[PAP 81] PAPERT S., *Mindstorms: Children, Computers, and Powerful Ideas*, Basic Books, New-York, 1981.

[PER 99] PERAYA D., "Vers les campus virtuels. Principes et fonctionnements techno-sémio-pragmatique des dispositifs de formations virtuels", *Hermès*, vol. 25, pp. 153–168, 1999.

[PIC 17] PICQ P., *Qui va prendre le pouvoir ? Les grands singes, les hommes politiques ou les robots*, Odile Jacob, Paris, 2017.

[RIN 96] RINAUDO J.-L., "Les histoires de Gaëtan, production d'hypertextes au cycle des approfondissements", *Revue de l'EPI*, vol. 81, pp. 93–100, 1996.

[RIN 02] RINAUDO J.-L., *Des souris et des maîtres*, L'Harmattan, Paris, 2002.

[RIN 11] RINAUDO J.-L., *TIC, éducation et psychanalyse*, L'Harmattan, Paris, 2011.

[RIN 12] RINAUDO J.-L., "Approche subjective du non-usage", *Recherches & éducations*, vol. 6, pp. 89–103, 2012, available at: http://rechercheseducations .revues.org/1055.

[RIN 15a] RINAUDO J.-L., "Rapport au temps et à l'espace dans les échanges numériques en formation", *Conférence Séminaire IMPEC*, Lyon, France, 25 September 2015, available at: https://impec.sciencesconf.org/resource/page/id /25.

[RIN 15b] RINAUDO J.-L., "Imaginaire éducatif et technologies numériques", *Interfaces numériques*, vol. 4, no. 2, pp. 251–267, 2015.

[RIN 16] RINAUDO J.-L., "Entretien avec Jean-Luc Rinaudo", *Distances et médiations des savoirs*, vol. 13, available at: http://dms.revues.org/1370, 2016.

[ROU 08] ROUSSILLON R., *Le jeu et l'entre-je(u)*, PUF, Paris, 2008.

[SEA 60] SEARLES H., *The Non-Human Environment in Normal Development and in Schizophrenia*, International Universities, Madison, 1960.

[SHE 18] SHELLEY M.W., *Frankenstein; or, The Modern Prometheus*, Lackington, Hughes, Harding, Mavor & Jones, London, 2018.

[TIS 15] TISSERON S., *Le jour où mon robot m'aimera. Vers l'empathie artificielle*, Albin Michel, Paris, 2015.

[TOR 16] TORDO F., *Le numérique et la robotique en psychanalyse. Du sujet virtuel au sujet augmenté*, L'Harmattan, Paris, 2016.

[TUR 84] TURKLE S., *The Second Self: Computers and the Human Spirit*, Simon & Schuster, New York, 1984.

[TUR 11] TURKLE S., *Alone Together: Why We Demand More of Technology and Less of Each Other*, Basic Books, New York, 2011.

[VAN 02] VANHEULE S., "Qualitative research and its relation to lacanian psycho-analysis", *Journal of the Psychoanalysis of Culture and Society*, vol. 7, no. 2, pp. 336–342, 2002.

[WIN 00] WINNICOTT D.W., *La crainte de l'effondrement et autres situations cliniques*, Gallimard, Paris, 2000.

[WIN 58] WINNICOTT D.W., "La capacité d'être seul", *De la pédiatrie à la psychanalyse*, pp. 325–333, Payot, Paris, 1958.

[WIN 71] WINNICOTT D.W., *Playing and Reality*, Tavistock, London, 1971.

A Telepresence Research Set-up in a Doctoral Seminar: the "Digital Presences" Workshop

9.1. Introduction

The conditions for participating in scientific demonstrations have tended to evolve over the past few years under the combined effect of individual hypermobility and the digital possibilities that enable new forms of presence at a distance. In the more specific framework of a doctoral seminar, the dispersal of the participants abroad, particularly young doctorates, often deprived of any possibility of connections with their former research teams, makes the potential for allowing them to attend, via screen, a form of exchange regarding their work or that of others, very useful, even though from a distance.

It is on such a context that this chapter is focused, that is, a doctoral seminar comprising two audiences: an F2F audience and a remote audience. This chapter aims to demonstrate a research approach by explaining the context and the primary research questions. At the time of this writing, while the research corpus is complete, the analysis has hardly been started, and will therefore not provide us with results strictly speaking, but rather findings in terms of results, supported by the experiences felt by actors in

Chapter written by Christine DEVELOTTE.

this educational scenario. The general idea of the approach was to design a system that would allow us to conduct an empirical study of what telepresence engenders in a doctoral seminar and what impact it has on the participants and on the dynamic of exchanges that takes place there. Another important goal of this research is to produce data that will be, in short order, accessible to all researchers via the Ortolang platform.

9.2. Context: reflexive research

The Multimodal Interactions seminar presented by ÉCran (IMPEC) began in 2013 at the École normale supérieure in Lyon[1]. It is a monthly seminar dedicated to the study of screen-based communication and telepresence (as defined by Weissberg, that is, as one of the forms of presence at a distance; the author notes that digital engineering confers an intensification of presence to telepresence (physical sensors, etc.) [WEI 99, p. 41]) that traditionally invites presentations of the progress of in-process theses and conferences by invited researchers. Less traditionally, this seminar was attended by young doctors who wanted to continue to attend the seminar remotely. At the beginning, the involvement of these participants remotely was realized via the Skype program or on the Google Hangouts platform. A computer was placed in the middle of an oval table around which the F2F participants were seated, and we took the responsibility of manually turning the computer in the appropriate direction, depending on what was happening (facing the wall, in the case of the projection of a presentation, or facing the participant who was speaking, in the case of oral conversation). This patched-together system, while it allowed the participants to be present at a distance, was not very comfortable for the F2F participants, who had to remember to turn the computer so the webcam would always be correctly oriented for the remote participants, who were sometimes left oriented, because of the F2F participants' forgetfulness, towards a white board or some other unimportant angle.

Hence, in 2016, we sought, on the one hand, to improve this system and, on the other hand, to combine it with the construction of a corpus dedicated to studying different aspects of screen-based interactions, which were from

1 Available at: https://impec.sciencesconf.org/resource/page/id/4.

the beginning the object of the seminar's inquiries. The initial idea was therefore to accommodate remote participants at the beginning of the 2016 school year to use different methods in order to be able to analyze the effects of the degree of the autonomy of the artifacts within the seminar's dynamics. We therefore brought in a Beam telepresence robot, a Kubi[2] robot and a videoconference platform, which varied from session to session depending on the documents to be shared (Adobe Connect, Google Hangouts or Skype). In order to facilitate visuals for the remote participants via Adobe Connect, a remotely controlled webcam was used in the seminar in order to be able to orient (or zoom) more easily based on what was happening during the seminar. We must therefore specify here that the Beam robot was not selected, but was rather already there, and we therefore took advantage of its presence at the Institut français d'éducation (IFE). This 1.58-meter-tall robot is equipped with an LCD screen that allows us to view the face and bust of the participant controlling it remotely. Furthermore, its wheels allow this robot to move. One of the seminar participants, Dorothée Furnon, who is working on her thesis on the use of the Beam robot in an educational system (see Chapter 7), facilitated its integration into the seminar by helping the users to take charge of the robot and by organizing an orientation session for the seminar participants with the robot at the École centrale de Lyon in September 2015.

The videoconferencing tools were chosen for convenience in each session (number of remote participants, availability of tools). Therefore, there were three communication tools that allowed remote participants (between three and five depending on the session) to interact with the number of participants physically in Lyon, in the framework of the JMPEC seminar in 2016–2017. We use the expression "communication tools" as an umbrella term for designating both videoconferencing platforms and software programs or artifacts.

While organizing the work planned for the year, it was decided that the half-days for building the corpus and collecting data would be called the "exploratory workshop on digital presences" and to bring together for this

---

2 This is an iPad that works with Skype and is connected to a rotating arm, which allows it to be oriented laterally as well as vertically; available at: https://www.revolverobotics.com/.

seminar the approximately 15 research-instructors or future researchers whose names are given in the note below[3].

A few details about the seminar's ambiance: conversations were considered to be favorable for nurturing all of the participants, primarily doctoral students, and therefore particular attention was paid to creating a climate of goodwill for the collective construction of knowledge, in order to encourage the participation of the least scientifically advanced individuals among the group as much as possible. In this way, we align ourselves with those who associate teaching efficacy with sustaining "a classroom ambiance that is both organized and pleasant, positive and warm" [TAL 12]. All of the participants were informed of the study's objectives and even participated in their development: it was, in effect, a co-constructed study based on the initial idea proposed by Christine Develotte.

In order to accumulate data concerning different aspects of a doctoral seminar, we chose to collect them in a variety of situations, as shown in the following five sessions (initial presentation and interactions):

– a "data session" style presentation by Morgane Domanchin, a doctoral student in Lyon (45 min), about her thesis work (concerning a corpus of Skype-based interactions between students in Lyon and at MIT in Boston), then interactions with both the F2F and remote participants (45 min);

– a presentation by sociologist Évelyne Lasserre (université Lyon-1) and Axel Guïoux (université Lyon 2): "Fixed mobility – presence beyond obstacles" at Lyon (45 min), and their interactions with both the F2F and remote participants (45 min);

– a presentation from the United States by Susan Herring of Indiana University: "Discourse Pragmatics of Robot Mediated Communication" via

---

3 The "Digital Presences" exploratory workshop is composed of the following participants: Amélie Bouquain (doctoral student, ICAR), Tatiana Codreanu (PhD, Imperial College London, associated with ICAR), Christelle Combe-Celik (MCF, Aix-Marseille, LPL), Christine Develotte (P.U., ENS Lyon, ICAR), Morgane Domanchin (doctoral student, Lyon-2, ICAR), Mabrouka El-Hachani (MCF, Lyon-3, Elico), Dorothée Furnon (doctoral student, Lyon-2, ECP), Jean-François Grassin (MCF, Lyon-2, ICAR), Yigong Guo (doctoral student, ENS de Lyon, ICAR), Samira Ibnelkaïd (ATER, université de Franche-Comté, associated with ICAR), Françoise Poyet (P.U., Lyon-1, Elico), Joséphine Rémon (MCF, Lyon-2, ICAR), Caroline Vincent (post-doctoral researcher, IFÉ, EducTice), Liping Zhang (MCF, Hangzhou, China, associated with ICAR).

Beam and Adobe Connect (45 min), then interactions with both the F2F and remote participants (45 min);

– a "data session" presentation by Christelle Combe Celik via Kubi and Adobe (45 min): "From an imagined ethos to an ethos produced by beginning tutors online", and their interactions with both the F2F and remote participants (45 min);

– a group work session with the participants in the "Digital Presences" workshop in Lyon and remotely, intended for reflection about how to graphically represent the work situation being studied (45 min). This session was initially focused primarily on Morgane Domanchin's illustration presented in Figure 9.1.

No particular scenario was planned in advance for any of these sessions since we had chosen to operate in the most "natural" way possible, notwithstanding the presence of cameras. The 15 participants were not always present at every session; the average being approximately 10–12 depending on the session. In such a system, exchanges between participants could function according to different modalities, of which we can distinguish:

– oral exchanges: these were the most anticipated and the ones whose quality was the most important for the fluidity of conversation. Regardless of the communication tool, the poor functioning of the audio channel (with regard to reception as well as production) became a group problem to be resolved;

– visual exchanges: the visual channel includes the image of the participants and the robot's mobility; while it is very important to be able to see the person to whom we are speaking, the absence of an image for a remote participant (e.g. in the case of a problem with the webcam) did not invalidate the participation of this non-visible speaker by others;

– written exchanges: these can occur on the Adobe Connect platform in public or private mode between two or more remote participants via Adobe Connect. We were also able to, in the cases of some technical difficulties, send texts via a remote participant's phone to try to resolve the problem without interrupting the discussion taking place in the seminar.

Studying the multimodality of the interactions between the participants was complicated by the fact that different exchanges could take place at the same time and between different people.

One of the intrinsic difficulties of studying telepresence lies in the need to maintain the confidentiality of the data. In effect, if we want to precisely analyze exchanges that take place in a hybrid seminar, it is necessary to have the right to use the participants' images to be able to detect signs of discomfort, pleasure, facial expressions, gestures and so on. On the other hand, it is often clearly difficult to obtain this right from individuals who do not want to be filmed or do not want their images to be used, even only for research purposes. The ethical procedures involved in such research therefore make data collection all the more difficult when it is a question of repeated collection, as in the case that will be presented below.

It is therefore an important obstacle that arises when all of the participants not only authorize the use of their images but also see the scientific utility of doing so.

9.3. Technical-physical system

The five sessions that were chosen for data collection took place in a room adapted for pedagogical experiments, namely the facilities of the *Laboratoire d'innovation pédagogique et numérique* (LIPéN) at the *ENS de Lyon*.

Techno-methodological support was provided by the Cellule de corpus complexes (CCC) associated with Labex ASLAN[4]. A team of research engineers and technicians allowed us to create a plan for capturing the data that included different angles with the intention of recording as much of the complexity of the situation as possible. A camera was placed in front of the Kubi, a GoPro was used and there were four video streams generated for each recording.

Moreover, the remote participants recorded their screens (dynamic screen capture) and their bodies in front of the computer (by a camera at the feet).

---

4 Labex ASLAN includes two labs in Lyon (DDL and ICAR) for "Advanced studies about the complexity of language", available at: http://aslan.universite-lyon.fr/.

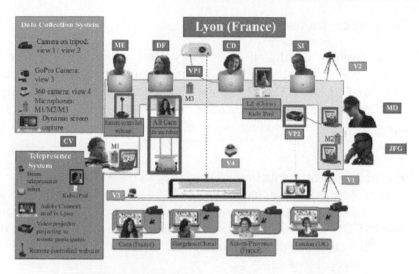

Figure 9.1. *Illustration of the layout in the LIPéN room by Morgane Domanchin (ICAR, université Lyon-2). For a color version of this figure, see www.iste.co.uk/rinaudo/telepresence.zip*

With regard to the room diagram, we tried to represent the F2F speakers (in red) and the remote speakers (in blue), as well as the technical equipment: the cameras (V1 and V2, GoPro 3 and 360), the microphones and wall-mounted video projectors (VP1 and VP2): the first video projector served to project PowerPoint presentations by presenters (or any other participant) and the second allowed us to project the participants' images onto the wall via Adobe Connect.

Figure 9.2. *Photo of the session with the remote presenter participating via robot and displaying his presentation via Adobe Connect projected on the wall. For a color version of this figure, see www.iste.co.uk/rinaudo/telepresence.zip*

9.4. Theoretical framework

The integration of digital technology into education provides an opportunity for a number of modifications to professional practices [ALB 02, MET 11, POY 11]. The more specific topic of telepresence began to be studied from a general viewpoint in 1997 [FOW 97] and was then developed in domains including the teaching of medicine [KAU 99] and languages [COD 10].

The types of teaching situation in which research has been done related to telepresence experiences include TP [GAL 14], webinars [IBN 16] and language class sessions that connect students in a telecollaboration framework [ODO 07]. This telecollaboration often only relates to the part of the course that takes place in a "hybrid" fashion, that is, with part in person and part by videoconference.

Recent studies centered on screen-based interactions conducted by the JMPEC group are based on a phenomenological approach to the digital such as the one proposed by Stéphane Vial. He has developed an analysis of the digital from the techno-phenomenological viewpoint and proposed the idea of digital ontophany (way in which beings appear), arguing from the fact that the digital "influences the way in which the real appears to us" [VIA 11, p. 99]. For Vial, it is the very phenomenology of beings that is redefined and renegotiated by technical culture. This work has exposed the modalities of intersubjectivity in digital interaction [IBN 16], depending on the features provided [HOT 01] by the communication tool being used.

Studies related to telepresence connected to robots are even more recent and are found in the study of languages [OHH 10], as well as in events such as scientific colloquia. Neustaedter et al. [NEU 16] recently studied the same Beam robot as the one we used in the JMPEC seminar to collect recommendations concerning its use in a conference context and to point out some difficulties such as those associated with the construction of the identity of the person using the robot and his difficulties in interacting with the other participants. They also asked themselves the question of how many robots can be used in the same conference (their experiment was conducted on three robots simultaneously used during the same conference). They finally specified that no research has yet been published about the use of robots in such an academic context.

These recent studies are valuable for our research, as are those that were presented in May 2017 in Denver using the framework of interdisciplinary research (psychology, media studies and computing), in which Choi et al. [CHO 17] focused on the effects of gestures and facial expressions for 36 robot users during interpersonal communication. Although they determined that a positive role is played by the slow movements of the telepresence robot for the feeling of proximity perceived by his interlocutor, they came to see the need to compare more carefully the facial expressions produced by speakers, via videoconference systems, and "by the robot". This is effectively one of the scientific stakes of knowing whether these results can be applied between different systems: in a study comparing in-person interpersonal exchanges on the one hand and by videoconference on the other hand, Cosnier and Develotte [COS 11] showed that facial expressions were more emphatic and held longer in videoconferences than in person. To the extent that we can consider robots as "enriched video conferences" because of their mobility, it makes sense to ask are the previous results transferable to the Kubi robot? To the Beam robot? Or to both?

All of the work concerning videoconferences, as relevant to collaborative work as to interpersonal social relationships, to the construction of identity and to the expression of emotions (facial expressions), must be revisited.

To orient the research, from the beginning, during the discussion regarding the experiment that would be conducted, the members of the "Digital Presences" group determined three topics that seemed of interest for study:

– attention management (see the polyfocalization of attention [JON 04]) and capacity management;

– bodies and spaces, agency of tools;

– politeness and the protection of faces, the affective and emotional dimensions of presence via screen.

It is therefore around these first topics that the initial research will develop, leading to the production of a collective work whose definitive form we have not yet chosen. However, a number of other directions are possible depending on the discipline (psychology, educational sciences, sociology, language sciences, information and communication sciences), given that this kind of corpus is targeted using an interdisciplinary approach.

The unusual situation that leads to interactions with nearby participants and with others mediated by various communication tools is associated with difficulties in managing speech turns and the orchestration of interactions, without mentioning the technical problems that can occur at any time.

9.5. Techno-methodological choices

Since the JMPEC seminar is pluridisciplinary, the initial stance was to privilege a naturalist approach in order to be able to collect analyzable data using different approaches depending on the disciplines addressed by the different researchers participating in the seminar. More personally, my analytical approach is based on comprehensive ethology [COS 11, p. 4], an empirical approach that consists of cross-referencing behavioral and perceptual data from participants at different times during data collection. "Ethological methodology is particularly heuristic in approaches where observation is essential, for example in the clinic, developmental psychology, and social psychology, that is to say anywhere where interindividual communication constitutes a privileged object of study" [HOT 01]. The remote participants particularly drew our attention and were asked to participate in different kinds of interviews, most often explanatory interviews [VER 94] or auto-confrontation style interviews.

The construction of a well-thought-out corpus was designed based on the following data collection methods: videos (for behavioral analysis), interviews (for the analysis of experience) and texts written by participants. The written texts included both Google Forms (see the questionnaire in Appendix 9.9.2) for evaluation of each session and more developed writing to collect the participants' feelings about the seminar after more careful thought.

A file on Google Drive allowed us to categorize the different aspects related to each session (the Google Docs serving as minutes, the calendars and use tables of the communication tools, the theoretical articles associated with each of the three axes, etc.). This tool, as practical as it could be made, was nevertheless not accessible from China by Liping.

The complete corpus is composed of the five sessions that were filmed in October and November 2016 and then in January, March and April 2017. The set of recorded data for the five sessions constituted 9 hours 16 minutes of recording. To this data related to the participants' behavior, the post-activity data concerning their subjective perceptions is added. The method of collection of post-activity data varied depending on the sub-groups' themes: semi-directed interview for some, explanation for others and questionnaires for another were thus collected from interviews (18 audio or video interviews lasting 45 minutes on average; see the table in Appendix 9.9.1) and written texts. Two kinds of written texts were collected:

– first, at the end of each session, the participants were invited to fill out an online questionnaire designed to collect their feelings "in the heat of the moment";

– then, in June 2017, each participant explained their perceptions at the end of the exploratory workshop on digital presence based on the following four questions posed to them:

- What were the notable points of the experience you had this year in the workshop?

- What "habituation" did you feel you underwent?

- What were the things that remained sensitive/difficult?

- What advice would you give to someone who wanted to use a mixed in-person/remote system?

9.6. Technical work on video data

Before they could be submitted to an actual analysis, the data had to be digitized, edited into multiscope videos and standardized in order to be stored on the data-sharing site (Ortolang).

The five sessions were provided with video subtitles lasting about 90 minutes each[5], with each recording including four video streams (including one from a 360° camera), four audio streams and three screen captures from the remote participants' computers. The data were filmed in MOV and MP4 formats. They was digitized and stored in a private space in Ortolang. It

---

5 Specifically, first session: 48 min, second session: 1 h 37 min, third session: 1 h 40 min, fourth session: 1 h 41 min and fifth session (double): 1 h 20 min + 1 h 50 min.

should be noted that the presentation of the "Digital Presences" corpus is now available.[6]

The goal of pre-processing the video data is to be able to provide to all of the researchers a multimodal transcript of this corpus (encoded on ELAN). It is effectively necessary to use software that allows us to collect data about multimodal (gestural, verbal, visual, etc.) and plurisemiotic (textuality, orality, actions on screen, etc.) interactions in order to be able to very precisely identify the points of difficulty or discomfort from facial expressions, prolonged silences and so on. Moreover, in order to facilitate analysis, it is useful to proceed with multiscope video editing (sound synchronization for the different audio and video channels chosen based on the goals of the analysis). All of these complex video documents must be of excellent quality in order to make it possible to conduct qualitative research because their degree of clarity is connected to that of the studied corpus.

All of these data-processing activities that took place before the data was shared on a site are technical and time-consuming and require the efforts of several members of the team and of the JCAR[7] laboratory in order to maintain the established schedule for posting data online.

At the time of this writing, at the end of 2017, video data collection and interviews have been completed. We have begun transcriptions and are beginning to analyze the data.

9.7. Discussion

The experiment we conducted, which constitutes an object of study by making (future) researchers-instructors the subjects of a study about presence in a doctoral seminar, raises a number of questions. We will list some of them below.

The first question refers back to the reflexivity of the work of the researchers about themselves. This process is similar, in a certain way, to the activity clinics [PRO 07], where one seeks to take a more distanced look at his own practice. In what way does the presence of cameras modify speech

---

6 Available at: https://www.ortolang.frL/market/corpora/impec.

7 Christelle Celik, Morgane Domanchin, Julien Gachet, Justine Lascar, Gerald Nicolaï and Daniel Valero.

acts? This omnipresent question in the field of interaction analysis is sharpened by the fact that the participants knew that they and their colleagues would work later on this data.

Can we still talk about an ecological approach when a field is sufficiently involved in the captured material? As far as we are concerned, we think yes: for us, the claim of this approach relies on the fact that our intention for the participants was for the seminar to operate as much as possible in the same way as when it is not being filmed. The seminar seemed to us, at the level of the perceptions that we had the opportunity to share among ourselves, to take place in a similar way whether it was filmed or not. The research highlights the perceptions that each had about the instrumentation of this seminar. With the improvements in the technical recording tools, we could imagine a system for data capture that would be invisible; it remains to be seen whether the fact of knowing that one is being filmed will have the same repercussions for participants.

What are the variables to take into account? In a complex situation of academic training, many factors may explain the dynamics of exchanges that take place. Technology certainly plays a non-negligible role (cameras and robots), but speaking and speech acts are equally dependent on the position of participants and their knowledge and their habituation to the way of operating in this seminar. In other words, sociological and psychological variables also play a crucial role in the degree of participation from each member.

The ultimate objective of making the data shareable with the scientific community so that it can take advantage of it was also the reason for questions relative to the standardization of the data.

What choices characterize this data, which will be subsequently usable by others, in an indeterminate amount of time?

Clarifications and attitudes were taken as a group, for example, during the discussion concerning the non anonymization of the data. The question discussed at that time is as follows: in our future work presentations, should we mask with a beep the first names of the participants who appear on the audio recording? Do not the researchers who want to work with this data know us already, for the most part? In the final account, what were the disadvantages that stemmed from our interactions? The exchanges concluded with the agreement of all participants to not anonymize the visuals or the sounds of the videos we produced.

Recent decisions also were related to the interviews: initially collected as audio or video recordings, we chose to transcribe them all as simple transcripts, that is, without taking into account the JCOR standards, which are usually adopted by our lab[8] (with a degree of precision, including different elements such as the length of silences) and to have them re-read by the interviewee in order to validate the text that will be shared with the research community. We therefore have interviews in two formats: video and audio files reserved for the researchers in our group and their textual transcriptions, which will be put online for other researchers to use.

For a researcher, agreeing to become the object of study creates problems [GOF 74] at different levels of research that we continue to try to negotiate in the group each time they come up.

The last series of questions that we want to share concerns the research questions in educational sciences related to this data. They can be both more or less general (at the level of the session's contents, for example) and more or less reliant on technology.

How do the transmission of knowledge, collaborative work and stimulation of discussions between participants take place?

Is there a playful dimension added by the presence of robots in the seminar for the participants in Lyon (or for those who used them)?

In order to bring in elements of responses to the phenomena of habituation and discovery, we sought to make sure that each tool was used by the same person during at least half a day and to have the Kubi and the robot used by all of the remote participants. What are the details of participation by Beam robot? By Kubi? By Adobe Connect? What different perceptions are there (if any) between these communication tools for those who used all of them? What is the level of involvement of the different participants depending on the tools used? Can they distinguish a degree of involvement specific to each tool? Are there contributions in terms of

8 Available at: http://icar.univ-lyon2.fr/projets/corinte/documents/2013_Conv_ICOR_250313 .pdf.

learning for the participants who use the robots? More generally, what limits and what advantages are there for each configuration?

These few questions, proposed here as examples, are situated at the micro level (interpersonal interactions) or even at the middle level (at the level of the doctoral seminar that hosted this exploratory workshop). Self-testing (here the doctoral seminar) of a system that can later, depending on the results, inspire changes to other educational situations is part of the objective of this research. The questions linked to the transferability of the results of this study for other audiences must necessarily be asked. It is important, nevertheless, not to lose sight of the macro, more institutional level, which largely predetermines what can or cannot happen with regard to the integration of robots in the educational context. If university education can claim a certain liberty of action and locations that are favorable for this kind of experiment, primary and secondary educational contexts are much more closely supervised and constrained in their modes of operation. The favorable reception of a robot by a teacher in his middle- or high-school class does not mean that all teachers at the same establishment will receive this robot with equal enthusiasm, because it may be considered intrusive. Educational policies therefore must aid in the development of such telepresence systems if they seem to be useful for integrating all students, particularly those who are incapacitated or distant. Studies taking into account this macro level in educational science will also be useful for explaining the numerous educational, technical, economic and administrative obstacles that can impede an institution's interest in this innovation.

9.8. Conclusion

This exploratory workshop about digital presences seems to us to be representative of the current round of research, ranging from the sophistication of technological tools and those linked to research (for reception, preprocessing and processing of data) to accessibility, since, if the constituted corpus conforms to standards, then it will be able to be shared with the scientific community. It is also a context that relies on the proximal zone of learning by the youngest in a new way: depending on whether they find themselves remote or not, via a robot or another, their presence in the doctoral seminar presents itself differently. This is what has already emerged from the different interviews that were conducted with the remote participants after having used different communication tools.

This experiment illustrates the virtues of operating with "collective intelligence" insofar as everyone is involved in this group work, and therefore solidarity is formed among its members, which allows us to collect this data. In the background, there effectively appear many decisions and divisions and many interindividual regulations that themselves could also be interesting to conserve with the goal of documenting the genesis of the workshop. The limits of "off" and "on" are themselves negotiable according to the degree of anthropological research one seeks to conduct.

9.9. Appendices

9.9.1. *Appendix 1. Explanatory interview*

Sample interview from the "Bodies and spaces, agency of tools" group. The questions below were directed to the participants *in situ* (with video recording of the interview).

Ask the person to recall specific moments from the experience and to try to describe everything he remembers regarding that moment. To help the person put himself into an evocative frame of mind, hypermnesia instructions can be given (say absolutely everything that you remember: odor, temperature, feelings, who was there, what you saw, what was said, etc.). Researchers should only focus on these experiential dimensions (emotion, cognition, activity, perception, etc.) or on specific moments, but not on speech. Researchers should try to lead the person to not generalize, but to focus on the experienced moment (avoiding the generalizing "we" or "you", as, for example, "when you are there you do this..." and "I always do this...").

We are going to focus on the body, the way in which it experiences remote interaction. We can therefore let the person know what we are seeking is his physical experience, the way in which it was felt during interaction.

Avoid closed questions and, especially, avoid asking "why": emphasize rather "when you say this, can you tell me more?"

First part of the interview: pre-interaction reminder

Can "pre-interaction" be temporally situated by the person himself: at what time does this preparation begin for him? The same morning, the day before, two days before...? Based on what he feels, did he think beforehand about the place he would occupy for the video? The clothes he is wearing? When did you think about this? And describe this moment.

Then, the structure of the seminar can be followed: before connection, during connection and afterwards.

1) "Perceptions":

- Expectations? What perceptions?

- Stress?

- Physiological state? (How did you feel?)

Example questions: "When you awoke on the morning of the seminar, can you tell us what you thought about?", "If you thought about the seminar, can you tell us when that was?", "Do you remember thinking anything specific at that time?", "Can you tell us how you felt?"

2) "Facts":

- What physical preparation did you do?

- Where did you set up?

- Did you try to see all of the participants (*in situ* and *ex situ*)?

- Organization with other participants?

Example questions: "Can you talk about the way you prepared before joining the seminar?", "Can you describe how you chose the location where you placed yourself to participate in the seminar?", "What did you think about, what did you tell yourself?"

Second part of the interview: mentioning the class and the interaction

1) "Perceptions":

- Visual/auditory access?

- Impression of having been sufficiently seen/heard by all? And having sufficiently heard/seen all of the other participants?

- Feeling of having been able to communicate? Feeling of being an inconvenience?

- Did you feel that you had lost control of your perceptions?

- Where did you perceive the bodies of the remote participants to be?

- What did you feel was your relationship with the objects and the other participants (in person and remote)?

- What emotions did you feel or perceive other remote participants to be feeling?

Example questions: "Can you describe a time when you felt heard or, on the contrary, a moment when you felt that the other participants did not listen to you, or anything else?", "Can you describe a moment when you felt that others saw you or, on the contrary, that they did not see you?"

To the question "Did you feel you lost control of your perceptions?", we can ask further: "Can you describe a moment when you wanted to do something but did not do it?", Can you explain what was happening for you at that time?", "What did you do at that time?" (to see if there was mission creep).

2) "Facts":

- What did you do to make yourself present and to make the remote participants present?

- What actions did you perform to make yourself seen and heard by the remote participants and to make it possible for you to see and hear them?

- Did you ask for/give help? Did you work with other participants to make yourself present/to make them present?

Third part of the interview: post-interaction reminder

1) "Perceptions":

- What did you feel when the remote participants disconnected?

- How did you feel after they disconnected?

- Did you feel tired? Physically, mentally?

2) "Facts":

- Did you change your physical posture when they disconnected? Your location?

- What recovery did you require (in relation to potential fatigue)?

9.9.2. *Appendix 2. Questionnaire*

This is the questionnaire that was administered to participants in the "Digital Presences" group at the end of each session.

– In which situation did you find yourself? (in-person/Adobe Connect/Kubi/Beam)

– How did you experience the communication situation (data session/conference and discussion)?

– Can you list everything you felt during this session?

– Can you identify a moment when your attention waned?

– Can you identify an event that bothered you?

– Can you identify an event that particularly interested you?

– What kept your attention?

– What could be improved? (frustrations)

– Were you able to participate the way you hoped?

– With regard to speaking?

– Note taking?

– Gestures?

– Did you feel included?

– Did you seek to conceal anything during the session?

– To what end?

– For you, who was the most "present" during this session (one or more people)? Name and reason.

– Was there an irritating situation (misunderstanding, tension, conflict, confusion) during this session?

– Was there anything that made you laugh or smile?

– After this session, was there a practice established that allowed for improvements in communication?

– Did you engage in any anticipatory behaviors connected to the means of communications used?

9.10. References

[ALB 02] ALBERO B., DUMONT B., Les technologies de l'information et de la communication dans l'enseignement supérieur : pratiques et besoins des enseignants, Survey, Ministère de l'Éducation nationale et ministère de la Recherche, Paris, 2002.

[ALB 09] ALBERO B., THIBAULT F., "La recherche française en sciences humaines et sociales sur les technologies en éducation", *Revue française de pédagogie*, vol. 169, pp. 53–66, 2009.

[CHO 17] CHOI M., KORNFIELD R., TAKAYAMA L. *et al.*, "Movement matters: Effects of motion and mimicry on perception of similarity and closeness in robot mediated communication", *CHI*, Denver, United States, 6–11 May, 2017.

[COD 10] CODREANU T., DEVELOTTE C., "Enseigner par visioconférence poste à poste : cadre méthodologique pour l'analyse de pratiques tutorales", in SIDIR M., BRUILLARD E., BARON G.-L. (eds), *Acteurs et objets communicants. Vers une éducation orientée objets ?*, pp. 60–71, INRP, 2010, accessed December 2017 at: http://halshs.archives-ouvertes.fr/hal-00510826/fr/.

[COS 11] COSNIER J., DEVELOTTE C., "Éthologie compréhensive de la conversation en visioconférence poste à poste", in DEVELOTTE C., KERN R., LAMY M.N. *et al.* (eds), *Décrire la conversation en ligne*, ENS Éditions, Lyon, 2011.

[DEV 10] DEVELOTTE C., GUICHON N., VINCENT C., "The use of the webcam for teaching a foreign language in a desktop videoconferencing environment", *ReCALL*, vol. 23, no. 3, pp. 293–312, 2010.

[FOW 97] FOWLER C.J.H., MAYES T., "Applying telepresence to education", *BT Technology Journal*, vol. 15, no. 4, pp. 188–195, 1997.

[GAL 14] GALLON L., "Immersion dans un TP en téléprésence", *WPRT 2014 : 3e Workshop pédagogique Réseaux & Télécoms*, Saint-Pierre de la Réunion, France, 2014.

[GOF 74] GOFFMAN E., *Les rites d'interaction*, Éditions de Minuit, Paris, 1974.

[GUT 10] GUTH S., HELM F. (eds), *Telecollaboration 2.0: Language, Literacy and Intercultural Learning in the 21ˢᵗ Century*, Peter Lang, Bern, 2010.

[HOT 01] HOTIER H., "Entretien avec Jacques Cosnier", *Communication et organisation*, no. 19, 2001, accessed December 2017 at: http://journals .openedition.org/communicationorganisation/2537.

[HUT 01] HUTCHBY I., *Conversation and Technology: From the Telephone to the Internet*, Polity Press, Cambridge, 2001.

[IBN 12] IBNELKAÏD S., DEVELOTTE C., "Le webinaire, ou quand communications distancielle et présentielle s'articulent", *Distances et Médiations des Savoirs : actes du colloque Jocair à Amiens*, 6–8 September 2012, vol. 1, pp. 51–71, 2012.

[IBN 16] IBNELKAÏD S., Identité et altérité par écran : modalités de l'intersubjectivité en interaction numérique, PhD thesis, université de Lyon-2, available at: https://transphanie.com/, 2016.

[JON 04] JONES R., "The problem of context in computer mediated communication", in LEVINE P., SCOLLON R. (eds), *Discourse & Technology Multimodal Discourse Analysis*, pp. 20–33, Georgetown University Press, Washington, 2004.

[KAU 99] KAUFMANN C., RHEE P., BURRIS D., "Telepresence surgery system enhances medical student surgery training", *Studies in Health Technology and Informatics*, vol. 62, pp. 174–178, 1999.

[MET 11] METZER J.-L., "Internet et pratiques professionnelles dans l'enseignement secondaire : quelles évolutions ?", in POYET F., DEVELOTTE C. (eds), *L'éducation à l'heure du numérique : état des lieux, enjeux et perspectives*, pp. 49–70, INRP, Lyon, 2011.

[MOE 05] MOEGLIN P., *Outils et médias éducatifs. Une approche communicationnelle*, PUG, Grenoble, 2005.

[NEU 16] NEUSTAEDTER C., VENOLIA G., PROCYK J. *et al.*, "To beam or not to beam: A study of remote telepresence attendance at an academic conference CSCW '16", The 19th ACM Conference, San Francisco, United States, 27 February–2 March 2016.

[ODO 07] O'DOWD R. (ed.), *Online Intercultural Exchange*, Multilingual Matters, Bristol, 2007.

[OHH 10] OH-HUN KWON, SEONG-YONG KOO, YOUNG-GEUN KIM, "Advanced robotics and its social impacts (ARSO)", *2010 IEEE Workshop on Advanced Institute of Science and Technology*, pp. 305–701, IEEE, New York, 2010.

[POY 11] POYET F., DEVELOTTE C., *L'éducation à l'heure du numérique. État des lieux, enjeux et perspectives*, INRP, Lyon, 2011.

[PRO 07] PROT B., ROGER J.-L., "Refaire son métier. Essai de clinique de l'activité", *L'orientation scolaire et professionnelle*, vol. 36, no. 3, 2007, accessed December 2017 at: http://osp.revues.org/1513.

[TAL 12] TALBOT L., "Les recherches sur les pratiques enseignantes efficaces", *Questions Vives*, vol. 6, no. 18, 2012, accessed December 2017 at: http://questionsvives.revues.org/1234.

[VER 94] VERMEERSCH P., *L'entretien d'explicitation*, ESF Éditeur, Montrouge, 1994.

[VIA 11] VIAL S., *L'être et l'écran*, PUF, Paris, 2011.

[WEI 99] WEISSBERG J.-L., *Présences à distance*, L'Harmattan, Paris, 1999.

Conclusion

Concluding a collective work is often a difficult task. Intermingling different disciplinary perspectives [ANN 13] and interweaving points of view makes writing a conclusion even more delicate.

The development of digital technologies makes it possible for telepresence systems to advance in the field of education and training. Building on Geneviève Jacquinot's concept proposed 25 years ago [JAC 93], telepresence contributes to modifying the antagonism between presence and absence, and fostering the feeling of presence [HAD 16] for remote learners. It therefore becomes practically impossible to know whether the person in training is present or remote. The telepresence learner, teacher and researcher are all simultaneously present and absent. We can even write present-absent with a hyphen. With telepresence robots, it is no longer only a question of identifying how F2F actors can be psychologically present all the while being physically absent, but also how they can be physically absent and mentally present when represented by a tool that extends their own bodies. This impossibility of separating distance and presence may also evoke the potential spaces between inside and outside as theorized by Donald Winnicott [WIN 71]. These spaces, which exist between physical reality and psychic reality, are kinds of creations that allow actors to overcome both the constraints of physical reality (the outside) and the contradictions of psychic reality (the inside). The preceding chapters have shown that telepresence systems modify spatial and temporal distances, as well as transactional distances and some forms of social distances, by counteracting isolation.

Conclusion written by Jean-Luc RINAUDO.

Does this modify pedagogical distance? It is likely that telepresence systems, for example virtual classes or robots, have an effect on methods of teaching and learning. If different actors do overcome distance [JAC 93], it is not certain that they deeply modify the practices of teaching-learning. On the contrary, these telepresence systems can be considered as analyzers of pedagogical practices and learning modalities in distance learning as in F2F learning. Here we return to Daniel Peraya: "Yes, most of these distances do not specifically characterize the pedagogical relationship of distance: it seems to me, on the contrary, that all training systems can share them. They are therefore transposable, undoubtedly with some changes, to F2F or hybrid training systems" [PER 14].

At the same time that they modify the presence-absence relationships, telepresence systems also contribute to redefining what are ordinarily called hybrid training systems. These hybrid systems rely most often on alternating between moments of F2F training and moments of distance learning, whether they are synchronous or asynchronous. Now, telepresence systems, which offer distance within presence, transform the idea of hybridization.

Thus, we believe that the analysis of telepresence in training allows not only for the attribution of meaning to systems that implement it but also for readdressing the questions that originate in distance education. Nevertheless, if we study the effects, we will not use the expression "reduce the distance," which seems to us full of contradictions in the educational domain. In effect, if telepresence systems allow for actors to cross spatial, temporal or social distances, it is probably not possible or desirable to completely reduce pedagogical distance or the distance to learning. If pedagogical distance is completely reduced, there would no longer be any asymmetry between the instructor and the learner, which, Philipe Meirieu reminds us, is essential to the educational relationship [MEI 97]. Similarly, if the distance to knowledge managed to be completely resolved, the desire for knowledge that stems from a lack of it [BEI 14] would come to fade. In other words, telepresence systems modify training situations; however, despite that, they do not reduce the pedagogical triangle, theorized by Jean Houssaye [HOU 88], to a single straight line or a single point.

References

[ANN 13] ANNOOT E., BERTIN J.C., "Quel homme @ distance ?", in *L'homme @ distance : innovation et développement*, pp. 171–178, CNRS Éditions, Paris, 2013.

[BEI 14] BEILLEROT J., "Désir, désir de savoir, désir d'apprendre", *Cliopsy*, vol. 12, pp. 73–90, 2014, accessed January 2018 at: http://www.revuecliopsy.fr/wp -content/uploads/2014/11/RevueCliopsy12-Beillerot-désir-073.pdf.

[HAD 16] HADDOUK L., *L'entretien clinique à distance*, Éditions Érès, Toulouse, 2016.

[HOU 88] HOUSSAYE J., *Le triangle pédagogique*, Peter Lang, Bern, 1988.

[JAC 93] JACQUINOT G., "Apprivoiser la distance et supprimer l'absence ? ou les défis de la formation à distance", *Revue française de pédagogie*, vol. 102, pp. 55–67, 1993.

[MEI 97] MEIRIEU P., "Praxis pédagogique et pensée de la pédagogie", *Revue française de pédagogie*, vol. 120, pp. 25–37, 1997.

[PER 14] PERAYA D., "Distances, absence, proximités et présences : des concepts en déplacement", *Distances et médiations des savoirs*, vol. 8, 2014, accessed January 2018 at: http://journals.openedition.org/dms/865.

[WIN 71] WINNICOTT D.W., *Playing and Reality*, Tavistock, London, 1971.

Postface

Introduction

My French dictionary lists about 60 terms beginning with tele but not (yet) the word "telepresence". However, we can refer to Wikipedia to find a definition. "The term telepresence refers to several techniques that allow an individual to have the impression of being present, to give the impression of being present, or to have an effect at a place other than one's actual location".

A sort of "presence at a distance", as several authors mentioned about the emergence of synchronous systems for FAD (distance education) several years ago.

The work clearly conveys the beginning of the domestication of this telepresence in training and education. The phase of ecstatic lingering dissolves in favor of a decreasingly experimental approach, which has become practically routine.

The fact that most of the chapter authors have also contributed and are engaged instructors in these practices bears witness and reinforces this impression, even though this sometimes reduces the "critical distance".

We should also note that if, in these approaches to the space/time of training, most of the situations are synchronous, it is conversely the proxemics that are at play.

Postface written by Jacques WALLET.

Digital ontophany and the haptic dimension

For some researchers, the real/virtual boundary does not exist. For example, as quoted by Françoise Poyet in her chapter, Stéphane Vial thus presents his work *L'être et l'écran (The Being and the Screen)*:

> *Le temps est venu d'analyser "l'ontophanie numérique" dans toute sa complexité. La prétendue différence entre le réel et le virtuel n'existe pas et n'a jamais existé. Nous vivons dans un environnement hybride, à la fois numérique et non-numérique, en ligne et hors ligne, qu'il appartient aux* designers *de rendre habitable* [VIA 13].

> The time has come to analyze "digital ontophany" in all its complexity. The so-called difference between the real and the virtual doesn't exist and has never existed. We live in a hybrid environment, simultaneously digital and non-digital, online and offline, which designers must render livable [VIA 13].

This point of view is opposed to the "distinctionist" tradition, which is found among most authors working on media; it is present in numerous disciplines, with a variety of theoretical frameworks. This situation is not new; as stated thus by Geneviève Jacquinot: "It was necessary (and still is) to work against the impression of reality, against the illusion of transparency, and to learn to see in every image a discourse about the work, an organization of forms where I read the world as much as I read the world in myself" [JAC 98].

In a postface, I am not going to bring up too many theoretical ideas; the chapter authors have done so and the showdown of (French and English) bibliographies presents a multitude of approaches. Because, irresistibly, I think of my first contact with telepresence, long before my own use of online systems: reading of an author of science fiction novels named Albert Robida, whose prophetic dimension on the benefits and ravages of progress extends, in my opinion, beyond those of Jules Verne, despite the fact that the latter are more well known.

Thus, years after the invention of the telephone, while film was still in search of its industrial format, he imagined in advance, among other things, the Internet and videoconferencing, using a robotized system (the word did not yet exist) which he called a Telephonoscope (capitalized). What is fascinating is that, beyond his technical intuition, he foresaw the use and socialization that emerged in social practices, leisure and education.

As an example, here are two passages that return to the question of telepresence; everything is said by the word "almost" in the first extract and in the curious cognitive conflict of "distance versus presence" described in the second extract:

> The invention made it possible not only to converse over long distances with everyone in the world connected electrically to the network, but also to see one's interlocutor in a particular framework, in his faraway home. A happy suppression of absence, which pleases families that are often scattered throughout the world in our busy era, and nevertheless all reunited in the evening in the communal center if they want to be – dining together at different, distant tables, but forming nevertheless almost a family table [ROB 92, p. 8].

> Since she was 12 years old, Estelle attended courses at the Zurich Institute, without leaving home, completely remotely. A valuable benefit for families who live far from any town center, who are no longer forced to commit their children to regional schools, isn't it? Estelle had therefore done all of her classes remotely, without leaving her home, without leaving Lauterbrunnen. She also attended classes at the École centrale d'électricité in Paris and also review via phonogram by several renowned masters.

> Unfortunately, she wasn't able to take her exams remotely, since the rules did not allow it, and, before the master examiners, a timidity she got from her father impaired her [ROB 92, p. 25].

But let us return to the topic at hand: even though the learners are no longer sheep since, as affirmed by all of the chapters in this work, the participants in training interact among themselves or with the instructor or referring tutor.

The present communicational stakes progressively fade in all of the texts most of the time, in order to focus not only on the relational but also the cognitive stakes. The question of the feeling of telepresence is not easy.

If acoustic and optical dimensions are henceforth normalized, two comments from students extracted as examples from different chapters highlight the issues of the haptic dimension, or at least that of the haptic illusion, and, more specifically, the one connected to the use of the robot:

> "I really had the impression of being together with everyone [...] I didn't feel separate even if I was in my living room" (This is a transcript) (N.B. Thanks to the robot...) I could even go to the coffee break with my friends/so that was good.

> Physically I'm not there and I yet I'm present physically, it's stupid but I'm in two places at once and I have a real environment and an unreal environment where I'm driving and it's really disconcerting; suddenly I have trouble getting into it, and as soon as I hear interference it brings me back to reality and it's difficult and then you have your eyes focused on the screen the whole time.

This training in telepresence involves emotion and affect, but virtual encounters exclude the body and provoke a form of relational misunderstanding. The reading of some chapters explicitly highlights that telepresence provokes a reinforcement of the desire for a real encounter: some of the authors have highlighted the benefits of collective meetings in training ecosystems in which they have participated or observed.

In order to make progress in the domain, we are tempted to propose that a "mechanistic" scale or coefficient of telepresence be objectified for the writing of specifications for future hybridized training. The tools or environments (virtual classes, robots, videoconferences, social networks), or combinations of several technologies, do not all provoke the same effects, the same uses, the same interrelationships, which have been clearly underlined in the different chapters, even though sometimes some of the terms used are similar.

The specificity of the teaching/learning dimension

One of the chapters mentions the term "pedagogical distance" without completely explaining the polysemy of the expression. This brings us back to long-standing empirical observations: teaching is also a communication situation in which everyone knows that one can be present in a class without really paying attention to, listening to or understanding it.

For example, the causes of inattention in traditional F2F situations bring us back to multiple explanatory factors and theoretical frameworks. Perhaps some authors, in their comparative approaches to "remote/distant students", forget them a little, in wanting to compare the "comfort" or the "motivation" of remote students. Attending class in person does not necessarily mean paying attention to the contents of the course. Educators and educational software designers have shown this to us with scores of theoretical frameworks relating to the observation of teaching practices or to the types of knowledge in play in teaching/learning. Moreover, the presence of the teacher does not signify his capacity to mobilize listening and to involve his listeners.

It is this "feeling of presence/coefficient of presence" that Geneviève Jacquinot already highlighted during a conference about presence at a distance:

> Contrary to what has often been said and written, these "real" new technologies do not reinforce abstraction, but they embody them more and more [...]. We can also speak about a "coefficient of presence". In teaching, particularly, we are prisoners to this experience of presence reduced to "physical" presence and therefore to this idea that as soon as there is no longer physical presence, there is no longer any authentic communication. It is already progress to recognize that physical presence is "one" of the dimensions of presence, and that there is a whole range of presences that range from complete absence to co-presence. We can even add... To what we can call "F2F presence", because one can be present in person and completely absent, as we all know. When one speaks of these technological systems and the "distance" they introduce, and which concerns us, we often implicitly compare an ideal situation in which, in person, there is

real intercommunication and, on the other hand, a situation via technology that is as big of a failure as we can imagine.

Finally, we must undoubtedly think about this "presence/ absence" dichotomy and to try to think about and work on the modifications that can occur in our perceptual phenomena, since the intrusion of these technologies requires or allows us to imagine a presence, the "benefit of a presence" [...]. Our relationships with space and time are changed and, as a consequence, our ways of seeing, and doubtless, of knowing... [JAC 06].

The series of texts presented bear witness to contemporary developments in training, which raise the question of the hybridization of genres. One of the major criticisms of distance learning, that of the isolation of learners, is henceforth behind us; several years ago, in a report entitled "Affective distance and pedagogical proximity", the challenge posed to telepresence, even though this term was not yet in use, was: "In developing this notion of pedagogical distance, is it possible to imagine distance learning systems that are more appealing and even more 'warm'?" [THO 10].

In our view, this is a necessary but not sufficient condition, because it should be connected to wide-reaching questions about the motivation of learners, whether they are remote or physically present during training.

In conclusion, technological advances in the service of telepresence in training, and, more generally, in online relationships and socialization, will continue. For instructors, the challenge of "tele-empathy" is undoubtedly generalizable, because the hybridization of training and learning will accelerate its possible standardization, constituting, in another register, a completely different challenge.

References

[JAC 98] JACQUINOT G., "Cinéma et dernières technologies", in BEAU F., DUBOIS P., LEBLANC G. (eds), *Du cinéma éducateur aux plaisirs interactifs, rives et dérives cognitives*, pp. 153–168, INA/De Boeck, Paris/Brussels, 1998, accessed January 2018 at: http://edutice.archives-ouvertes.fr/file/index/docid/1606 /filename/index.html.

[JAC 06] JACQUINOT G., "Le sentiment de présence", *Actes des deuxièmes rencontres Réseaux Humains/Réseaux Technologiques*, Poitiers, France, 2006, accessed January 2018 at: http://rhrt.edel.univpoitiers.fr/document.php?id=773.

[ROB 92] ROBIDA A., *Le vingtième siècle la vie électrique*, Librairie illustrée, Paris, 1892, accessed January 2018 at: http://gallica.bnf.fr/ark:/12148/bpt6k101948n /f3.image.

[THO 10] THOT CURSUS, "Dossier Distance affective et proximité pédagogique", 2010/2011, accessed January 2018 at: http://cursus.edu/article/7454/distance -affective-proximite-pedagogique/#.WldecUxFzwo.

[VIA 13] VIAL S., *L'être et l'écran*, PUF, Paris, 2013.

List of Authors

Gustavo ANGULO
Education Department
Université Teluq
Quebec
Canada

Stéphanie BOÉCHAT-HEER
HEP Béjune
Switzerland

Romaine CARRUPT
HEP Valais
Switzerland

Ann-Louise DAVIDSON
Université Concordia
Montreal
Canada

Brigitte DENIS
Crifa
Université de Liège
Belgium

Christine DEVELOTTE
ENS-IFÉ
Lyon
France

Dorothée FURNON
ECP
Université Lyon 2
France

Nadia NAFFI
Université Concordia
Montreal
Canada

Cathia PAPI
Curapp
Université Teluq
Quebec
Canada

Françoise POYET
Elico
Université Lyon 1
France

Jean-Luc RINAUDO
Cirnef
Université de Rouen Normandie
Mont-Saint-Aignan
France

Jacques WALLET
Cirnef
Université de Rouen Normandie
Mont-Saint-Aignan
France

Index

Other titles from

in

Innovations in Learning Sciences

2018

BARTHES Angela, CHAMPOLLION Pierre, ALPE Yves
Evolutions of the Complex Relationship Between Education and Territories
(Education Set – Volume 1)

LARINI Michel, BARTHES Angela
Quantitative and Statistical Data in Education: From Data Collection to
Data Processing
(Education Set – Volume 2)

2015

POMEROL Jean-Charles, EPELBOIN Yves, THOURY Claire
MOOCs: Design, Use and Business Models